COURAGEOUS
CONVERSATIONS
ABOUT
RACE

This book is dedicated to Wendell "E. J." Singleton,
who deserves success in school.

A
Field
Guide
for
Achieving
Equity
in
Schools

COURAGEOUS CONVERSATIONS ABOUT RACE

GLENN E. SINGLETON
CURTIS LINTON

Foreword by Gloria Ladson-Billings

CORWIN PRESS
A SAGE Publications Company
2455 Teller Road
Thousand Oaks, CA 91320-2218

For information:

Corwin Press, Inc.
A Sage Publications Company
2455 Teller Road
Thousand Oaks, California 91320
www.corwinpress.com

Sage Publications Ltd.
1 Oliver's Yard
55 City Road
London EC1Y 1SP
United Kingdom

Sage Publications India Pvt. Ltd.
B-42, Panchsheel Enclave
Post Box 4109
New Delhi 110 017 India

Printed in the United States of America

Library of Congress Cataloging-in-Publication Data

Singleton, Glenn E. (Glenn Eric)
Courageous conversations about race: A field guide for achieving equity in schools / by Glenn E. Singleton & Curtis Linton.
        p. cm.
Includes bibliographical references and index.
ISBN 0-7619-8876-9 (cloth)—ISBN 0-7619-8877-7 (pbk,)
    1. Educational equalization—United States. 2. Academic achievement—United States. 3. United States—Race relations. I. Linton, Curtis. II. Title.
LC213.2.S58 2006
379.2'6'0073—dc22

                                    2005014862

This book is printed on acid-free paper.

06   07   10   9   8   7   6   5

Acquisitions Editor:	Rachel Livsey
Editorial Assistant:	Phyllis Cappello
Production Editor:	Melanie Birdsall
Copy Editor:	Jacqueline A. Tasch
Typesetter:	C&M Digitals (P) Ltd.
Indexer:	David Luljak
Cover Designer:	Michael Dubowe

Contents

Foreword

When I was first approached to write the foreword for this book, my inclination was to decline. Like many people, I have an impossible schedule that hardly allows for any additional tasks. However, when I had an opportunity to read the manuscript, I understood why I had to make room in my schedule to write this foreword. Almost all of the conversations about schools today focus on the need to be more rigorous, to be more accountable, and to close the achievement gap that exists between the United States and her international peers, between rich and poor children within the United States, and between White and Black students (and other students of color) in this nation. Of those concerns, only the last one seems to deal directly with the question of race. In truth, all of them deal with race—just as almost everything in our society does.

One of my reasons for wanting to write this foreword is quite personal. I live in a city that prides itself on its tolerance and activism on behalf of people who have experienced discrimination, disadvantage, and exclusion. It is one of the few places in the country that started study circles on race where scores of community members came together week after week to discuss race and racism in the city. However, once the school district decided to take a serious look at racism, we began to see just how difficult it is to engage with notions of race and racism. Let me be clear—the district is filled with teachers, administrators, and others who have good intentions and goodwill toward all students, regardless of their race, language, and ethnicity. But those good intentions (and goodwill) do not help teachers and other educators deal with the problems of race and racism that pervade our schools at every level.

Another reason I was prompted to write this foreword is the result of having recently viewed the feature film *Crash*. This is a film about the intersecting racial, ethnic, and class lives of people in Los Angeles. It is dramatic, compelling, and raw, and yet for all its intricacies, it leaves out the most salient intricacy—the way power organizes and deploys race and racism. Instead, in *Crash*, we have a story of multiple levels of prejudice and bigotry—everyone is complicit. We have no way to think about the structural and symbolic systems that make race so available to us. We can leave the theater believing that "it's everybody's fault" and not clearly examine how systems of power are operating to keep the current social order intact. As elegantly as the film is crafted, at base, *Crash* leaves us with a sense of despair about race and ethnic relations in the United States. It reinscribes the notion that individual actors bear sole responsibility for our current racial state and that there is little we can do about it. However, this volume offers another vision for educators.

Race is the proverbial "elephant in the parlor." We know it's right there staring us in the face—making life uncomfortable and making it difficult for us to accomplish everything we would really like to do—but we keep pretending it isn't. As one African American community activist once said, "Don't you realize how much better we could be, how much farther along we could be, if we didn't invest so much time and energy into racism?"

From my perspective, this volume, *Courageous Conversations About Race: A Field Guide for Attaining Equity in Schools,* is an attempt both to expose the elephant and to get it moved out of the parlor. The beauty of this volume is that it is designed to help lay people—teachers, administrators, parents, community leaders, and even university professors—begin to engage in the emotionally and psychically difficult conversations about race.

Some people believe that talking about race only "makes it worse." We have all heard those who say, "If you would only stop talking about race, people wouldn't be racist," or "You're the racist because you keep bringing it up!" That's akin to saying, "I wouldn't have cancer if I didn't go to the doctor!" Glenn Singleton and Curtis Linton have offered us an important book, providing us with empirical data and well-constructed exercises to help us think through the ways that race affects our lives and our professional practices.

One of the surprising aspects of the book is how freely the authors offer assistance for which they could be handsomely compensated. Much of the work in this book reflects their ongoing professional practice, and yet, they have seen fit to make it widely available. This is a testimony to their passion and concern about healing the racial divides that pervade our schools, communities, and the nation.

I love the notion of "courageous conversations." Think about what it implies. I can think of numerous times in my life when I have had to have a courageous conversation. Typically, I have had such a conversation with someone in whom I am deeply invested—my spouse, my children, my parents—and I deeply care about the outcome of that conversation. When I needed to talk to a teenaged son about steering clear of drugs, it was a courageous conversation. I did not want to appear cavalier—that is, "Just say no"—because I wanted him to take me seriously. I did not want to be a stern, disciplinarian—"If I ever catch you using drugs I will ground you for a year"—because I didn't want him to feel he could never come to me with questions and concerns. I needed to have an honest conversation about how he could address peer pressure and take his own stand and about how much his staying healthy and pursuing his life dreams meant to our entire family.

I think the same thing obtains in a school setting. Singleton and Linton are suggesting that teachers have to be willing to have courageous conversations with people with whom they share their professional lives. They have to care about the people and the environment. They cannot continue to make polite conversation or issue polemic dictums. They need to have real, authentic, hard conversations—courageous conversations—if they are ever to address the disease of racism that is so prevalent in U.S. life.

In the recent book *Color Mute: Race Talk Dilemmas in an American School* (Pollock, 2004), the author describes how people in one U.S. high school struggle to talk about race—at the most basic levels. We do not know what to call each other or if we should call each other anything that has a racial designation. But Pollock demonstrates that even when we avoid talking about race, we are talking about race; that is, even in our avoidance of the subject, we are engaging it. This is similar to David Roediger's (1999) assertion in his book, *The Wages of Whiteness*, that even in his all-White German American neighborhood, race was never absent. Furthermore, in a study of teachers teaching early literacy (Ladson-Billings, 2005), my colleague and I observed teachers regularly talking about students' failure to read without ever mentioning race. Almost all of the struggling students were Black or Latino. It was not until six months into the project that teachers recognized the salience of race in the students' achievement. At this point, we were able to deal honestly deal with the students' academic issues.

Each of the authors referenced above provides theoretical, conceptual, and empirical evidence about the ways race operates, both in the school and in the society at large. Singleton and Linton complete the circle by providing practical and practice-based strategies for confronting race in open and honest ways. However, it is important to point out that this is not a recipe book. This book requires the readers to think critically and confront their own deeply held ideas and perceptions about race. My sincere desire is that after you have had an opportunity to read this volume, you will, indeed, engage in some courageous conversations about race.

—Gloria Ladson-Billings
University of Wisconsin–Madison

REFERENCES

Ladson-Billings, G. (2005). Reading, writing, and race: Literacy practices of teachers in diverse classrooms. In T. McCarty (Ed.), *Language, literacy, and power in schooling* (pp. 133–150). Mahwah, NJ: Lawrence Erlbaum.

Pollock, M. (2004). *Color mute: Race talk dilemmas in an American school.* Princeton, NJ: Princeton University Press.

Roediger, D. (1999). *The wages of whiteness* (Rev. ed.). London: Verso Press.

Preface

This book is dedicated to Wendell "E. J." Singleton, the youngest member of co-author Glenn Singleton's extended family. Three years ago, the family lovingly sent a precocious, inquisitive boy off to school for the first time. E. J. arrived with pride and joy, but—like so many young African American boys—he was greeted by a system that did not expect much from him, yet had already determined much for him. In two short years of formal schooling, E. J. has been labeled a failure, special needs, at-risk, and ADD. History suggests that E. J. will find it virtually impossible to shake loose from these deficit descriptors.

We are writing this book because E. J. deserves qualified and skilled teachers who love him instead of fear him, as do his many friends in Baltimore public schools and students of color like them throughout this nation's schools. These youngsters deserve competent instructors who understand, value, and affirm their colorful African American, Latino, Asian, and other cultures. They are owed a procession of teachers who will be skilled in drawing out their innate brilliance, curiosity, and creativity.

Roughly 30 years ago in the very same public school system, Mrs. Hall, Mrs. Sandifer, and Mrs. Thomas, to name only a few, effectively taught Glenn Singleton in the way his cousin E. J. deserves to be instructed. Why is it that E. J.'s teachers are not capably meeting his academic, social, and emotional needs?

Every day, Glenn and his family worry about E. J.'s spirit as he travels the mean streets of Baltimore into the meaner hallways of his public school. The daily affirmations E. J. recites each morning are becoming a weak defense against a system that predetermines him to be incapable of achieving at a high level. Rather than point out all that is wrong with our schools and the adults who inhabit them, however, this book has been written to support educators and assist them in meeting the needs of E. J. and the thousands of other students of color like him.

Based on publicity generated by the No Child Left Behind Act, educators are acutely aware of the statistical gaps in achievement between White students and most students of color groups. We believe that the primary and essential way of addressing these gaps is to create a culture that encourages educators, both Whites and people of color, to discuss race safely and honestly in the school environment. Contrary to popular assumption, this is an issue of concern not only to educators and families who are people of color but to all; the welfare of all students—no matter what their color—depends on *all of us* succeeding at this conversation.

This is a book about race. In schools, race plays a primary role in sustaining if not widening the achievement gap. But educators have not been very good at talking about race and its impact on learning. We write this book to provide a strategy—Courageous Conversation—that educators can use to open up the conversation on race in their schools.

With so much written in the arena of achievement disparity, the last thing the field needs is another book pointing out the obvious—that we have not quite figured out how to educate all children well. What we offer, instead, is a detailed, thoughtful, ongoing, and influential strategy for having conversations about race that deepen our understanding about how and why the racial achievement gap persists in most schools and at all economic levels. It is precisely because few educators have explicitly investigated the taboo intersection of race and achievement that we offer this book. Our rationale is quite simple: We will never eliminate the racial achievement gap unless we have conversations about race.

We, the authors—Glenn Singleton, who is Black, and Curtis Linton, who is White—have used this strategy to guide our own mutual racial discovery. Within this context, we have worked closely to come to a better understanding of our own and our separate individual racial experiences. Glenn was already very aware of his own racial identity as an African American, but growing up White, Curtis was unaware of his equally powerful racial identity until he began working with Glenn while producing and writing a program for *The Video Journal of Education* entitled "Closing the Achievement Gap."

Curtis's initial engagement in this work came at the end of the first day of one of Glenn's seminars, Beyond Diversity. For many in the room, it was the first time they had ever been encouraged to openly discuss race with someone of a skin color different than their own. At the end of the day, Glenn offered the participants some concluding thoughts. He said that White people, emotionally moved by what they have heard, often approach him at the end of these seminars and ask, "So what do I do now?" "How can I be anti-racist?" "How can you forgive me for having been racist?" "How can I fix this?" Glenn's answer is simple but profound: "Just believe me."

Just believe me—is that all? Believe Glenn when he says that he experiences racial profiling almost daily. Believe him when he says that his

White neighbors treat him differently. Believe that he is a victim of lowered expectations, that he is accused of succeeding only because of affirmative action, and that he actually has a lifetime of racist and racially discriminatory experiences.

To believe and trust this person of color was Curtis's first level of understanding. He acknowledged that even though his experiences as a White man have been very different, he does not have the right to reinterpret Glenn's life, to justify the actions of others who are White, or to claim that Glenn does not actually experience what he claims he does. Curtis feels obliged to believe Glenn, to listen to him, and to treat him like the equal human being that he is.

Since that time, as we have worked together, we have deeply and personally reflected on, examined, and discussed the impact of race, first in our own lives and then in the culture at large. Curtis is White. Glenn is Black. The two of us exist on opposite ends of the American racial binary. Because of this, our individual racial experiences are dissimilar, and yet we are friends and colleagues. The key to our successful friendship and collaboration is our willingness to communicate openly, honestly, and respectfully about race. And in believing and trusting each other across racial categories, we can begin addressing the issue of race within our schools.

For nearly two decades, Glenn Singleton has guided thousands of educators in examining themselves racially, and he has worked closely with hundreds of school systems throughout the United States, helping them develop the culture and structure necessary to close the racial achievement gap. Over the past 10 years, Curtis Linton has visited hundreds of the most effective schools and school systems across North America, documenting on video their effective practices and creating training resources that help to duplicate those successes elsewhere. In writing this book, we have drawn on both of our experiences and related expertise to provide educators with a research-based strategy that they can use to understand race and address racism in their schools.

Courageous Conversation, as a strategy, begins with the premise that initially, educational leaders collectively view themselves and the schooling enterprise to be inherently non-racist. In fact, their tightly held beliefs and understandings regarding the significance of race make it difficult for teachers to comprehend, examine, and rectify the very ways in which race dramatically impacts achievement.

Unfortunately, the racial situation in schools only mirrors what takes place in the larger society. John Dewey suggested that schools must be the engine of social transformation. In *Courageous Conversations About Race: A Field Guide for Achieving Equity in Schools*, we have set out to redefine the educational context and then provide the content and process for educators to grapple personally with race as a critical sociopolitical construct. In our work with a variety of schools, districts, and regional programs, we have found that Courageous Conversation effectively enables educators to develop and operate from a transformed racial philosophy that guides their policy analysis, institutional restructuring, and instructional practice reform.

As educators engage in, sustain, and deepen interracial dialogue about race with each other and with students and their families, systems then can truly support all children in achieving at higher levels. As schools work toward equity, they will narrow the gaps between the highest- and lowest-performing groups and eliminate the racial predictability regarding which groups achieve in the highest- and lowest-performing categories.

Courageous Conversations is divided into three parts reflecting the three essential characteristics of anti-racist leadership: *Passion*, *Practice*, and *Persistence*. In *Passion*, the book begins by exploring the landscape of educational reform and exposing the issue of race as a most devastating phenomenon impacting the lives and learning of all children. We go on to help the reader focus on race in lieu of the traditional topics, such as poverty, language, and learning disabilities, which have long occupied our attention and resulted in only unsatisfactory incremental systemic changes. The next series of chapters, *Practice*, takes the reader on a step-by-step journey into the race conversation, providing the language, markers, tools, and insights necessary to begin and stay in the dialogue. Finally, in *Persistence*, educators will learn about the leadership that is necessary to close racial achievement gaps. They will finish the book by investigating the work of the Lemon Grove School District and its success in implementing a systemwide Courageous Conversation.

This book provides a foundation for those educational leaders at the system and school level who are willing and ready to begin or accelerate their journey toward educational equity and excellence for all children. This includes superintendents, board members, district administrators, principals, team and teacher leaders, and engaged members of the community. It is designed to assist in facilitating effective dialogue about the racial issues that impact student achievement. As you progress through each chapter, you will be prompted to reflect on your learning and, in particular, your own racial experience. At the end of each chapter, you will find implementation activities that you can use with your staff to lead them in discussing the impact of race in the classroom. As a school or system-level leader, this book will guide you in engaging your staff in a conversation on race as a first step in closing the racial achievement gap.

Preface

As you address the prompts and complete the exercises we have carefully embedded in each chapter, you will feel a surge in your own will, skill, knowledge, and capacity to lead others through the same journey. Although we urge you to avoid involving others too soon in your own developmental process, at some point, you will not be able to resist ushering your friends, family, and colleagues into a Courageous Conversation. We have witnessed this process unfold for thousands of educators over the past decade.

Closing the teaching and learning gap requires that teachers think about their craft differently. E. J.'s teachers certainly have their work cut out as most of them need to envision and practice pedagogy in ways that they have never seen nor experienced before. But a teacher's hope in the unseen, along with an unwavering belief that our families really do want the best schooling for our children, can sustain them in this work.

We are writing this book in the hope that our readers embrace what we view as a moral imperative to arrive at a deeper understanding of race and racism. We suspect most educators already believe that racism is morally wrong. The challenge for us is to advance our shared moral position into a realizable and comprehensive foundation for challenging institutional racism. Our students deserve nothing less.

Given the magnitude of race as a topic and the long history of racial achievement disparities, no one book can solve this educational problem and the broader societal issues that underlie it. What this book can do is get us pointed in the right direction by engaging, sustaining, and deepening the conversation about race, racial identity development, and institutional racism. It is our hope and belief that having Courageous Conversations will create the lasting foundation on which magnificent new relationships between teacher and student are built and higher achievement is gained.

To our ancestors and elders who have provided a historic foundation on which our contemporary understanding and insights about race are built, we thank you. We also recognize that without the patience, practice, and persistence of our partner districts and other educational leaders throughout this nation, we could have never discovered the deep and lasting impact of Courageous Conversation in today's schools. Our most sincere acknowledgment of the many who have contributed greatly to this book is seen in our efforts to capture their work and words in a thoughtful and thorough way. Writing about these transformative dialogues represents our hardest work yet. But the greatest learning also occurs as we engage, sustain, and deepen the interracial conversation about race in schools and districts. Through this transformative work, student success will increase, the racial achievement gap will close, and you will personally be impacted as you discover yourself racially. And now, it is time for you to join us in this journey of possibility!

Acknowledgments

We would like to acknowledge the following for their generous assistance, support, and dedicated efforts in helping all students succeed:

Chapel Hill-Carrboro City Schools

Cherry Creek Schools

Lemon Grove School District

Pacific Educational Group, Inc.

Oak Grove School District

San Jose State University, Urban High School Leadership Program

The Video Journal of Education

Jamie Almazan

J. Brooks

Phyllis Cappello

Nettie Collins-Hart

Andy Garcia

Donn Griffits

Glenn Heath

Yvette Irving

J. Lagoo

Blanch Linton

John Linton

Melody Linton

Rachel Livsey

Jere McInerney

L. McLean King

Graig Meyer

Pamela Noli

Neil G. Pedersen

Janet L. Perkins

Jackie Thompson

Tracy Tyler

Pablo Vega

Frank Wulftange

Frederique Wynberg

The contributions of the following reviewers are gratefully acknowledged:

Stephen Bergen
Principal
Lab School for Creative Learning
Ft. Collins, CO

Dr. Karen Hayes
Assistant Professor
Department of Educational Administration and Supervision
University of Nebraska
Omaha, NE

Elizabeth J. Lolli
Superintendent
Barberton City School District
Barberton, OH

Franklin CampbellJones
Associate Professor of Education Leadership
Rowan University
Glassboro, NJ

About the Authors

 **Glenn E. Singleton** is the executive director of Pacific Educational Group, Inc. (PEG). He introduces PEG's Framework for Systemic Equity/Anti-Racism Transformation to K–12 district administrators and higher education executive leadership. In 1992, he founded PEG to address systemic educational inequity by providing support to districts in meeting the needs of underserved students of color.

Singleton designs comprehensive support for partner school districts throughout the nation. PEG helps educators heighten their awareness of institutional racism and develop effective strategies for closing the racial achievement gap. In 1995, Singleton developed Beyond Diversity, a nationally recognized training center aimed at helping educators identify and examine the powerful intersections of race and schooling. Beyond Diversity introduces Courageous Conversation and provides the foundation for all PEG-led programs.

Singleton has appeared on ABC's *Good Morning America* and has written numerous articles on the topics of equity, institutional racism, and leadership and staff development for national journals, magazines, and newspapers. He serves on the annual conference planning committee for the National Staff Development Council. He is the 2003 recipient for the Eugene T. Carothers Human Relations Award for outstanding service in the fields of human rights and human relations.

Singleton is adjunct professor of Educational Leadership at San José State University. He is founder of Foundation for a College Education of East Palo Alto, California. Singleton earned his master's degree from the Graduate School of Education at Stanford University and his bachelor's degree from the University of Pennsylvania. He is a native of Baltimore, Maryland, and currently resides in San Francisco, California.

About the Authors

**Curtis Linton** is a co-owner of The School Improvement Network where he is co-executive producer of *The Video Journal of Education* and *TeachStream*. He has spent the last 10 years documenting on video and in print the improvement efforts and best practices of the most successful schools and school systems across North America. Each year, he visits more than 100 classrooms and schools, capturing what they do to succeed with all students at the classroom, school, and system levels.

Linton has written or produced dozens of award-winning video-based staff development programs. His areas of expertise include closing the achievement gap and improving minority student achievement, using data, leadership, effective staff development, brain research, differentiation, action research, and coaching. With the goal of delivering results-based professional development efficiently to large numbers of educators, he works with school systems to design comprehensive school improvement plans that integrate workshops, video, electronic media, and other resources. As a part of this, Linton conducts workshops on effective classroom practices.

Linton also works extensively in the community, including serving on the Davis School District Equity Committee. Linton received his master's degree in fine arts from the University of Southern California and currently resides with his wife, Melody, in Salt Lake City, Utah. They have a son.

1

Breaking the Silence

Ushering in Courageous Conversation About Race

Of all the civil rights for which the world has struggled and fought for 5000 years, the right to learn is undoubtedly the most fundamental. We must insist upon this to give our children the fairness of a start which will equip them with such an array of facts and such an attitude toward truth that they can have a real chance to judge what the world is and what its greater minds have thought it might be!

—W. E. B. DuBois (1949)

What is a child's right to learn? This is a fundamental question that we pose to you, the reader of this book. Our assumption is that most educators enter the profession believing that *every* child has the right to learn, whatever the child's race, culture, or economic class.

In reaction to the preceding quote, Linda Darling-Hammond (1997) asks, "How [can we] reinvent the system of U.S. public education so that it ensures a right to learn for all its students, who will enter a world in which a failure to learn is fast becoming an insurmountable defeat?" (p. 2). There is no time left for educators in the United States to let this question linger.

Of particular interest to us is the topic of race and its role in the education of this country's children. We believe that race—and thus racism, in both individual and institutionalized forms, whether acknowledged or unacknowledged—plays a primary role in students' struggle to achieve at high levels. We are writing this book with hopes that the reader shares our moral understanding of this issue and is willing to engage with us to come to a deeper understanding of race and racism. Most educators inherently believe that racism is morally wrong. The challenge is to advance that moral position into real, comprehensive, cognitive, and intellectual foundations of understanding that will allow us to challenge racism in our everyday personal interactions and professional practices.

THE RACIAL ACHIEVEMENT GAP

The significant achievement gap that exists between Black and Brown students and their White and Asian counterparts has been publicized more than ever due to the impact of the federal No Child Left Behind legislation. This is indeed a *racial* achievement gap because the variance in performance exists between students of different skin colors. To begin addressing this *racial* gap—intentionally, explicitly, and comprehensively—is the purpose of this book.

With all of the recent attention to the achievement gap, which has been thoroughly investigated and evidenced in the work of Kati Haycock, Ruth Johnson, Belinda Williams, and countless other esteemed colleagues in the field, we are not asking *if* the achievement gap exists. Our intention is to move educators beyond acknowledging the reality of the racial gap toward developing a strategy for eliminating it. We want to illuminate a primary reason why the gap persists and propose a strategy for its elimination. Our primary and essential question to you is as follows:

> To what degree do you and your system have the will, skill, knowledge, and capacity to understand and address issues of race as they relate to existing racial achievement disparities?

Based on our experience, few classrooms, fewer whole schools, and far fewer entire school districts can offer up educators who are truly willing and prepared to address the racial achievement gap head-on. Considering that the racial composition of our student population is rapidly changing, how will educators who are the racial inverse of the emerging student population arrive at a new and necessary level of cultural proficiency and instructional effectiveness? Whereas the number of students of color continues to increase dramatically, the number of teachers of color is actually dropping. The 2000 census indicates that more than 72% of five-year-olds enrolled in preschool in our most populace state, California, are non-White. Thus, there is a dramatic need to build interracial knowledge and understanding so that the adults in schools comprehend the needs of their children.

Essential Questions

Related to the aforementioned systemic preparedness question are three essential questions, adapted from *Understanding by Design* by Grant Wiggins and Jay McTighe (1998, p. 179), that all educators need to address in their work in school:

1. What is it that students should know and be able to do?

2. How will we know when students know it and are able to do it?

3. What do we do when we discover that students don't know it and are not yet able to do it?

In this book, we take these questions further by framing them in terms of the personal and professional inquiry and action educators must consider as they address the racial achievement gap:

1. What is it that educators should know and be able to do to narrow the racial achievement gap?

2. How will educators know when they are experiencing success in their efforts to narrow the racial achievement gap?

3. What do they do as they discover what they don't yet know and are not yet able to do to eliminate the racial achievement gap?

Without asking these questions, educators are left searching—knowing there is a problem, but not knowing what to do about it.

External Factors

Frustrated by the racial achievement gap's existence, educators often blame social, economic, or political factors external to the school and unrelated to the quality of learning and teaching. We have found this kind of blaming to be insufficient at best and destructive at worst when trying to address racial achievement disparity. Families send their best children off to school each day, and it is the educators' responsibility to greet students with the highest quality instruction and emotional support possible.

In his article "The Canary in the Mine," Mano Singham (1998) disputes common and simplistic explanations that educators invoke to explain the persistence of the racial achievement gap. Among these are

The *"liberal interpretation,"* which claims that "educational disparities are caused by socioeconomic disparities" (Singham, 1998, p. 10). However, as has been well documented elsewhere and will be evidenced later in this book, racial achievement gaps exist even among students within the same socioeconomic levels. In other words, poverty alone cannot explain the gap. Specifically, if this poverty explanation were valid, most students at similar family income levels would be performing at nearly the same level in school. In our work, we have discovered that poor White students, on average, outperform poor Black students, and this pattern persists at the middle and upper income levels as well. Even more alarming are data that indicate poor White students may outperform middle-income Black and Brown students.

The *"conservative" or "sociopathological model,"* which says that because the Civil Rights Movement removed legal barriers to Black advancement, "various social pathologies within the Black community (lumped under the euphemism 'Black culture') must be at fault" (Singham, 1998, p. 10). Thus, supporters of this model "tend to lecture Black Communities constantly about the need for a wholesale spiritual awakening to traditional virtues and the work ethic" (Singham, 1998, p. 10). The problem, however, with this approach is that the White critics are—in essence—asking the Black community to just "act White." As Singham (1998) continues, "Given the behavior of Whites during the time of slavery, to ask Blacks to regard Whites as role models for virtuousness seems presumptuous, to put it mildly" (p. 10).

The *"genetic model"* is the third view put forth to explain the achievement gap. For example, Herrnstein and Murray's (1994) *The Bell Curve* concludes that "educational disparity is a fact of nature, the result of long-term evolutionary selection that has resulted in Blacks' simply not having the genetic smarts to compete equally with Whites" (according to Singham, 1998, p. 10). Singham strongly refutes this view. Furthermore, this argument has been thoroughly debunked by extensive research, such as that presented by Kati Haycock (2003).

Educational Responsibility

To move beyond these refutable and hotly debated explanations and arrive at a deeper and more useful understanding of the racial achievement gap, educators need to stop placing blame on the places and people beyond their control. By doing this, they will avoid faulting children for who they are and what their background is. We advocate a new strategy because it encourages educators to engage in difficult self-assessment and to take responsibility for what they can control: the quality of their relationships with colleagues, students, and their families, both in the classroom and throughout the school community.

According to Linda Darling-Hammond (1997),

The fundamental problem is that we have pushed the current system as far as it can go, and it cannot go far enough. If we care about all students and about the fate of the society as a whole, we cannot ignore real problems or merely seek to "get around" the present system. We must re-create it so that it, in turn, reshapes the possibilities for the great majority of schools. (p. 27)

Two decades earlier, Tomas A. Arciniega (1977) put it this way:

Public education has successfully shifted the blame for the failure of schools to meet the needs of minority students on to the shoulders of the clients they purport to serve. They have pulled off the perfect crime, for they can never be held accountable, since the reason for failure in school is said to be the fault of poor homes, cultural handicaps, linguistic deficiencies, and deprived neighborhoods. The fact that schools are geared primarily to serve monolingual, White, middle-class and Anglo clients is never questioned. (p. 123)

We believe that the racial achievement gap exists and persists because fundamentally, schools are not designed to educate students of color, and educators continue to lack the will, skill, knowledge, and capacity to affirm racial diversity. Consequently, educators need to begin a deep and thorough examination of their beliefs and practices in order to "re-create" schools so that they become places where all students do succeed.

Change is tough—any change! Thus, another primary challenge to addressing racial achievement disparity is that school systems struggle with change. If school systems truly care about *all* children, then why have they not been more willing to address the achievement gaps? How can educators in good conscience allow a racial achievement gap to persist? Are they unaware of some of the inherent racial inequities or racial biases in the system? Or are they perhaps conscious of the inequities but unwilling to address them? It certainly seems easier not to deal with the hard work of change because it requires educators to be innovative in their search for a new solution and courageous in the face of those who wish to at least maintain and perhaps even perpetuate the status quo.

Janice E. Hale (2004) wrote recently that "it is hypocritical to talk about 'equal opportunity' when the system ensures never-ending advantages for upper-income White students" (p. 34). The disparity is easy to see; what remains invisible is a focused and concerted effort to adequately and successfully address the racial achievement gap.

THREE CRITICAL FACTORS

Through our fieldwork and research, we have defined three critical factors necessary for schools systems to close the racial achievement gap: passion, practice, and persistence. Without these critical factors, a system quickly disengages from an intentional desire to change how students are taught and supported in their learning. The three factors for closing the racial achievement gap can be described as follows.

Passion

Passion is defined as the level of connectedness educators bring to anti-racism work and to district, school, or classroom equity transformation. One's passion must be strong enough to overwhelm institutional inertia, resistance against change, and the system's resilience or its desire to maintain the status quo. Furthermore, passion is required to confront these challenges because our society as a whole—despite what may be said—continuously proves unwilling to support schools financially or politically to the degree that is needed to bring about deep and lasting change. But passion is insufficient if it is not translated into transformed relationships and practices that in turn prompt improved teaching and learning for every child, in every school, every day.

Practice

Practice refers to the essential individual and institutional actions taken to effectively educate every student to his or her full potential. Substantial knowledge and research-based practices exist about what works in the classroom for students of color. Educators need to develop and engage these skills. Because the most effective practices are infrequently amplified, the racial achievement gap might legitimately be seen as a teaching gap, even a racial teaching practice gap. Specifically, achievement disparities among White, Black, and Brown student groups can be defined as much by teachers' inability to recall and engage effective strategies as it is by students' inability to master the standards. Again, our work in schools provides evidence that educators have an insufficient repertoire of instructional practices to effectively teach students of color.

Persistence

Persistence involves time and energy. Rarely do we dedicate sufficient time to address the racial achievement gap. Persistence at the institutional level is the willingness of a school system to "stick with it" despite slow results, political pressure, new ideas, and systemic inertia or resistance to change. A persistent school system institutionalizes real school change with effective leadership, classroom implementation, and community partnerships. Individual educators who are persistent remain focused on equity and closing the racial achievement gap regardless of which direction the educational reform wind is blowing.

THE STRATEGY OF COURAGEOUS CONVERSATION

These three critical factors provide a philosophical context within which we will introduce to you Courageous Conversation, a strategy for addressing the various impacts of race on student achievement. Engaging the strategy of Courageous Conversation begins with a deep-seated *passion* to address a multitude of race matters in education and a commitment to the Four Agreements of Courageous Conversation. Beyond this, educators will *practice* the Six Conditions of Courageous Conversation, which provide a road map for participating in and facilitating interracial dialogue about race. Finally, as an anti-racist leader, you will exercise *persistence* in exploring the role of Courageous Conversation in systemic equity anti-racism transformation, which creates the lasting structures within which to achieve equity in your classroom, school, or school system.

Organization of This Book

Courageous Conversations is divided into three parts reflecting the three essential characteristics of anti-racist leadership: Passion, Practice, and Persistence. Part I, "Passion: An Essential Characteristic of Anti-Racist Leadership," explores the landscape of educational reform and exposes the issue of race as a phenomenon that affects the lives and learning of all children. In these chapters, we help the reader to focus on race in lieu of the traditional topics—such as poverty, language, and learning disabilities— that have long occupied educators' attention and have resulted in only unsatisfactory incremental systemic changes.

Part II, "Practice: The Foundation of Anti-Racist Leadership," takes the reader on a step-by-step journey into the race conversation, providing the language, markers, tools, and insights necessary to begin and stay in the dialogue.

Finally, in Part III, "Persistence: The Key to Anti-Racist Leadership," educators learn about the leadership that is necessary to close racial achievement gaps. Specific strategies for teachers, schools, and districts to use in the implementation of systemic equity anti-racism transformation, are provided, including organizational ideas that help teachers develop better ways to teach and help schools to embrace the communities they serve. The book concludes with a description of the work of the Lemon Grove School District and its success in implementing a systemwide Courageous Conversation.

We have included in each chapter prompts and exercises designed to help readers personally reflect on what they've learned. Use these questions to guide deeper examination of your own attitudes, beliefs, and actions. You might also ask a trusted friend or colleague to join you in conversations that help you reflect on your own thoughts and feelings. These are critical in helping you to deepen your understanding of race, its impact on students, and your own abilities to engage in anti-racist leadership.

Likewise, at the end of each chapter are implementation exercises for focused school- and systemwide professional learning. These will guide you and your colleagues in the immediate and effective application of the Courageous Conversation strategy. Follow the guidelines to conduct safer and more productive dialogues and activities. We encourage you to provide Courageous Conversation Journals for each participant in the activities so that they can reflect back on their learning, growth, and challenges.

This book provides a foundation for those educational leaders at the system and school level who are willing and ready to begin or accelerate their journey toward educational equity and excellence for all children. This includes superintendents, board members, district administrators, principals, team and teacher leaders, and engaged members of the community. It is designed to assist in facilitating effective dialogue about the racial issues that impact student achievement.

Language of Race

The language that we use in this book to define and discuss racial matters is the language that we have discovered to be most effective in our work with thousands of educators in this country and other parts of the world. We believe our language of choice will help you gain access to and find your voice in Courageous Conversations about race. Because language is at the heart of culture, it is essential that we establish common language around race while at the same time remain open to how our varied racial experiences shape our own vocabulary and comfortableness with the conversation in general.

The language surrounding racial issues has remained elusive precisely because constructive and Courageous Conversations about race occur infrequently in American culture. To address race, the language of race must become concrete so that school leaders can effectively guide the conversations that will assist them in eliminating the racial achievement gap.

As you enter into this conversation, please accept a certain degree of ambiguity regarding our use of language that defines and describes race. Working through the Six Conditions of Courageous Conversation in Part II, you will come to understand why we often refer to people's skin color rather than to their culture or ethnicity. Furthermore, we capitalize racial descriptors such as White, Black, and Brown. This is to acknowledge and place racial identity on a par with ethnic identity, such as Asian American and African American. Pay attention to when you experience personal dissonance with the terminology and take time to clarify what the words mean to you. Willingly use racial terms in your conversations to deeply examine race and its impact.

By using our framework, you can come to understand race in a personal and profound way. After this, you will discover how we translate these personal insights about race into practices that effectively narrow the racial achievement gap.

We are all learners, to some degree, in this examination of race. It matters not where you are on the continuum of racial understanding. What is important is your willingness to deeply explore your own racial identity and better empathize with the corresponding perspectives and experiences of the racial other. Consequently, we invite you, the reader, to join with us in this journey toward racial equity and anti-racist leadership.

PART I

Passion

An Essential Characteristic of Anti-Racist Leadership

> *The key here is not the kind of instruction but the attitude underlying it. When teachers do not understand the potential of the students they teach, they will underteach them no matter what the methodology.*
>
> —Lisa Delpit (1995a, p. 175)

Teaching is a demanding profession. It requires remarkable skill, substantial knowledge, and significant effort. It would take little effort to describe the technical requirements of teaching, but teaching is not a technical job. The very best practitioner in education will fail without the right attitude. Attitude underlies everything necessary in successful teaching. But what is the right attitude for engaging in the effort to close the racial achievement gap?

Passion is the key. Having worked with thousands of educators, we have observed that those teachers and administrators who are most proficient at teaching *all* students of *every* race also have a tremendous amount of passion for the work they do.

For us, equity is a characteristic to foster. In a school that strives to close the racial achievement gap, educators work toward promoting high achievement among all students and equitably providing the type of

11

instruction that each student needs. When considering your own attitude, the following question should be posed: Is equity really your passion?

Just as people can become anti-racist once they begin to develop an authentic need to include people of many races in their personal life, school leaders can become truly passionate for equity work as they discover a will to succeed with students of color in their school. This will or desire manifests itself as the driving and emotional force behind the work they do. Leaders with such a passion will begin to see equity as an essential characteristic of their school's success. They will clearly notice inequities where they exist and willingly focus on correcting them.

Educators need to locate this passion in order to transform schools. Observing schools with leaders who are truly passionate about equity is an incredible experience. These are amazing and dynamic schools that exude a great sense of community and enthusiasm. In these schools, continuous learning by all and high expectations for everyone—including the teachers—are everyday experiences. Conversely, in schools lacking that sense of passion for equity, feelings of pessimism, failure, and hopelessness are omnipresent. These buildings are full of toxic adults who stave off meaningful reforms, and they are deadly places for the large numbers of children of color who typically attend them.

School leaders need to decide where they stand in relation to equity, and if they do not yet have passion for it, they must find some; passion is a prerequisite to succeeding in a school with a diverse racial population. Nowhere in our description of passion for equity do we suggest that the educator must be a person of color. Culturally proficient and courageous educators of all races can succeed with *all* students, but only after they locate and nurture their passion for equity work.

The essence of passion is engagement and willingness to change. There is little honor in holding back, limiting participation, accepting mediocrity, and finding comfort in the status quo. With passion, we engage our soul and our being in this work, along with our mind and our body. With passion, we reclaim our hope and belief in the possibility of a future devoid of racial injustice—a future governed by equity and anti-racism. With passion, we will survive the conflict, the lack of support, and the passive resistance that comes with challenging institutionalized racism in our schools. And with passion, we will have the strength not only to *stand up for* what is right for our children, but to *do* what is right for them as well.

Passion is the cornerstone of anti-racist leadership. Emboldened with *passion*, enabled with *practice*, and strengthened by *persistence*, we can create schools in which *all* students achieve at higher levels, achievement gaps are narrowed, and the racial predictability and disproportionality of high and low student achievement are eliminated.

What's So Courageous About This Conversation?

I Dream

I am from a clash of Color,
From an idea of love, modeled for others' perception.
I see me as I am, but am hidden from others' views.
I am who I am, but a living contradiction to my peers.
I see life as a blessing, a gift granted to me.
Why should my tint describe me?
Why should my culture degrade me?
Why should the ignorance of another conjure my presence?
Too many times I've been disappointed by the looks,
By the sneers and misconceptions of the people who don't get me,
Who don't understand why it hurts.

I dream of a place of glory and freedom,
Of losing the weight of oppression on my back.
I dream of the enlightenment of people,
Of the opening of their eyes.
I dream for acceptance,
And for the blessing of feeling special just once.
One moment of glory . . . for the true virtue in my life.
For the glimmer of freedom, and a rise in real pride.

—Used with permission of Pablo Vega, Junior, Chapel Hill
High School, Chapel Hill, North Carolina

Reflection

What are your initial reactions to Pablo's poem? What parts of the poem resonate most for you? What parts of the poem present confusion for you? Judging from his work, what type of student do you believe Pablo to be? If Pablo were a student in your school, how might you respond to his voice? To what degree do you believe "Pablos" are attending your school?

Implicit in this poem are the moral reasons that schools need to address the gap in student achievement that exists among racial groups today. This poem was written by Pablo Vega, a student of Latino heritage, in roughly 15 minutes. His schoolwork indicated he was an average student. Yet, when given the opportunity during a Courageous Conversation workshop to share his personal feelings about his perceived place in society and the opportunities placed before him, he eloquently and effortlessly composed a poem that provides evidence of his extraordinary level of knowledge, skill, and intellect.

Pablo attended Chapel Hill High School in Chapel Hill, North Carolina. The Chapel Hill-Carrboro School District has been among the highest-performing school systems in North Carolina for many years. According to one local news outlet, WRAL (2003), Chapel Hill schools are among the very best. The district's reputation was well-known and publicized throughout the state and especially in the community. Using aggregated data, its average achievement scores consistently ranked in the top five in North Carolina in every subject.

Then, Chapel Hill took the courageous step of disaggregating the data and looking at the performance indicators by race. Students of color accounted for roughly 20% of the district's students, and the new data showed they were scoring far below their White and Asian counterparts (Singleton, 2002).

Nettie Collins-Hart, an assistant superintendent in the district, described the newly revealed gap this way:

> The discrepancy is more glaring because we are so high performing. We are the number one school district in the state. However, if you compared African American students, not only was there an achievement gap here—as there certainly is in most school districts—but our African American children were not, in many cases, performing at par with other school districts that didn't have the resources and the reputation that we had. (Singleton, 2002)

In fact, whereas the district's White students were ranked at the top statewide, the district's Black students scored below the average for all Black students in North Carolina.

Faced with this reality, some educators in Chapel Hill admitted several years ago that they might not be quite as great as they had thought they were when it comes to educating *all* students. They embraced the understanding that a truly first-rate school district is one where all students succeed, not just those of a certain race or background. At that time, they began to incorporate into their system the strategy of Courageous Conversation—a process that would help them foster success of *all* their students, no matter what they look like or where they live.

Today, the vast majority of stakeholders in the district, including board members, administrators, teachers, families, and community members, have participated in Courageous Conversation to build racial understanding and discover what they can collectively do to close the achievement gap. Chapel Hill embarked on a rigorous equity program with great success and has persisted in these efforts. As a result, the achievement gap between all groups is closing rapidly, as shown in recent district reporting (Chapel Hill-Carrboro School District, 2004).

Increasingly, every student in Chapel Hill-Carrboro city schools is guaranteed access to a successful education, including Pablo Vega and Black and Brown students like him. Pablo has experienced "the glimmer of freedom and a rise in real pride" described in his poem. He took valuable time in his senior year to participate in the professional development of educators in Chapel Hill; then, he graduated to attend a four-year college, and he intends to become a teacher.

Reflection

What achievement similarities and differences exist between your school system and the Chapel Hill-Carrboro City School District? In what ways could your system benefit from similar equity efforts?

COURAGEOUS CONVERSATION

To exercise the passion, practice, and persistence necessary to address racial achievement gaps, all of the members of the school community need to be able to talk about race in a safe and honest way. Courageous Conversation is a strategy for school systems to close the racial achievement gap. By engaging in this strategy, educators develop racial understanding, conduct an interracial dialogue about race, and address racial issues in schools. According to Margaret Wheatley (2002), "Human conversation is the most ancient and easiest way to cultivate the conditions for change—personal change, community, and organizational change" (p. 3).

As schools engage in open and honest dialogue about achievement disparities, they can effectively address the obstacles to success that exist for all students. This dialogue is an educational necessity. Speaking about what needs to happen to begin closing the achievement gap, Julie Landsman (2004) writes,

> Teachers need to meet with parents, members of the community, students, and colleagues to discuss racism in our schools, our cities, and our states. Through dialogue with our students and their communities, we may find ourselves looking at learning, cooperation, and achievement in a more complex, interesting way. (p. 29)

Defining Courageous Conversation

We have labeled the formal structure that exists for this type of dialogue Courageous Conversation, defined as

> utilizing the agreements, conditions, and compass to engage, sustain, and deepen interracial dialogue about race in order to examine schooling and improve student achievement.

Specifically, a Courageous Conversation

- *engages* those who won't talk.
- *sustains* the conversation when it gets uncomfortable or diverted.
- *deepens* the conversation to the point where authentic understanding and meaningful actions occur.

Courageous Conversation is a strategy for deinstitutionalizing racism and improving student achievement. It was created and developed by Glenn Singleton while he was directing a statewide California project aimed at redesigning the admissions process in the state university systems to align with high school restructuring. Recognizing that school reform initiatives and traditional diversity training fail to consider the impact of race and racism on student achievement disparities, Glenn created Courageous Conversation so that K through 12 and higher educators could examine why students of color were not gaining access to effective schooling and, subsequently, admission to college.

If we understand the need for dialogue about the racial achievement gap, the question becomes how we open ourselves up to have a Courageous Conversation about these questions:

Why do racial gaps exist?

What is the origin of the racial gaps?

What factors have allowed these gaps to persist for so many years?

Some educators may say, with reason, that today, people are talking about race and student achievement more than they ever have. The challenge, however, is to move beyond a basic awareness of the racial patterns found in student achievement data to ask *why* the data show a gap.

An additional question also needs to be asked: If it had not been for the federal No Child Left Behind legislation, would educators be talking about racial gaps in achievement at all? If the answer is no, what does this suggest about willingness to investigate the intersections of race, teaching and learning, and achievement? Absent Courageous Conversation, we have found that the authentic, sustainable transformation of beliefs, expectations, and practices cannot occur.

Four Agreements of Courageous Conversation

The initial action for educators entering into Courageous Conversations is to commit to practicing the Four Agreements. Educators must agree to

1. stay engaged.

2. speak your truth.

3. experience discomfort.

4. expect and accept non-closure.

In our professional development work with school leaders, we often establish norms to guide difficult dialogue. We have discovered, however, that these norms typically fall apart once race is put on the table. Specifically, when race surfaces as a topic for conversation, educators quickly become silent, defiant, angry, or judgmental. Courageous Conversation participants soon recognize that normal rules and guidelines for dialogue are insufficient in interracial discourse about race. Thus, the agreements serve as the bridge to engaging, sustaining, and deepening conversations about race.

Recognizing that these agreements exist as a foundation for the conversation enables those who would normally feel unsafe in such a conversation to feel safer, even while experiencing discomfort. Specifically, the agreements offer a safer space so that educators can engage their fears: for example, a White teacher who is afraid of offending or appearing racist or a principal of color who fears becoming angry or being labeled as oversensitive or too emotional. Collectively, the agreements serve as a conduit for more meaningful interracial dialogue.

The Four Agreements of Courageous Conversation are explored in greater detail in Chapter 3.

Six Conditions of Courageous Conversation

To support the Four Agreements that define *how* we are to have the conversation, the Six Conditions of Courageous Conversation guide participants through what they are supposed to talk about and what they need to be mindful of during the interracial dialogue. Consequently, the agreements define the process while the conditions outline the content and progression of Courageous Conversation.

The Six Conditions are as follows:

1. Establish a racial context that is personal, local, and immediate.

2. Isolate race while acknowledging the broader scope of diversity and the variety of factors and conditions that contribute to a racialized problem.

3. Develop understanding of race as a social/political construction of knowledge and engage multiple racial perspectives to surface critical understanding.

4. Monitor the parameters of the conversation by being explicit and intentional about the number of participants, prompts for discussion, and time allotted for listening, speaking, and reflecting Use the Courageous Conversation Compass (see Figure 2.1) to determine how each participant is displaying emotion—mind, body, and soul—to access a given racial topic.

5. Establish agreement around a contemporary working definition of race, one that is clearly differentiated from ethnicity and nationality

6. Examine the presence and role of Whiteness and its impact on the conversation and the problem being addressed

The Six Conditions are somewhat sequential as the First and Second Conditions serve to *engage* a conversation about race that previously had not existed. It is the way in which we "test the waters" to determine how ready we are to dialogue with others. The Third and Fourth Conditions *sustain* the conversation and help to keep it moving once we have established a willingness to engage. The Fifth and Sixth Conditions *deepen* the interracial dialogue about race by guiding us into the most difficult and least examined subject matters related to how we live and understand race and racial dominance in our society. The conditions serve as an important scaffold for an increasingly more difficult, provocative, and authentic interracial conversation about race.

These Six Conditions of Courageous Conversation are explored individually and in greater detail in Chapters 5 to 10.

The Courageous Conversation Compass

Linda Darling-Hammond (1997) has said, "In order to create a cohesive community and a consensus on how to proceed, school people must have the occasion to engage in democratic discourse about the real stuff of teaching and learning" (p. 336). Part of this "democratic discourse" is providing enough time and space in the Courageous Conversation so that every educator's perspective and experience can be listened to and affirmed. The Fourth Condition of Courageous Conversations asks us to use the Courageous Conversations Compass to determine the place of engagement at which each participant in the dialogue is processing the content.

We created the compass as a personal navigational tool to guide participants through these conversations. It helps them know where they are personally as well as to recognize the direction from which other participants come. Collectively, it leads them to a mutual understanding of their varied beliefs and opinions and helps them locate the sources of their emotion.

On the Courageous Conversation Compass, we have identified four primary ways that people deal with racial information, events, and/or issues: Emotional, Intellectual, Moral, and Social. These are the four points or cardinal directions of our compass.

Figure 2.1   The Courageous Conversation Compass

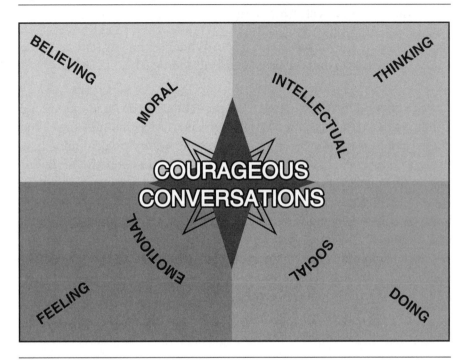

- *Emotionally,* we respond to information through *feelings,* when a racial issue strikes us at a physical level and causes an internal sensation such as anger, sadness, joy, or embarrassment.
- *Intellectually,* our primary response to a racial issue or information may be characterized by personal disconnect with the subject or a steadfast search for more information or data. Our intellectual response is often verbal and based in our best *thinking.*
- *Morally,* we respond from a deep-seated *belief* that relates to the racial information or event. This belief has to do with the rightness or wrongness of a given racial issue. The justifications for one's moral views are often situated in the "gut" and may not be verbally articulated.
- *Socially,* we connect and respond to racial information through our *doings* or what is most often characterized as specific behaviors and actions.

In a sense, emotional responses are seated in the heart, intellectual in the mind, moral in the soul, and social in the hands and feet. This compass together with the Six Conditions and Four Agreements fulfills the complete definition of Courageous Conversations.

Reflection

For the purposes of better understanding and personalizing the Courageous Conversation Compass, consider the following topics:

- Affirmative action
- Bilingual education
- O. J. Simpson trial
- Indian gaming

As you say each of the aforementioned phrases and think about its significance, where do you initially locate yourself on the compass? As you ponder the topic for a longer period of time and begin to connect it to your own personal experience, where do you travel on the compass? Do you experience significant or minimal movement?

A DIFFICULT CONVERSATION

Margaret Wheatley (2002) has asked, "What would it feel like to be listening to each other again about what disturbs and troubles us, about what gives us hope, about our yearnings, our fears, our prayers, and our children?" (p. 3). To gain full access to her question—*what would it feel like?*—we need to venture into a difficult conversation, one that clearly troubles educators and can make everyone downright uncomfortable. We believe that the ability to truly listen to and converse with each other will help educators improve education for *all* children—White included—and to better understand the racial experiences that impact their learning.

Educators typically have not examined and discussed race in their schools because they have feared not knowing how to go about this process correctly. Some justify inaction on racial achievement disparities by suggesting that no one knows how to impact them. Saying "we don't know how" allows educators to claim that they have done all they can do. Such suggestions do not produce improved results.

We suggest that the problem of educators not knowing what to do about racial achievement gaps or how to talk about race is not as devastating as the problem of educators failing to seek solutions to the gaps.

Implementation Exercise

Got Passion?

Time required: 45 minutes

Materials required: Courageous Conversation Journal for each participant and the following worksheet

1. Introduce the concept of Courageous Conversation with the following definition:

    Utilizing the agreements, conditions, and compass to engage, sustain, and deepen interracial dialogue about race in order to examine schooling and improve student achievement

2. Briefly describe the agreements, conditions, and compass and inform the group that they will explore these in further depth later.

3. Based on the explanation in Part I of this book, describe *passion* as it relates to equity work.

4. Divide staff members into small groups of three or four people with whom they work closely and give each member a copy of the following activity worksheet.

5. Have each member of your group fill out Box 1 of Figure 2.2 in response to the prompt

    What is a non-school-related activity about which I am truly passionate?

    Post these responses around the room to establish a large community.

6. Have each member fill out Box 2 in response to the prompt:

    What is it that I feel and that you would see as I engage in the activity about which I am passionate?

    Briefly share responses in the small groups.

7. Have each member fill out Box 3 with the following prompts:

   What is my personal definition of equity/anti-racism?

   What is our collective definition of equity/anti-racism?

   Briefly share responses in the small groups.

8. Determine as a large group a collective definition for both equity and anti-racism. Make sure that the educators address both terms.

9. Have each member fill out Box 4 with the following prompts:

   When I am engaging in equity/anti-racism work, what do I feel and what do you see?

   What qualities and characteristics are exhibited by school leaders who are engaging in equity/anti-racism work?

   In what ways do I personally exhibit these qualities and characteristics of equity/anti-racist leadership?

   Have participants discuss in their small groups what they have determined about personal passion for equity/anti-racism in their work in the school.

10. Have the larger group share reflections from small-group discussions.

11. Encourage participants to keep this exercise and future equity/anti-racism work in their Courageous Conversation Journal.

Figure 2.2   Got Passion?

1. My Passion	2. Looks and Feels Like
3. Equity/Anti-Racism	4. Leadership

Why Race?

Most of us remain trapped in the narrow framework of the dominant liberal and conservative views of race in America, which with its worn-out vocabulary leaves us intellectually debilitated, morally disempowered, and personally depressed. . . .

Our truncated public discussions of race fail to confront the complexity of the issue in a candid and critical manner. The predictable pitting of liberals against conservatives, Great Society Democrats against self-help Republicans, reinforces intellectual parochialism and political paralysis. . . .

We confine discussions about race in America to the "problems" Black people pose for Whites rather than consider what this way of viewing Black people reveals about us as a nation.

This paralyzing framework encourages liberals to relieve their guilty consciences by supporting public funds directed at "the problems"; but at the same time, reluctant to exercise principled criticism of Black people, liberals deny them the freedom to err. Similarly, conservatives blame the "problems" on Black people themselves—and thereby render Black social misery invisible or unworthy of public attention.

Hence, for liberals, Black people are to be "included" and "integrated" into "our" society and culture, while for conservatives they are to be "well behaved" and "worthy of acceptance" by "our" way of life. Both fail to see that the presence and predicaments of Black people are neither additions to nor defections from American life, but rather constitutive elements of that life.

—Cornel West (2001, p. 2)

> **Reflection**
>
> In what ways are the "presence and predicaments of Black people . . . constitutive elements of [American] life"? Does this also apply to other groups of color? How have the condition and experiences of Black people in America influenced your conservative and/or liberal views about race?

A rguably, great divisions exist between racial groups in the United States because we lack understanding that each group possesses a unique racial perspective, and we struggle to empathize with the racial others' unique racial experience. To expand on what West (2001) wrote, White Americans expect that people of color should be "integrated into White society and culture" and become "worthy of acceptance by the White way of life" and establish Whiteness as the acceptable standard.

The collective message from the dominant racial group to people of color is that the problem of race stems from their inability to thrive in "mainstream" society. Although individual responsibility is an admirable American ideal, people of color face an enormous challenge as they attempt to find a foothold in a nation that has never fully respected them or granted them equality.

THE PROBLEM OF THE COLOR LINE

The existence of a racial achievement gap is not shocking when you consider the day-to-day schooling reality for students of color. During their formative years, they must negotiate the psychological turmoil prompted by oppression and different status, while at the same time they are viewed by the school system and the larger society as a problem. Until teachers discover a love, empathy, and authentic desire to reach their students of color, these children will not develop to their full social, emotional, and academic potential. Likewise, as educators engage in racial equity work throughout the school system, they discover that their souls are nourished by the heightened engagement of their students of color.

According to W. E. B. DuBois (1903), "The problem of the twentieth century is the problem of the color line, the relations of the darker to the lighter races of men in Asia and Africa, in America and the islands of the sea" (pp. 15–16). This rings as true in the 21st century as it did when Dubois's text was first published in 1903. Without question, great strides have been made to establish equality through politics and law, but true racial equality in our habits of heart and mind remains elusive. To work toward equality requires tremendous effort on the part of all racial groups—the racially advantaged and the racially disadvantaged.

Racial inequality is not just a "Black problem" or a "Brown problem." It is a problem that impacts all of us. Thus, for White educators to claim rightfully that they are not racist, they must take action in bringing about true racial equality and insist on racial justice always and everywhere.

Education for All Students

The aim of this book is to help educators improve the achievement of *all* students while narrowing the gaps between the lowest- and highest-performing groups and eliminating the predictability and disproportionality of which racial groups occupy the highest and lowest achievement categories. To achieve this aim, educators, families, and community leaders must embrace the motto that is included in the pledge we ask our students to repeat each morning: . . . *with liberty and justice for all.*

If we truly want liberty and justice for everyone, we *all* must work toward attaining equality. People of color must continue to draw individual and institutional attention to racial inequity and demand racial equality. As recipients of racial advantage, White people must embrace their responsibility to challenge the awarding and acceptance of privilege. Absent these essential and interconnected actions, racial inequality, and thus tension and racial divisiveness, will continue to erode our aspiring democracy.

To quote Cornel West (2001) once again,

> To establish a new framework, we need to begin with a frank acknowledgement of the basic humanness and Americanness of each of us. And we must acknowledge that as a people—
> *E Pluribus Unum*—we are on a slippery slope toward economic strife, social turmoil, and cultural chaos. If we go down, we go down together. (p. 4)

Racial Responsibility

If White people are the primary guardians and recipients of racial privilege, they also bear significant responsibility for the perpetuation of racial inequality or racism. This is no insignificant prognosis for public education, given that the overwhelming majority of teachers, principals, superintendents, and board members are White. Despite the extraordinary and groundbreaking efforts of civil rights leaders to bring about racial equality, sustainable reform will occur only when White people individually and collectively embrace and encourage change. At the very least, White educators must allow change to happen. Without their active participation in this way, racial injustices will continue to be viewed by White people as a primary concern only for people of color.

Here is an excerpt from an Asian parent's letter to a Los Angeles elementary principal in reaction to tense discussions among parents and staff as to whether or not they would hire another staff member of color:

> The most hurtful racially charged comment said to me in my entire life wasn't *Jap* or *Chink* or *gook* or any of about a dozen things in my life I've been called. The most hurtful thing came from someone I liked and respected a great deal; someone who I thought was smart and compassionate. We were arguing about a hiring decision in which race was a factor. My argument was that she was in a position to help the cause of people of color and that it was incumbent upon her to do so. She told me that, "Racism is a big problem; it's a global problem. I resent you for trying to make it my problem."
>
> The translation to my ears? "I'm White. Racism is your problem, not mine. I don't have to deal with it if I don't want to." What infuriated me was the contrast in our situation—people of color have to deal with racism whether they want to or not. The conversation turned sour after that and I've never been able to forget that when push came to shove, that was what she felt.
>
> That comment stuck with me for years. That argument contains the underlying resentment many people of color feel towards White people; the feeling that *racism is your problem, not mine.* And, I assume, it's an underlying feeling many White people feel towards people of color: *Stop trying to make racism my problem.* I feel that sentiment lies beneath some of the parents' unwillingness to go along with the changes [at the school].
>
> I submit that with racial inequities continuing to worsen and with de facto segregation continuing to worsen, we're slouching towards another race riot or worse—something as inevitable to me as the next earthquake. And at that point, it will become obvious that racism is all of our problem.

Reflection

What are your initial reactions to this Asian parent's voice? Do you believe that these sentiments may be shared by parents of color in your school system? What data might you use as evidence to support your belief? What personal action might you take in response to this parent's letter and other people of color's related concerns?

The words that this Asian parent chose to engage the principal of her child's school are central to addressing racial achievement gaps in schools. The most productive and progressive society is one in which every member has full and unencumbered access to academic success and emotional security. When one group feels marginalized, everybody is affected—including those who are in positions of power and privilege, who often perceive themselves to be unaffected by the experiences of the underserved. White Americans are born into a social position in which they must assure people of color and students of color that the dominant society has their best interests at heart. The cost of not offering this assurance is a continuation of the present racial division, de facto segregation, and disparate educational outcomes. In important discussions about how to improve our society and how to better our schools, race matters.

THE RACIAL GAP

The most troublesome achievement gap is the racial gap—the difference in student achievement between White and Asian students and their Black, Latino, Native American, Southeast Asian, and Pacific Islander counterparts. Without question, poverty and wealth impact student achievement as well. Statistically, however, even within the same economic strata, there is an achievement gap based on race. The University of California (1998), together with the College Board, prepared a study that vividly captures the racial gaps that appear when average SAT scores are broken down both by family income and by race/ethnicity (see Figure 3.1). While this study involves only applicants to the freshman class at one large public institution, the findings seem to hold more far-reaching implications about the intersection of race, income, and achievement across the nation.

Some readers might wonder whether these data from 1995 reflect the current situation. While we would have preferred to use more current data, the College Board and most educational institutions rarely provide

Figure 3.1   Average SAT Scores by Parental Income and Race/Ethnicity

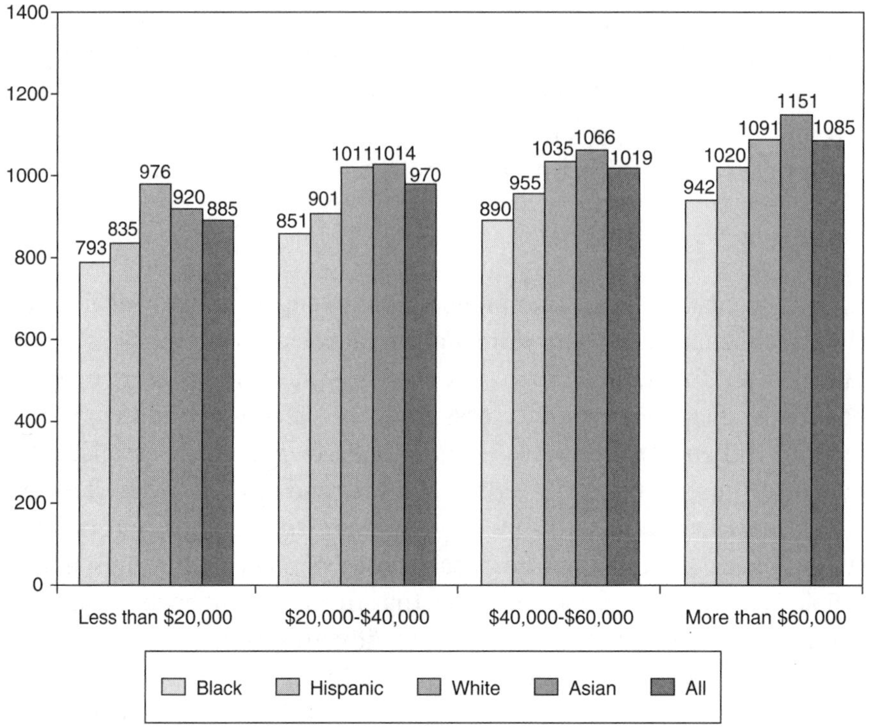

Source: National Center for Education Statistics, U.S. Department of Education.

data for public consumption that compare by race, income, and achievement. The University of California (UC) study was quite rare, and, in spite of the intervening decade, we believe that the study continues to offer relevant information about today's racial and income achievement patterns. For those who remain unconvinced, we ask what significant racial reforms have occurred in the K through 12 system and in the American economic structure over the past 10 years that would create a dramatic shift in the data.

As clearly shown in Figure 3.1, income does impact achievement: The scores of all races improve as their family income increases. However, wealth or poverty alone fails to fully explain the racial achievement gap, which persists irrespective of income level.

In most studies and reports, achievement gaps are addressed in terms of economic differences with little or no connection made to race. The UC data, which shows the intersectionality of race and income, reveals important subtleties about racial achievement gaps. First, at every income level, Black and Brown students are outperformed by White students. Specifically, Black students are predictably the lowest-performing group at every level. Second, such data help us to see the astonishing achievement disparity existing between Black and White students who are equally poor. Third, we see that poorer White students actually outperform middle-income Black and Brown students. Consequently, even if we were to project the data to students in families with incomes of $200,000—clearly a greatly diminished pool of Black and Brown families—the racial gap would most likely persist.

To suggest that the achievement gaps evidenced in the UC study of SAT scores has nothing to do with race or racism stands in the way of a complete explanation of the disparity within and between income levels. Of course, the study also provides potential evidence of the inherent cultural biases in the SAT and suggests that institutional racism is deeply imbedded in the American education. White students achieve scores that are quite similar across a broad income spectrum—differing by slighty more than 100 points. By comparison, the scores of all groups of color show substantial change from lowest- to highest-income groups: for Blacks, approximately 150 points; for Latinos, by almost 200 points; and for Asians, more than 230 points. In addition, White students predictably and measurably have higher achievement at the lowest-income level. Why is this so? To address this question, we must consider ways in which the SAT and other standardized assessments of educational progress favor White students.

Socioeconomics and Race

When discussing socioeconomic background, it is important to consider the full weight of the descriptor. The primary emphasis in considering socioeconomic background is placed on financial status—the *economic* half. Equally important, however, is the *socio* status, the aspect related to broader cultural nuances located in a person's current and previous environments. Exploring students' socioeconomic status is an invitation for educators to dialogue about their cultural and economic background, where culture must include racial identity.

For people of color, the concepts of culture and race are virtually synonymous if not deeply overlapping. Furthermore, people of color are often identified by their racial/cultural identity first and then by their economic background. Although author Glenn Singleton is a middle-class Black man, he is seen in society's eyes as Black first and perhaps middle class second. The *socio* or racial/cultural status will always outweigh or trump the *economic* status in our race-conscious society; nevertheless, members of the dominant racial culture tend to search for and acknowledge primarily economic differences when explaining social stratification and academic achievement disparities. Why is it that educators struggle to recognize that students' economic status is influenced, modified, and governed by their families' racial/cultural identity?

Furthermore, according to longitudinal academic data, the students' *socio* or racial/cultural background appears to have a more powerful impact on participation and performance than their economic status. We believe this is because these racial/cultural factors significantly impact students' vision of the future and their expectations about what school will and will not offer them. We hold that these racial/cultural elements are primary factors in the persistence of the racial achievement gap. Later in this book, we will explore the notion of racial/cultural status in greater detail.

Addressing the Racial Gap

Courageous Conversation serves as a strategy to eventually eliminate these racial achievement gaps. Furthermore, such conversations help build the passion educators, students, and families need to address systemic racial inequities and the resulting achievement inequality. Based on our partnerships with numerous school systems, we have found the racial achievement gap to be the most difficult gap to address. However, we have witnessed that when educators make dramatic progress toward narrowing the gaps between students of different races, they also succeed at closing all related gaps, for example, linguistic and economic gaps.

Consider the evidence in the most recent report from the Chapel Hill-Carrboro School District (2005) in North Carolina. This district has engaged in Courageous Conversation for five years as a primary strategy for addressing racial achievement gaps. Not only has the Chapel Hill-Carrboro School District shown tremendous improvement in reducing racial achievement disparities, but it has made significant progress toward closing other gaps as well. In 2002, when schools were first required to meet federal Average Yearly Progress goals, only four schools in the Chapel Hill district were successful. Just two years later, 14 of the 15 schools in the district met the national goals and were recognized as "distinguished schools" on statewide rankings. According to the Chapel Hill-Carrboro School District (2004), "The district as a whole showed a 94.2 percent proficiency rate, a statistic which included the district's students with exceptional education needs (Special Education) and students with limited

English proficiency. In five schools, more than 95 percent of the students demonstrated proficiency on the tests."

RACE AS A FACTOR IN EDUCATION

As expectations, opportunities, resources, and access become equitable across all racial groups, the gaps close because all students are supported in the differentiated ways necessary to achieve success. It is our belief that the most devastating factor contributing to the lowered achievement of students of color is institutionalized racism, which we recognize as the unexamined and unchallenged system of racial biases and residual White advantage that persist in our institutions of learning.

Reflection

To what degree do you and your colleagues believe race impacts student achievement? To what degree has race been a factor that is investigated in your school system's effort to address achievement disparity? Has this been an effort embraced by *all* educators—White included?

When schools address the issue of race head-on, dramatic results occur. Take, for example, Del Roble Elementary School in San Jose, California, a school of primarily Black, Latino, White, and Asian students. Del Roble, like many schools throughout the country, is characterized by a high rate of student transience and a large population of English language learners. Predictably, Del Roble has little if any categorical funding to support efforts in developing teachers to deliver a culturally responsive instructional program.

After disaggregating school data and discovering significant gaps between the various subgroups of students, the staff at Del Roble joined with the community to begin using the Four Agreements, Six Conditions, and Compass of Courageous Conversation. This new language enabled teachers to examine instructional practices, a hallmark of creating an equitable school environment. In the case of Del Roble, educators, students, and families have successfully reduced their school's achievement gaps by focusing primarily on how students of different races experience teaching and learning. Evidence of their dramatic improvement is shared in the official school description written by the school's principal, Yvette Irving:

It is said that, in dreams, an oak tree symbolizes longevity, stability, strength, tolerance, wisdom, and prosperity. "Del Roble" is Spanish for "of the oak." It also names our school and represents all of the characteristics of the students, staff, and community in which it resides. Del Roble has its roots in local history having just celebrated its 30th year in existence. It is a stabilizing force for the community acting as a community center for adult education, neighborhood meetings, youth sporting events, and an evacuation site in times of need. The tree trunk is created by the staff who work inside the walls of the school, with support from the Oak Grove School District central office, and a community of parents, neighbors, and businesses that give it strength. Wisdom, emanating from the intentional and unwavering commitment to equity in access and outcomes for all students, is found in the Del Roble branches. The result—academic excellence—is achieved through acceleration in place of remediation, and differentiation rather than homogeneity. The core values of Quality Performance, Life-long Learning, Respect, Positive Interdependence, and Integrity are practiced by staff and student alike, and act as the leaves that blanket the children as they enter the school. These core values bring with them a tolerance for those who are different in ways both visible and unseen

When you look at the accurate but impersonal statistics reflecting the Del Roble community you will find the following: 53% or 278 students participate in the NSLP (National School Lunch program), and we have a 23% mobility rate. 36% or 185 students are English Learners (EL). 48% of students have a primary language spoken at home that is not English, and 24 different languages are spoken on campus. Our racial diversity is reflected in 12% African American, 39% Latino, 20% Asian, 20% White, and 9% Other. Nationally, research implies that these statistics put the school at a disadvantage. The staff and community of Del Roble Elementary look at these statistics as our prosperity. With such diversity in the students who enter the doors of the school, the staff demonstrates innovation, collaboration, and determination as they educate and nurture the whole child.

The results of seizing this opportunity and implementing a comprehensive, standards aligned program in conjunction with an equity focus resulted in another set of "cold hard facts." Last year, 2002–2003, the school's Academic Performance Index (API) based on the state Standardized Testing and Reporting (STAR) results demonstrated a 43 point schoolwide growth from 712 to 754, compared with the prior year. Some subgroups exceeded overall school gains, with a 59 point growth for Latino students, 51 for Asian students and 23 for White students. The API also documented a 59-point growth for socioeconomically disadvantaged students. The school has the vision of *accelerating the rate of achievement of Latino and Black students, while sustaining the continued growth of their White and Asian counterparts.* This has been accomplished within the parameters of a limited school budget, since Del Roble receives no federal Title I funding, and with a staff wherein 65% of the teachers have 5 years or less experience. The school has also demonstrated success in increasing parent and community involvement, bringing back former Del Roble students as volunteers, developing partnerships with local businesses, and reducing disciplinary referrals. In addition we have created systemic change with racial representation in GATE (Gifted and Talented Education) now proportionate to the school enrollment, as it is in special education. The school's passionate belief is its responsibility to educate the whole child. Thus, the staff pursues professional development that not only supports them in effective teaching with standards aligned instructional materials, but that also helps them to foster a safe, happy, and healthy student. The school models what it hopes to teach its pupils. With the determination of staff, students and parents, the vision becomes a reality.

The shared goal of staff and community is that each child who enters Del Roble leaves as a well-rounded, well-developed, life-long learner. This success is measured not only by the school's test results, but also in what each child becomes. By both measurements Del Roble has proven to be a success. "From little acorns, great oaks grow."

—Yvette Irving

In addition to standardized test data, Del Roble uses a second statistical analysis to measure whether student achievement growth is equitable across all racial groups. Using district and state data already disaggregated by race, Del Roble teachers calculate an *opportunity gap*, a statistic that compares rates of progress toward proficiency among racial subgroups. The opportunity gap measures the percentage of students in each grade who have already reached proficiency in comparison to the percentage of students who seem to be progressing too slowly to reach proficiency by the time they finish elementary school. As shown in Figure 3.2, Del Roble's opportunity gaps from the 2001–2002 school year ranged from 42.5% in second grade to 25.5% in fifth grade.

During those years, Black and Latino students were progressing at a slower rate toward proficiency than their White and Asian counterparts by a minimum of 25%. The school's improvement goal was to have all students reach proficiency by the end of sixth grade, and—as shown by these statistics—that did not seem likely to occur. At least that was the case

Figure 3.2   2001–2002 Del Roble Math Proficiency Versus Opportunity Gap

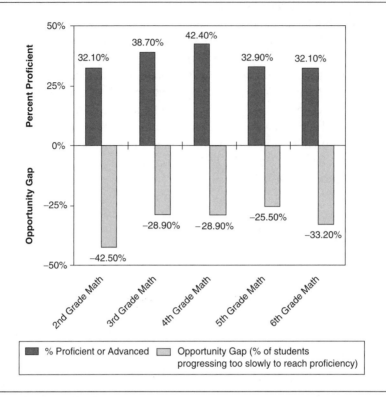

Source: Oak Grove School District.

until Del Roble educators began addressing the institutionalized racial challenges inherent in their school culture, climate, program, and structures.

The administrators and teachers at Del Roble created a dramatic turnaround in student achievement by acknowledging that racial biases existed in their own work and that these biases made it difficult for some students of color groups to succeed. The staff found these biases to be most pervasive in special education and GATE designation, hiring practices, and the teacher-classroom assignment process. In further addressing racial bias, teachers examined the curriculum used in their classrooms to see if the literature, for example, related to the culture of all students. The staff began to surface and share methods used by teachers who were succeeding with all students and to replicate those practices throughout the grade levels. Furthermore, Del Roble staff members actively fostered and nurtured relationships with families of color who had not traditionally been involved in school affairs. Most important, through the use of Courageous Conversation, the entire staff became honest about their racial beliefs, expectations, judgments, and fears.

As a result of these efforts, the Del Roble community completely eliminated the opportunity gap in only one year's time. Concurrently, they also raised overall proficiency by an average of 15% per grade. This is not to say that all students suddenly were performing at the same level. What it does say, however, is that every student, regardless of racial background, was accelerating toward proficiency at an acceptable rate—the gaps closed because traditionally lower-performing student groups began progressing rapidly toward mastery of the standards, as shown in Figure 3.3.

By closing the opportunity gap, the school could now boast that by sixth grade, every student would have the knowledge and skills necessary to succeed in middle school. In other words, no children would be left behind. By promoting equitable/anti-racist education in their school, Del Roble closed the poverty gap, gender gap, and English language learning gap. By addressing race as an essential and foundational issue, Del Roble dealt effectively with *all* known factors impacting student performance.

Figure 3.3   2002–2003 Del Roble Math Proficiency Versus Opportunity Gap

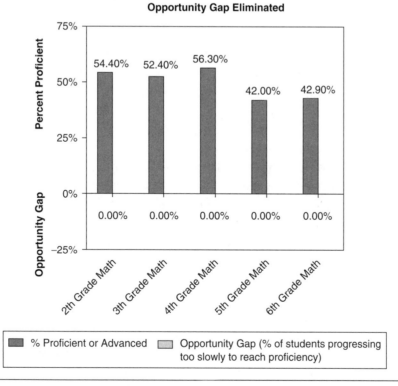

Source: Oak Grove School District.

> **Reflection**
>
> Based on what you have read, what would you suspect to be the cultural (i.e., attitudes and behaviors) and structural (i.e., programs and policies) reforms that enabled Del Roble Elementary School to eliminate the racial gap? To what degree do you see similar reforms being instituted in your school system?

DEALING WITH RACE

Recognizing that race is a significant factor impacting achievement requires that educators establish common understandings around racial issues. Too often, however, it seems that educators are reluctant to develop such understandings and instead blame the students themselves for the racial achievement gaps. Mano Singham (1998) explains this phenomenon in the following way:

> There is no real problem in the delivery system as such [especially in their own classroom] but only in the way that is received by different groups: that is, Black students don't respond to education in the proper manner. An alternative explanation is that the primary problem lies not in the way Black children view education but in the way we teach all children, Black, White, or other. (p. 12)

Many educators struggle to take personal and professional responsibility when it comes to meeting the needs of students of color who are not succeeding. Instead, they tend to focus on factors external to the school for explaining students' low achievement rather than examining their own instructional practices.

When dealing with issues of race, educators must become culturally proficient in relationships with students and families of varied racial backgrounds, experiences, beliefs, and understandings. As characterized by Lisa Delpit (1995a), teachers need to recognize "the haze of [our] own cultural lenses" (p. xv). Accordingly, as educators persist in Courageous Conversation and learn to address race more effectively, they will discover the limitations of their own views and recognize the validity of others'—even if some perspectives are radically different than their own. These different viewpoints, however, are not necessarily proof of racial division.

More often, they merely serve as evidence that a person's racial/cultural lens encourages him or her to view the world accordingly and perhaps differently than someone of another racial background.

Addressing the impact of race in education is not a "feel good" experience. Nor is it an attempt to make White educators feel guilty, promote pity for people of color, or extract revenge on their behalf. The use of Courageous Conversation provides the foundation for a systemic strategy to build responsibility through more thorough and authentic personal inquiry and engagement by educators, students, families, and the broader community. Educators participate in this difficult work for the sake of their students. Schools need to become places where effective education is guaranteed to every child. Ruth Johnson (2002) puts it the following way:

> It is about educators, students, and parents understanding the consequences of under preparation. It is about pointing out how and why some groups are under-prepared. Ultimately, it's about transforming the expectations and behaviors currently present in many schools and systems so that there are high-level options for all students. (p. 32)

ESTABLISHING COMMON LANGUAGE AROUND RACE

Developing and using common language in conversations about race helps establish critical understandings around how racial issues impact schooling. This is not to suggest that a single definition is available or even that one must be embraced. We do, however, believe that it is important that we provide a clear understanding of the meanings we intend when we use racial terminology.

Race, Racism, Racist

We refer to *race* as the socially constructed meaning attached to a variety of physical attributes including but not limited to skin and eye color, hair texture, and bone structures of people in the United States and elsewhere. Thus, *racism,* generically speaking, can be defined as beliefs and an enactment of beliefs that one set of characteristics is superior to another set (e.g., white skin, blonde hair, and blue eyes are more beautiful than brown skin, brown eyes, and brown hair). Continuing with this decontextualized definition, a *racist* would be any person who subscribes to these beliefs and perpetuates them intentionally or unconsciously.

Reflection

Do you personally resonate with our definitions of *race, racism,* and *racist?* How are these definitions similar to or different from your own?

The aforementioned definitions work on the level of pure theory, but when we view *race, racism,* and *racist* through the prism of historical and contemporary American culture, and perhaps more broadly through tenets of Western culture, we can introduce a far more exact definition of *racism.* We believe that racism is the conscious or unconscious, intentional or unintentional enactment of racial power, grounded in racial prejudice, by an individual or group against another individual or group perceived to have lower racial status.

The scholars Gerald Pine and Asa Hilliard (1990) implicate far more people in perpetuating the debilitating realities of racism:

> Racism describes the combination of individual prejudice and individual discrimination, on the one hand, and institutional policies and practices, on the other, that result in the unjustified negative treatment and subordination of members of a racial or ethnic group. By convention, the term racism has been reserved to describe the mistreatment of members of racial and ethnic groups that have experienced a history of discrimination. *Prejudice, discrimination, and racism do not require intention.* (p. 595)

What we find most powerful in Pine and Hilliard's definition is the fact that racism does not require *intent.*

Reflection

How does Pine and Hilliard's definition of racism compare to your own? Based on this definition, do you perpetuate racism? If so, how? If not, why?

In his article entitled *Racism,* Julian Weissglass (2001) broadly explores the nature of racism, its implications, and its distinction from the basic concept of prejudice:

Racism is the systematic mistreatment of certain groups of people (often referred to as people of color) on the basis of skin color or other physical characteristics. This mistreatment is carried out by societal institutions, or by people who have been conditioned by the society to act, consciously or unconsciously, in harmful ways toward people of color. Racism is different from prejudice. A person of color can hurt a White person because of prejudice. The difference is that in this country, people of color face systematic and ongoing personal and institutionalized biases every day. (p. 49)

This description expands racism greatly by establishing it as the systemic perpetration of prejudice toward members of a particular race. It is important to note that for these acts to become systemic, they must emanate from the dominant race. Other groups do not have the racial power, presence, and position necessary to maintain the prejudicial acts over time and throughout society without abatement. Weissglass (2001) concludes by quoting Shirley Chisholm, America's first Black congresswoman, who said that "racism is so universal in this country, so widespread and deep-seated, that it is invisible because it is so normal" (p. 49).

Reflection

What reaction do you have to Weissglass's and Chisolm's assertions that racism is systemic, universal, invisible, and perpetrated by the dominant race? In what ways does this suggest that only White people can be racist? What is your belief?

Institutionalized Racism

Racism becomes institutionalized when organizations—such as a school or a school district—remain unconscious of issues related to race or more actively perpetuate and enforce a dominant racial perspective or belief, for example, that racism is not a problem worthy of attention or redress. Despite efforts to reduce individual and collective racist acts, institutionalized racism persists in American culture and its educational systems due to educators' inaction as well as actions considered harmful to students of color. To serve students of color equitably, it is essential to challenge institutionalized racism and vigilantly reduce individual racial prejudices.

In explaining *institutionalized racism* in her landmark book, *White Awareness,* Judith H. Katz (2003) first quotes the *American Heritage Dictionary* definition of *racism:*

1. The belief that race accounts for differences in human character or ability and that a particular race is superior to others.

2. Discrimination or prejudice based on race.

And then adds the following qualification:

Prejudice plus power. (p. 53)

According to this definition, institutionalized racism equates to prejudice connected with the *power* to protect the interests of the discriminating racial group.

In further defining the nature of this power, Lindsey, Robins, and Terrell (2003), in their book *Cultural Proficiency,* define institutionalized racism as "the power to create an environment where that belief [racism] is manifested in the subtle or direct subjugation of the subordinate ethnic groups through a society's institutions" (p. 248).

It is important to consider this discussion of institutionalized racism as it pertains to schools. Rarely is intentional discrimination the central problem in the teacher-student relationship; rather, the discrimination includes unquestioned assumptions on the part of the institution within which these interactions take place. These assumptions—such as Asian students are better at math, Latino parents don't support their kids in school, or advanced placement classes are too difficult for Black students— are at the heart of the racial achievement gap. Thus, institutionalized racism means to allow these negative assumptions to persist unchallenged by those having positional power. Unquestioned assumptions about the attitudes and abilities of student of color and their families are the basis for detrimental instructional practices that foster and preserve racial inequities in schools.

Henze, Katz, Norte, Sather, and Walker (2002) provide a shorthand formula to describe this type of institutionalized racism:

Racism = racial prejudice + institutional power

They go on to establish a distinct difference between *individualized racial prejudice* and *institutionalized racism:*

Certainly, any individual can perpetrate acts of racial prejudice towards another individual. Thus, African Americans as individuals can be racially prejudiced against White people, Asians can be racially prejudiced against Latinos, and so on. But African Americans collectively do not have the social, political, or economic power in the United States to alter the collective racial experience of White people. So in that sense, no matter how much racial prejudice individual African Americans or other people of color might project towards White Americans, truly they cannot be said to be practicing institutional racism unless they are actively supporting the maintenance of racial power for White people. (p. 9)

Reflection

In what ways do you resonate with these scholars' definitions of *racism* and *institutionalized racism?* In what specific ways are their definitions similar to or different from your own?

The starting point in deinstitutionalizing racism is to believe first and foremost that racism exists. The vast majority of school administrators and school board members, past and present, are White. Consequently, most educators—even those of color—are supervised and evaluated by a White person. When this is the case in a particular school or school system, White educators experience a sense of racial superiority—whether consciously or unconsciously—manifested in their assumption that they uniquely possess certain skills and knowledge necessary for "appropriately" dealing with all students, parents, or even administrators and other teachers.

Because White educators feel connected to the person who has always been in charge, their support of the White racial status quo equates to normal operational procedure. An educator, parent, or student of color who challenges the White racial status quo is seen as a "troublemaker," "angry," or an "outsider." Through Courageous Conversation, educators are able to discover a more effective response in which the predominantly White-led system authenticates the criticism rather than viewing it as an attack or dismissing the people of color rendering the critique.

Institutionalized racism also leads to feelings of racial inferiority for students of color and racial superiority among White students. For example, when White students enter an advanced placement classroom and see few if any students of color, they are unconsciously indoctrinated into

White intellectual supremacy. These notions are typically unchallenged by educators, even as students of color learn about these classes, made up mostly of White students, and labeled as the "smart," "honors," "gifted," "advanced," "GATE," or "best" class. Not seeing others who look like them in these classes, the students of color will see themselves as being incapable of performing at equally high levels and feel unwanted in such classes or unworthy of taking them. Furthermore, because these classes are often taught by the more seasoned and respected teachers—the teachers who express passion for their work—the students of color are essentially taught by the system that they are *worth less* than White students.

According to Weissglass (2001), institutionalized racism fosters feelings of inferiority for students of color in the following ways:

(1) The incorporation into institutionalized policies or practices of attitudes or values that work to the disadvantage of students of color (for example, differential allocation of resources, or tracking practices that consign many students of color to low tracks with less experienced teachers, from which they can seldom escape).

(2) The unquestioned acceptance by the institution of White-middle-class values (for example, the scarcity of authors of color in many secondary schools' English curricula).

And (3), schools' being passive in the face of prejudiced behavior that interferes with students' learning or well-being (for example, not addressing harassment or teasing, or meeting it with punishment instead of attempting to build communication and understanding). (p. 49)

These unquestioned actions in schools are the most damaging aspects of institutionalized racism because they stigmatize and marginalize students of color, thus creating gross inequities between them and their White counterparts. To eradicate these harmful practices, school communities must focus their efforts on intentionally and explicitly addressing systemic racial disparities, wherever they may exist.

Reflection

Considering the aforementioned definitions of *racism* and *institutionalized racism*, where do you notice these phenomena most obviously and dangerously existing in your school system?

Anti-Racism

In coming to understand racism and institutionalized racism, it is not enough simply to become *non*-racist. Educators of all races should become *anti*-racists, which means to actively fight racism and its effects wherever they may exist.

Anti-racism can be defined as conscious and deliberate efforts to challenge the impact and perpetuation of institutional White racial power, presence, and privilege. It is critical that our examination of institutionalized White racism is not viewed as being against White people; rather, it is a way in which people of all races can gain the same level of access and privileges that White people tend to demand, to feel entitled to, and to take for granted. Anti-racism means working toward a realization of the ideals that the United States professes are true for all citizens. Specifically, anti-racism means that life, liberty, and the pursuit of happiness are guaranteed to people of color as well as White people.

To be anti-racist is to be active. Simply claiming to be non-racist and to "not see race in others" passively allows racism to continue. To close the achievement gap, educators need to be aggressively anti-racist. Anti-racism is a deep, personal, and ongoing analysis of how each and every one of us perpetuates injustice and prejudice toward those who are not members of the dominant race.

Weissglass (2001) calls schools in which there are active anti-racist efforts under way "healing communities." In these environments,

> a wide range of anti-racism work will be going on. Educators will be identifying how their unaware bias affects their students, challenging any attitudes of low expectations, working with parents to help them support their children's learning, and identifying how racism becomes institutionalized in policies and practices. They will be questioning their curricula and pedagogy and working to make them more engaging to students of different cultures. (p. 50)

Anti-racist schools teach the history of how oppressed peoples have been treated in this country and support students of color and their families to challenge and heal from internalized racism. Anti-racist schools move beyond the celebration of diversity and create communities in which it is possible for students to talk about how they experience unfairness and discrimination and to heal. In these healing communities, adults' highest priority is caring about students and their learning.

As White educators are prompted to examine race and practice anti-racism, they need to be aware that White privilege counteracts their engagement by offering the opportunity to walk away from this conversation on race at times when it gets tough or personally uncomfortable. People of color face racial injustice daily and simply cannot avoid dealing with racism. Consequently, it is perhaps the greater injustice toward their colleagues and friends of color when White people choose not to deal with racial issues. To willingly partake of White privilege and be a bystander to racial inequity is actually to participate in the perpetuation of racism. Likewise, White educators who actively disengage from conversations about improving the achievement of students of color are racist because anti-racism requires active challenges to institutionalized White racial power, presence, and privilege. There is no gray zone in anti-racist work.

As Oprah Winfrey has said, "Racism is the day-to-day wearing down of the spirit. Anti-racism is the day-to-day goin' after the little things."

Equity

Another critical term for educators to develop meaning around when doing anti-racism work in schools is *equity.* Achieving true equity for all students must be a central and essential component of any attempt to close the racial achievement gap. Lacking a focus on equity, educators might experience a widening disparity in achievement among students because the root causes of the gap remain unaddressed. In the long run, this will serve only to further disenfranchise students and parents of color. All students can benefit from a focus on equity because an equitable school system is one that works to address the needs of each individual child.

We have developed the following definition for equity:

Educational equity is raising the achievement of all students while

- narrowing the gaps between the highest- and lowest-performing students; and
- eliminating the racial predictability and disproportionality of which student groups occupy the highest and lowest achievement categories.

Reflection

How does this definition of equity compare to the definition you developed in the previous chapter?

Equity is far more than a state of being or an abstract ideal. Rather, it is an operational principle that enables educators to provide whatever level of support is needed to whichever students require it. In the classroom, this means providing each and every student with what each individually needs to learn and succeed.

Furthermore, there is a distinct difference between *equality* and *equity*. According to DeCuir and Dixson (2004),

> In seeking *equality* rather than *equity*, the processes, structures, and ideologies that justify inequity are not addressed and dismantled. Remedies based on equality assume that citizens have the *same* opportunities and experiences. Race, and experiences based on race, are not equal. Thus, the experiences that people of color have with respect to race and racism create an unequal situation. *Equity*, however, recognizes that the playing field is *unequal* and attempts to address the inequality. (p. 29)

Equity is not a guarantee that all students *will* succeed. Rather, it assures that *all* students will have the opportunity and support to succeed. In an equitable system, the barriers that inhibit student progress are removed. Students of color and their families can rest assured that the school will meet their needs to the same degree it meets White students' needs. Equity does not mean that every student receives an equal level of resources and support toward his or her educational goals. Rather, equity means that the students of greatest need receive the greatest level of support to guarantee academic success.

DO WE HAVE THE WILL?

As educators, we need to ask ourselves, Do we have the *will* to educate all children? As Asa Hilliard (1995) suggests, providing quality education for all children is not a question of educators' experience or academic degrees conferred; rather, it is a question of their personal willingness to fulfill their professional responsibilities.

> The knowledge and skills to educate all children already exist. Because we have lived in a historically oppressive society, educational issues tend to be framed as technical issues, which denies their political origin and meaning. . . . There are no pedagogical barriers to teaching and learning when willing people are prepared and made available to children. (p. 200)

> ### Reflection
>
> Do you believe that the knowledge and skills to educate *all* students already exist in education? To what degree do you feel that your school system has the will or passion to meet the needs of lower-achieving students of color?

Race matters in society and in our schools. The knowledge base to effectively teach all students—regardless of their race—already exists. Educators must decide whether to embrace this knowledge, examine their personal beliefs and practices, and engage in anti-racism for the benefit of their students. Hilliard (1995) continues, "If we embrace a will to excellence, we can deeply restructure education in ways that will enable teachers to release the full potential of all our children" (p. 200).

By understanding race and its impact on schooling, as well as by having a vision of equity and the courage to be anti-racists, educators will fortify their will. Only then can they truly recognize that to unleash the full potential of all children is within reach of any educator. As posed by Ruth Johnson (2002), "When asked what they would want for their own children, most educators inevitably say they expect the highest levels of education. Do other people's children deserve any less?" (p. 32).

To give all children the fair and equitable education they deserve, schools need to analyze how it is that they are serving or not serving their student of color populations. When addressing the racial achievement gap, race matters. It is critical that schools address issues around race to uncover whatever institutionalized biases exist to prevent students of color from reaching their fullest potential. Courageous Conversation serves as an essential strategy for educators in addressing racial matters and deinstitutionalizing racism in the educational arena.

Implementation Exercise

Equity Terms

Time required: 45 minutes

Materials required: Courageous Conversation Journal for each participant and the following worksheet

1. Make a copy of the following worksheet for each participant.

2. Before the discussion begins, have each educator answer 1a, 2a, 3a, and 4a by writing down what they believe each of the following terms means:

   Racism

   Institutionalized racism

   Anti-racism

   Equity

3. Ask for three to four volunteers to share with the entire group their personal definition for each term. Compare and contrast these definitions.

4. Present the definitions for each term based on what is presented in this chapter.

5. After the discussion, have each person answer 1b, 2b, 3b, and 4b by writing down a new definition for each term.

6. Divide all participants into small groups of three to four people. Have the groups discuss how their understanding of these terms has changed.

7. Bring the large group back together and allow people to share any conclusions.

8. Have the participants reflect on their personal learning and keep the worksheet in their journals for later reference.

Equity Terms

1a. I have defined **Racism** as

_____

_____

_____

1b. I now understand **Racism** to be

_____

_____

_____

2a. I have defined **Institutionalized Racism** as

_____

_____

_____

2b. I now understand **Institutionalized Racism** to be

_____

_____

_____

3a. I have defined **_Anti-Racism_** as

_____

_____

_____

3b. I now understand **_Anti-Racism_** to be

_____

_____

_____

4a. I have defined **_Equity_** as

_____

_____

_____

4b. I now understand **_Equity_** to be

_____

_____

_____

Agreeing to Talk About Race

Discussions and debates about racism create anxiety and conflict, which are handled differently by different cultural groups. For example, Whites tend to fear open discussion of racial problems because they believe that such discussion will stir up hard feelings and old hatreds. Whites tend to believe that heated arguments about racism lead to divisiveness, loss of control, bitter conflict, and even violence. Blacks, on the other hand, believe that discussion and debate about racism help to push racial problems to the surface—and, perhaps, force society to deal with them.

—Gerald Pine and Asa Hilliard (1990, p. 596)

Courageous Conversation is an ambitious attempt to break down the racial tensions and ignorance that hobble our progress as a nation. By engaging in this dialogue, those who possess the knowledge get the opportunity to share it, and those who do not have the knowledge yet learn and grow from the experience. In building mutual understanding, educators discover what they need to collectively foster equity and diminish both overt and more subtle racial conflict.

To ensure personal engagement, honesty, endurance, and persistence in the dialogue about race in schools, the first formal step in this process is to commit to the Four Agreements of Courageous Conversation: to stay engaged, experience discomfort, speak your truth, and expect and accept non-closure. As preparation for making this commitment, however, educators need to consider their own racial consciousness. White educators might ask themselves: Are we aware that racial inequity exists, and are we capable of addressing it? Educators of color might ask: Do we unwittingly support institutionalized racism in our system, and are we willing to speak up and confront the inequities?

RACIAL CONSCIOUSNESS

One of the most difficult aspects for those who engage in Courageous Conversations about race is admitting that they may not know all that they have claimed to know or honestly believed they knew. With limited racial consciousness, many educators—Whites especially—feel inhibited when conversing about race and racial issues and/or find themselves lacking in knowledge and understanding about the experience of those who have different racial backgrounds.

Pamela Noli is a White educator in the San Francisco Bay Area. In the early part of her career, Pam felt that she was doing an immense amount of good for the teachers, students, and families of color with whom she worked because she deeply cared about their welfare. It was this sense of empathy and caring that guided much of her decision-making process.

She began her teaching career in California's San Joaquin Valley and chose to work in schools that primarily served Latinos. She was there by choice, and she knew that she loved the children. However, she assumed that the love she felt could overcome her lack of actual knowledge about her students' lives. She thought that if cared enough, she could make the right decisions for her students.

At the time, she was married to a Latino, had a Latino last name, and lived in a Latino farming community. Even though she learned more and more about some of the people of color in her town and what created their sense of community, she came to realize how much more she had to learn. As she says,

> I still really didn't know what I didn't know. I thought that because I loved so much that I did know, till someone said, "You know Pam, you're the most dangerous person in this conversation, you White liberals." That was exactly what she said to me! She continued, "White liberals are the most dangerous people in the conversation about race because you think you know because you care, but *you don't know what you don't know.*" You don't know what you don't know!

    – It was so true for me.

    – When I was going to college at Fresno State I was on the march with Cesar Chavez in Sacramento, but I was completely there as a missionary. I didn't know at the time, but as I reflect back, I was there helping those *poor Brown people*. I didn't know what I didn't know, but I thought I did. (Singleton, 2002)

For Pam, acknowledging that *she did not know what she did not know* was the hardest realization in coming to terms with her racial consciousness and how it affected her work with students of color. A huge shift for Pam in her own consciousness was separating the fact that she cared from what she actually knew.

While educators of color often have the knowledge about their own racial experience, they may lack an understanding of how to advance interracial dialogue in a productive way.

Jamie Almanzán is a biracial former middle school teacher of Mexican American and White American descent, who worked hard to develop a profound sense of who he is racially. The more that Jamie developed his consciousness around how race was impacting him and the students he served, the more he felt the need to share his insights with his colleagues, who were predominately White. The staff's resistance to engage in dialogue about Jamie's important discoveries caused internal conflict and great tension between him and his colleagues. Like many teachers of color in similar situations, Jamie eventually chose to retreat to the privacy and solitude of his own classroom as he felt that it was no use trying to get his colleagues to understand his point of view or the viewpoints of many of his Mexican American students and families. Clearly, his inability to facilitate interracial dialogue with school-based adults did not serve his students' best interest either.

To overcome these challenges, both of these educators participated in the Courageous Conversation program. For Pam, this strategy provided her with a way of attaining the knowledge she needed to understand what the lives and thoughts of her students of color were really like. For Jamie, Courageous Conversation helped him to facilitate effective interracial dialogue in the school setting. Armed with these skills and knowledge, these two educators increased not only their capacity to care but also their effectiveness in the classroom and with colleagues. Courageous Conversation fortifies the persistence educators need to build racial consciousness and impact more profoundly their schools' learning environments.

I Don't Know What I Don't Know

The first step in developing racial consciousness is acknowledging that "I don't know what I don't know"—a simple phrase with profound implications. Consciously, we use what we think we know when we share with others our opinions and beliefs. Equally powerful, however, is what we don't know or what we incorrectly assume we know. These two domains of knowledge—*I don't know I don't know* and *I don't know but I think I do*—are ultimately the most limiting in the way we lead our own lives. When we function based on a set of assumptions without accurate funds of knowledge about what is real, we have a myopic and distorted view of others.

In terms of our own racial experience, we may have a limited understanding not only of the lives of people of a different race but even of how our personal racial identities impacts our own lives. White people struggle to recognize that they have a racialized existence and that their color, indeed, affords them privilege and opportunity in our society. Likewise, people of color may distrust the motives of White people collectively, without actually discussing this distrust with the individual White people in their lives. To develop racial consciousness is to address our assumptions and build our funds of knowledge. This will allow us to live more authentically within our own racial experience and deal more honestly with the existence of others.

To develop our racial awareness, as diagramed in Figure 4.1, the Racial Consciousness Flow Chart, we must deliberately move out of "I don't know I don't know" through the different stages of consciousness until we reach "I know I know."

Figure 4.1   Racial Consciousness Flow Chart

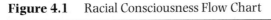

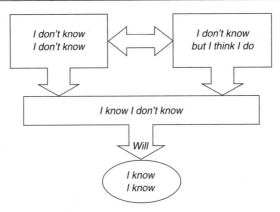

Moving Through the Stages

To advance through the stages as we confront racial issues on a daily basis is a consciousness-raising experience. When we act based on ignorance, we are functioning in the stage "I don't know I don't know." Likewise, if our assumptions guide us but they have not been verified, we are in the stage of "I don't know but I think I do." From either of these stages, we can experience an awakening of our consciousness by acquiring information that challenges our assumptions or equips us with new knowledge. At this point, we move into "I know I don't know." From here, we can exercise our *will* by actively engaging in the expansion of our knowledge and understanding. As we do this, we move into the final stage, "I know I know." Only at this point, do we begin to exist in full consciousness and become secure in our awareness that our fund of knowledge is sufficient.

The following story illustrates how we move through these different stages of racial consciousness awareness:

A White female teacher is asked whether or not Black students in the school are underrepresented in honors and Advanced Placement (AP) courses in comparison to White students. Having never considered this and being unaware of the racial enrollment in these courses, she responds no. Ignorant of the realities of White overenrollment in the honors and AP classes, her consciousness at this moment is in the stage of "I don't know I don't know."

– Next, the teacher expresses the belief that there is no racial achievement gap in the honors and AP program. This belief is in the stage of "I don't know but I think I do" because she is operating from an assumption that students of all races who qualify for these courses excel to the same degree.

– Following this, the teacher is presented with statistical data highlighting the achievement gap between Black and White students in honors and AP courses. This is now a consciousness-raising experience informing the teacher that her fund of knowledge related to the intersection of race and student course placement has been limited. At this point, she advances into the stage of "I know I don't know."

– Based on this experience, the teacher must exercise her *will and engage her passion* to discover the reality of the achievement gap, which might include discussing with honors and AP students of color why they succeed and don't succeed. This should lead her to explore other racial inequities that exist in her school. By doing this, she has elevated her consciousness into the stage of "I know I know." Secure in this newfound knowledge, the teacher becomes much more effective in her own classroom with all students.

Reflection

Think of an experience when your racial consciousness was developed. Name and reflect on the discovery, then trace it through the stages outlined previously.

It is important to reach this deepest level of racial consciousness to connect effectively with students, parents, and colleagues of different races. White educators should understand that the racial consciousness of people of color is acute, while an educator of color can likewise recognize how difficult engaging in this conversation is for a White person. Consequently, the productivity of interracial relationships, professional as well as personal, depends on how authentic we all become in our own racial consciousness.

This need to raise consciousness and advance from "I don't know I don't know" toward "I know I know" is more about where the adults are rather than the students. Educators eventually will need to determine the distance that exists between their own racial consciousness and that of the students. Large gaps in racial consciousness between teachers and students can create dissonance, especially when students feel that a teacher does not understand them. Consequently, what typically occurs in these situations of disconnect is that the student will disengage from learning before the adult attempts to raise his or her own racial consciousness and foster meaningful engagement.

As educators experience consciousness-raising opportunities in their schools with the overarching goal of rising to the stage of "I know I know" in their own racial consciousness, they prepare themselves to fully engage in Courageous Conversations about race.

FOUR AGREEMENTS OF COURAGEOUS CONVERSATION

To participate in effective interracial dialogue about race, the first step is to commit to the Four Agreements of Courageous Conversation. By committing to these, participants agree to

- Stay engaged
- Experience discomfort
- Speak your truth
- Expect and accept non-closure

Embracing these agreements will allow educators to engage, sustain, and deepen interracial dialogue about racial identity, racism, and the racial achievement gap that exists between White students and students of color.

The racial climate and culture in our country and our schools equip us with well-developed skills for disengaging from racial issues. Consequently, we have created lasting and hidden racial conflicts that impact all of us. These agreements, however, secure in participants the commitment and persistence needed to address these conflicts as they surface during Courageous Conversation. As described by Frederique Wynberg, a White staff developer and proponent of equity work in Vallejo, California,

> It takes Courageous Conversation to get to the point where you can actually think about race—as a White person—without feeling defensive. Or, for people of color, without feeling both defensive because you're now part of a White institution and also very angry because of what is going on in society and what's institutionalized. (Singleton, 2002)

For both White educators and educators of color, committing to the Four Agreements is the first step required to counter the problematic norms that occur during interracial dialogue about race. At the end of this chapter, you will have the opportunity to commit personally to these agreements and to try leading others in making the same commitment. With this accomplished, you will be ready to begin Courageous Conversation, assured by an understanding that all involved in the dialogue are fully committed to the process.

Stay Engaged

Participants in Courageous Conversation must stay engaged. This is a personal commitment each person makes, regardless of the engagement of others. Staying engaged means remaining morally, emotionally, intellectually, and socially involved in the dialogue. To stay engaged is to not let your heart and mind "check out" of the conversation while leaving your body in place.

This may be more difficult than it sounds because educators traditionally do not talk about race unless the racial challenge is unavoidable. Many White Americans have been conditioned to not talk about race. While Whites maintain this silence, many people of color—in the United States and beyond—converse about racial matters daily, if only among themselves. Consequently, little "before the crisis" interracial dialogue about race ever takes place. Collectively in the United States, racial topics tend to be "hot button" issues that either cause people of color to become vocally angry or make White people silently defiant or disconnected. Given this accepted pattern of interracial disengagement among the vast majority of Americans, it is no wonder so many racial challenges continue to exist.

Collective disengagement also exists in schools. When a dramatic racial achievement gap persists, the children of the school pay the ultimate price for the adults' unwillingness to engage in difficult interracial dialogue. Whenever the topic turns to race, many educators seem to disengage by (a) redefining the conversation to focus on poverty, family structure, or any of a number of diversity issues other than race or (b) becoming silent, perhaps staring off into space, and letting out a deep and drawn-out breath to signal lack of interest or discomfort with the conversation.

Reflection

Can you think of a time in a personal and/or professional circumstance when race became a topic of conversation and you either actively changed the subject or avoided the conversation altogether? What did you believe caused you to react in this manner?

The challenge is to resist the natural inclination to move away from the conversation. In our experience, most educators will not want to talk about racial issues. School leaders need to be aware of this as an initial step in creating the necessary safer space for staff to stay engaged. If this safety is not created, those at the table will stand up and walk away, whether literally or figuratively.

By individually committing to stay engaged in Courageous Conversations about race, educators can guard against the learned tendency to disengage. By collectively making this commitment, they can fully embrace the conversation and ensure that it deepens their focus on eliminating racial achievement disparity and propels their efforts to do so.

Speak Your Truth

Speaking your truth in Courageous Conversations about race requires a willingness to take risks. Speaking your truth means being absolutely honest about your thoughts, feelings, and opinions and not just saying what you perceive others want to hear. Too often, we don't speak our truth out of fear of offending, appearing angry, or sounding ignorant. But until we can become completely honest, the dialogue will remain limited and ultimately ineffective.

When it comes to racial matters in our society, we have learned to not say what's on our minds—to not speak our truth. This, however, often leads to deeper confusion, mistrust, and misunderstanding. Many beliefs concerning race are based on misconceptions and half-truths. This can occur when a member of one race believes that a member of another race agrees with or supports her simply because the other person said nothing. Without speaking his truth, the educator who has remained silent has allowed his own beliefs or opinions to be misinterpreted or misrepresented.

Lisa Delpit (1995b) has labeled this phenomenon the *silenced dialogue;* in it, teachers and parents of color tend to get quiet in the presence of more verbal White educators. In her essay, "The Silenced Dialogue: Power and Pedagogy of Educating Other People's Children," Delpit suggests that this silence occurs because educators and parents of color often feel their racial experiences are deprecated or invalidated by White educators. She goes on to write,

> [White educators] do not perceive themselves to have power over the non-White speakers. However, either by virtue of their position, their numbers, or their access to that particular code of power of calling upon research to validate one's position, the White educators had the authority to establish what was to be considered "truth" regardless of the opinions of the people of color, and the [educators and parents of color] were well aware of that fact. (p. 26)

This silence is likely to occur in faculty meetings, in the principal's office, and even during informal conversations when people of color describing a racist experience or situation are told, "Aren't you exaggerating it a little?" "that (White) person really didn't mean it that way," or "you probably just misunderstood them." As this happens time and time again, people of color grow silent, refrain from sharing their stories and opinions, and no longer speak their truth. This silence, however, is now seen as implicit agreement; others believe that the educators and parents of color actually agree with what is happening in the primarily White institution. Delpit (1995b) writes that when educators of color are silent, then "the White educators believe that their colleagues of color did, in the end, agree with their logic. After all, they stopped disagreeing, didn't they?" (p. 23).

For example, if only one Latino educator sits on a bilingual committee at a school, but—caught in the silenced dialogue—that educator says nothing as a policy is pushed forward, the school claims it has total support. Then, should the Latino community protest, the school points out that the Latino serving on the committee never said anything against the policy, which must be an indication that he or she supported it. What White educators in this and similar situations fail to take into account, however, is that the silence does not necessarily mean that the Latino educator agreed with the policy or felt safe to express his or her true feelings about it. It only means that he or she was silent.

The silenced dialogue can also occur among Whites. Henze et al. (2002) explain why educators may be afraid to address conflicts or tensions that have racial dimensions in an honest, forthright, and truthful manner:

> They may be afraid that doing so will lead to an increase in conflict or that they will then be targeted by the original perpetrators. They may simply not want to raise the issue because it is too painful to talk about or they know that other people will be uncomfortable. Many schools have a code of silence about race and ethnicity, a value system that says it's best to be color blind. In a color blind school, there is no safe place for someone [of color]. (p. 46)

In this "color blind school" where silenced dialogue is practiced among White educators, there may be a perceived lack of racial problems, but this is typically only because racial issues are redefined, ignored, avoided, and/or dismissed.

As Lena Williams (2000) writes in *It's the Little Things*, Whites often don't speak their truth in regard to racial issues because they are afraid of making a misstep and having to defend what they say, their actions, or their race. Consequently, White people may rarely share their own authentic racial stories and opinions, but rather they may talk about what happened to a White friend or tell a colleague of color what they believe he wants to hear. White people need to speak their own personal truth, as this is the only way for them to fully engage their racial consciousness. Even though they may fear appearing racist at first as they expose inner thoughts, speaking honestly is the way that White people can first become more fully cognizant of their own racial experience and subsequently develop deeper understanding of the racial perspectives and experiences of others.

Reflection

Can you recall a time when race was the topic of conversation and you became silent and/or shared something that was less than your truest feeling in fear of what other's response might be?

All educators—Whites and people of color—must share the responsibility to engage and speak their truth in Courageous Conversations about race. In fact, people of color will be more likely to open up when White people simply validate their experiences without shutting them down, interrogating them, or redefining their experience into more familiar diversity terms. A White person can never "own" the experience of a person of color, just as a person of color cannot "own" the White experience. We are only experts in defining our own experiences and personal realities. Part of our struggle is rooted in our inability to search for meaning in the racial perspective of others, no matter how different another's experience may be from our own.

When it comes to dealing with race, one of the greatest challenges in American culture and especially in our schools is that both White people and people of color don't share their honest feelings about race. For a Courageous Conversation to occur, we need to break our silence and speak our truth.

Experience Discomfort

Because of the problematic state of racial conditions in our society, Courageous Conversations necessarily create discomfort for participants. Rather than experience the discomfort in interracial dialogue, people often put an emphasis on how we are all alike instead of addressing our obvious differences. Typical diversity trainings are focused around not getting participants upset or too uncomfortable. Traditional diversity training, however, has been unsuccessful in helping schools close the racial achievement gap. The Courageous Conversation strategy, on the other hand, asks participants to agree to experience discomfort so that they can deal with the reality of race in an honest and forthright way.

In our work with school systems across the nation, we have challenged educators to deal openly and honestly with their racial challenges. On occasion, we have been accused of "dividing the staff." The reality is that we have simply brought into the open the troubles that already exist but have not been discussed. If educators experience division as they deal with issues of race and equity, we suspect that they were already silently divided. Although discomfiting, giving voice and meaning to this divide can begin the process of healing and transformation.

Likewise, it is disingenuous for school systems to address the achievement gap in a cursory or "feel good" way. Educators need to engage in this dialogue authentically. To do so, participants need to be personally responsible for pushing themselves into a real dialogue—the kind that may make them uncomfortable but also will lead to real growth. Such conversations require that people open up and examine their core racial beliefs, values, perceptions, and behaviors. But as people speak their truth, tremendous emotion and fear may surface, thus creating personal and collective discomfort. For White educators, discomfort unmasks their fear linked to offending people of color when expressing perceived biased or unsympathetic racial views and perspectives. On the other hand, educators of color most often avoid uncomfortable dialogue out of fear of expressing intense anger and being misunderstood, ignored, or even punished by their White colleagues.

To develop authentic interracial relationships, we must break our collective silence. Staying within the parameters of the Courageous Conversation strategy, however, allows participants to safely manage this dialogue. As they increase their tolerance for the discomfort, they will also increase their ability to address the most challenging institutional circumstances associated with racial achievement disparity.

Expect and Accept Non-Closure

The Fourth Agreement of Courageous Conversation encourages participants to recognize that they will not reach closure in their racial understandings or in their interracial interactions. The normal way of dealing with challenges faced by schools is to search for the "solutions." In Courageous Conversation, however, the solution is revealed in the process of dialogue itself. Simply put, we cannot discover a solution to a challenge if we have not been able to talk about it. Furthermore, the magnitude, complexity, and longevity of our racial struggle and strife in the United States rule out any possibility of discovering a "quick fix." In this conversation, the solutions discovered are ever forming and ever changing. Therefore, participants must commit to an ongoing dialogue as an essential component of their action plan. This is how to manifest the agreement to expect and accept non-closure.

Typical professional learning opportunities offer educators a binder in which specific steps and goals are listed. These seem concrete and may even appear sequential. The suggestion is that by the time each exercise or activity in the binder is completed, a solution will be found to the challenge being addressed. If such a binder existed for addressing racial achievement gaps, we would happily present it.

This, however, is not the case. Rarely has the issue of race been addressed in the traditional professional learning opportunities for educators, and it has never been presented as essential learning. We believe that much of this neglect is due to the fact that no neat and tidy tasks, processes, or timelines with guaranteed solutions exist. Courageous Conversation, however, triggers a moral, intellectual, social, and emotional shift that allows participants to revisit their many professional development binders of previous trainings with a newly developed racial lens and language. If people expect and accept non-closure in racial discourse, then the more they talk, the more they learn; and the more they learn, the more appropriate and promising will be their actions and interventions.

Reflection

As you reflect on the Four Agreements of Courageous Conversation, which do you believe will be the most difficult for you to embrace and practice? Why is this so? Which will be the easiest?

The strategy of Courageous Conversation is difficult but rewarding. Given that everyone enters this dialogue at a unique place, some will take longer to arrive at a basic understanding of what race is and how it impacts their lives, not to mention the time and readiness to talk about how race impacts student achievement. Others may be ready almost immediately to begin examining how race impacts the classroom, program, department, or schoolwide policies. Everyone, however, must stay collectively engaged throughout this continuous, challenging, and always evolving dialogue.

The Four Agreements of Courageous Conversation require commitment by each individual involved in the school improvement effort. These agreements prepare educators to authentically engage in Courageous Conversation. Furthermore, they allow stakeholders to manage the conversation as real change begins to occur. Some school systems engaged in race and equity work have added additional agreements to supplement these four. We encourage you to consider the culture of your school system and determine what other agreements might help your colleagues remain committed to Courageous Conversations about race.

Implementation Exercise

Four Agreements of Courageous Conversations

Time required: 45 minutes

Materials required: Courageous Conversation Journal for each participant and the following two worksheets.

Present the Racial Consciousness Flow Chart to your group and discuss the following:

- What does it mean to admit "I don't know I don't know"?
- What are the inherent weaknesses of "I don't know but I think I do"?
- How can admitting "I know I don't know" impact a teacher's efforts?
- What kind of *will* needs to be enacted to advance from "I know I don't know" to "I know I know"?
    1. Have each participant identify three areas where their knowledge exists for each stage of the Racial Consciousness Flow Chart. Reflect briefly with a partner.
    2. Share with the group the meaning and rationale for each of the Four Agreements of Courageous Conversation:
        a. Stay engaged
        b. Experience discomfort
        c. Speak our truth
        d. Expect and accept non-closure
    3. Divide the participants into small groups and have them discuss the Four Agreements using the following prompts:

- During a conversation about race, has anyone ever experienced *disengagement* from the conversation? How did it impact the dialogue?
- Has anyone ever felt *discomfort* during a conversation on race? If so, did you work through the discomfort successfully, or was it left unresolved?
- Which emotions prevent you from *speaking your truth* during inter-racial conversations about race? Which conditions can make it safer for you to deal with your racial fears and speak your truth?
- Why is it necessary to *expect and accept non-closure* when dealing with race?
    4. Have each participant complete and sign the following Four Agreements of Courageous Conversation document. After they complete this, have them keep the document in their Courageous Conversation Journal. Discuss with the group how having committed to these agreements will impact the staff's dialogue about student achievement in your school or school system.

Figure 4.2   Racial Consciousness Flow Chart for Exercise

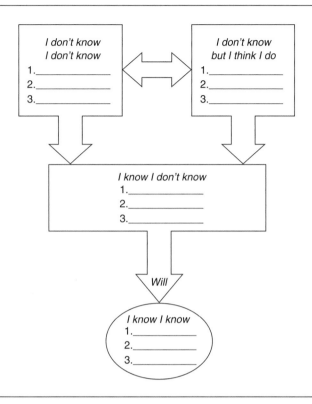

Four Agreements of Courageous Conversations

I agree to . . .

☐ Stay engaged.
☐ Experience discomfort.
☐ Speak my truth.
☐ Expect and accept non-closure.

My signature below indicates my commitment to engage, sustain, and deepen interracial dialogue about race.

_____
Educator's Signature

PART II

Practice

The Foundation of Anti-Racist Leadership

W hen a school system's educators have developed sufficient *passion* for addressing its racial achievement gap, leadership needs to develop the skills necessary to tackle institutionalized racism. For this reason, *practice* is the second quality of systemic equity/anti-racist transformation. By developing and implementing effective practices, educators find meaningful opportunities to use and enhance the knowledge, skills, and capacity they have gained through Courageous Conversation.

Educators who strive to achieve the vision of an equitable school system refrain from blaming underserved students for the system's failures. They see it as their professional and moral imperative to acknowledge where schooling is ineffective and specifically where instructional practices are unsupportive of student success.

We must aim to create a nation of high achievers regardless of background. Some Americans seem to believe that disparity and disproportionality in achievement among racial groups is inevitable—the result of obvious differences in the economic and educational resources that different groups can access. But this doesn't explain why some schools—indeed, some whole districts—serving poor children and large numbers of children of color achieve much better results than districts with comparable demographics do. Indeed, if the causes of underachievement rest primarily in families or the students themselves, these better results should not be possible. Perhaps it isn't poverty or racial/ethnic background in and of itself, but rather educators' response that suppresses educational achievement (Johnson, 2002, p. 6).

It must become unacceptable for educators to not guarantee equitable access and opportunity to all students groups. Student success cannot be left to chance. As described by Kati Haycock (2003), the "old way" of schooling leaves a great deal to chance because

- curriculum is left up to individual schools or teachers.
- teachers "broadcast" the content—a kind of one-size fits all approach.
- some students "get it" and some don't.
- teachers don't exactly know which students are really getting it . . . and they couldn't do much about those who aren't anyway.

The old way of schooling places sole responsibility for learning on the students and guarantees the same results we have always had. In the "new way" of schooling, however, educators accept full responsibility for teaching and *little is left to chance:*

- All teachers teach a common, coherent curriculum that clearly lays out what kids are supposed to have learned at each step of the way.
- Teachers use a variety of strategies to help students master a common set of knowledge and skills—individualized instruction.
- Teachers know which students aren't getting it the first time and which students are falling seriously behind.
- Teachers can tap into a variety of strategies for providing additional instruction to students who don't get it the first time or who are falling seriously behind.

The new way to educational success involves teachers acquiring the skills or *practices* they need to ensure that every one of their students succeed. Once again, *little is left to chance.* Teaching is centered and focused around getting each and every student to perform at or above the standards. When instruction is matched to the needs of the individual student, then education begins to transcend the perceived limitations of race, culture, and background.

We believe that language and communication provide the foundation of culture. Specifically, those ideas, thoughts, and perspectives that people are able to effectively exchange with members of their community become the basis for establishing shared values, attitudes, and behaviors.

In essence, only when educators have established both a language and process for communication about racial matters will they be poised to restructure their schools, classrooms, curricula, and relationships with students and families in ways that improve student engagement and performance.

In our work with schools, Courageous Conversation has served as that essential language and communication strategy. The Six Conditions of Courageous Conversation guide us through the essential content and processes of racial dialogue in a way that allows educators to feel safe as they examine the points at which race intersects schooling.

The conditions are progressive and intentionally build on each other. When educators cycle through the conditions, they add depth and complexity to the conversation. As you develop greater understanding of the conditions in the following chapters and engage in the suggested reflections, exercises, and activities, you will master the *practices* needed to internalize Courageous Conversation and subsequently enhance your focus and effectiveness in addressing racial achievement disparity in your school system.

The First Condition

Getting Personal Right Here and Right Now

It is pretty clear the achievement gap has roots in school and non-school factors, but if you tell teachers the gap has two sources, they want to fix the out-of-school stuff first. They never get around to doing the things they can do.

—Kati Haycock, director of The Education Trust
(Quoted in Barnes, 2004, p. 70)

Rather than blaming factors external to schools for causing the racial achievement gap, educators should address the critical factors within their control that influence student achievement, such as the qualifications, expectations, and cultural proficiency of educators, the rigor of the curriculum, and the effectiveness of instruction.

Closing the racial achievement gap begins with an examination of self rather than of others. For this reason, the First Condition of Courageous Conversation invites us to

establish a racial context that is personal, local, and immediate.

Specifically, educators need to address their own racial attitudes, beliefs, and expectations as they relate to their students of color as well as their White students. When the conversation focuses initially on the educators' own racial consciousness, identity, and experiences, they can better understand the way in which they may be interpreting their students' academic interests and engagement.

PERSONAL, LOCAL, AND IMMEDIATE

To develop a fuller understanding of race, we must first look deeply and introspectively at our own racial existence as a doorway to understanding the complexities of race in America. This is why the First Condition of Courageous Conversation prompts participants to examine their own personal, local, and immediate circumstances related to race. In doing this, they engage in the dialogue by carefully examining their personal racial identity development and experiences linked to racism.

Examining the impact of race in our own lives serves as a precursor to examining the impact of race in the larger context of a school. As we become personally aware of our own racialized existence, we can more deeply understand the racial experiences of others. Without doing this, we will continue to assess the racial experiences of others through our own distorted lens. The foundational level of racial awareness must be personal, local, and immediate. Thus, heightening racial consciousness begins with self-examination and is bolstered by continuous racial inquiry and reflection.

Reflection

Before you opened this book, how consciously aware of race were you?

As authors of this book, we could not have come from more different racial backgrounds. Precisely because Glenn Singleton is Black and grew up in Baltimore, Maryland, and Curtis Linton is White and grew up in Salt Lake City, Utah, we have experienced radically different racial realities. Both of us have led intensely racialized lives that we needed to analyze critically prior to understanding each other. One important difference, however, in our journeys toward personal racial consciousness—and a difference that we believe is reflective of the experience of our respective racial groups—is that Glenn has long been aware of the impact of race in his life whereas Curtis has only recently come to recognize himself racially. Given that our first step was to examine race in our own individual lives, Curtis needed to accelerate his racial examination while Glenn had to be patient during Curtis's process of inquiry and discovery. Having this kind of mutual introduction to race led us to a far greater understanding of and empathy for how race impacts our respective lives.

Between the chapters in which we explore the Six Conditions of Courageous Conversation are several *racial autobiographies.* These were written by Curtis, Glenn, and several of Glenn's current graduate students in the Urban High School Leadership Program at San José State University's College of Education. These are personal reflections on how race impacts individual lives. Racial autobiographies are a tool for developing and deepening personal understanding of and insights around race. They not only provide a process for racial discovery but also serve as examples of what it means to establish a racial context that is personal, local, and immediate. Highlighting the First Condition, the racial autobiographies also show the progression that each individual has followed to build his or her own racial consciousness. They can serve as models for your own work in equity and in racial self-definition.

Reflection

What can you recall about the events and conversations related to race, race relations, and/or racism that may have impacted your current perspectives and/or experiences?

THE IMPACT OF RACE ON MY LIFE

The First Condition of Courageous Conversation focuses on the way in which race impacts each of us, right here and right now. Imagine that a billboard sits above the road on your commute to work beckoning you to address the following question:

> *To what degree*
> *does race*
> *impact my life?*

The emphasis here is "my life" because to engage in Courageous Conversations requires making race personal. As the conversation becomes tough, the tendency is to become more impersonal. The pain of facing racism, coupled with the propensity of the dominant White culture to minimize or deny racist acts, might encourage people of color to generalize the personal impact of racism. In addition, many White people have a tendency to talk about racism only from the perspective of how people of color are oppressed rather than considering what role they might play in that oppression. We cannot talk about race collectively as a nation, family, or school until we have individually talked about race in our own lives—personally, locally, and immediately.

Reflection

To what degree and in what ways does race impact your own personal life?

Consider the billboard once again:

Race in my life?

0–100%

The billboard now asks for you to determine what percentage of your life is impacted by race.

Reflection

Determine the percentage of your life, from 0 to 100%, that is impacted by race.

As you examine this prompt further and begin to deeply investigate race personally, you will come to recognize that race impacts every aspect of your life 100% of the time. This total impact of race occurs whether you are conscious or unconscious of the impact and whether you spend time with people of the same race or of a race different than your own. Because people are defined by their racial identity in this society, race is constantly present and having an impact on your experience and perspective. This is to say that the impact of race disappears only when you no longer have your skin, and thus, the omnipresent skin that you are in defines your omnipresent racial impact.

What if you arrived at a percentage lower than 100? Most likely, you determined your level of racial *consciousness* rather than racial *impact*. People who answer the question with the lowest percentages typically do not view interactions with White people or White cultural experiences as racial. Low percentages are also derived by people who do not wish to characterize themselves racially, choosing instead to connect us all to one human "race." Although this idea may be noble and humans do belong to the same species, in the United States, as well as in other parts of the world, race is defined today by physical traits. Many White educators find it difficult and perhaps disturbing to consider themselves part of a racial group; ironically, the word *race* conjures up only images of and experiences with people of color. Educators of color, on the other hand, tend to quickly acknowledge the universality and omnipresence of race in their lives.

If you are White, it helps to think not only of outwardly racist comments or actions but of the ways in which race may play out in your personal relationships, opportunities, and sense of security throughout your community and beyond. Although author Curtis Linton grew up in a predominantly White community where race was rarely discussed, the impact of race on his life was still 100%: He felt racially secure in this society and benefited greatly from a schooling system that was geared to serve primarily White children.

Sometimes, people of color will list an impact percentage lower than 100 because they exclude time spent interacting with people of their own race. But race still dominates these interactions as people of color often feel safest, racially speaking, when spending time among those of their own race, just as White people do. If you are a person of color, consider how race plays into your life every day, how it affects the way others treat you, and whether it has had an impact on your schooling, career, and place in society. The racial impact is also 100% for author Glenn Singleton as he grew up in an all-Black neighborhood in Baltimore. Similarly, it was still 100% when he graduated from his all-Black elementary school and went on to attend a predominately White middle and high school.

This question is intended not so much to generate an assessment of race's impact but to initiate an ongoing conversation about racial consciousness and the degree to which educators are aware of how and when race permeates their personal and professional interactions. Once everyone realizes that race is always impacting our experience, the far more provocative question emerges: To what degree am I conscious of this 100% racial impact in my life?

Reflection

Based on your previous racial autobiography reflections, to what degree are you conscious of the 100% impact race has on your life?

Figure 5.1 Racial Consciousness Flow Chart

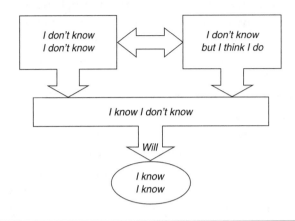

DEGREE OF RACIAL CONSCIOUSNESS

Discussing the role of race in our lives invites us to refer back to the Racial Consciousness Flow Chart introduced in the previous chapter and repeated in Figure 5.1.

In identifying how conscious you are about how race impacts your life, you are labeling the degree to which "I know I don't know" or "I know I know." This means that the difference between that percentage and 100 is how much "I don't know I don't know" or "I don't know but I think I do."

The percentage at which we believe that race impacts our lives can be viewed as our racial consciousness. The ability to effectively converse about race is determined by the degree to which we can consciously place the lens of race in front of us as we examine our own personal interactions with family and friends. Ultimately, educators need to view the experiences of students, work of colleagues, patterns in achievement data, school policies, and effective ways of engaging parents and the community through the lens of race. The success of Courageous Conversation, however, hinges on the willingness and ability of participants to examine *themselves* racially and not prematurely divert the dialogue to an examination of their students. Educators cannot effectively consider their students' attitudes and behaviors before they have carefully investigated their own.

RACIAL CONSCIOUSNESS
VERSUS RACIAL UNCONSCIOUSNESS

As shown here, if you consider your racial consciousness as a fraction, the denominator of 100 signifies the total impact of race and the acknowledgment that race permeates everything in modern American society. The numerator represents the degree to which you are racially conscious, locally and immediately. The difference between the numerator and the denominator is racial unconsciousness.

$$\frac{\text{Race in my life} = ?\% \quad (\textit{Racial Consciousness})}{100\% \quad (\text{Racial Unconsciousness} + \text{Consciousness})}$$

We need to challenge our racial unconsciousness in the conversation to reach a greater understanding of race in our own lives. This unconsciousness causes the greatest discomfort in interracial interaction, as often experienced by White educators working with colleagues, students, and families of color. This is because people of color tend not only to be more conscious of their own racial experience but to understand White racial culture as well because they have lived in a White-dominated society. Simply put, racial discomfort is maximized when people of lesser consciousness are required to interact with people of greater consciousness.

Over time, educators engaged in Courageous Conversation will better understand the inherent rises and dips in their own racial consciousness. It is precisely this movement that creates the sense of discomfort on which authentic dialogue is predicated. As educators practice these skills through Courageous Conversation, they will continually build their own racial consciousness and their ability to understand the racial reality of those with whom they interact. By arriving at their own personal, local, and immediate understanding of race in their own lives, they can begin to effectively address the omnipresent impact of race on the schooling of their students.

Reflection

Describe *race in my life* in terms of your perceived racial consciousness and racial unconsciousness. In which situations and circumstances do you believe yourself to be most racially aware? In which circumstances do you feel you would benefit from having greater racial consciousness?

Implementation Exercise

Race in My Life

Time required: 45 minutes

Materials required: Courageous Conversation Journal for each participant and the worksheet that follows

Introduce the First Condition of Courageous Conversations:

> *Establish a racial context that is personal, local, and immediate.*

Ask participants why it is important first to address race personally and individually before trying to understand it at a group or societal level.

1. Provide each individual with a copy of the worksheet and have them answer the prompt:

   How much is my life impacted by race?

   Have them consider, from 0–100%, the degree to which race impacts their life and write figure that in the box.

2. Divide the participants into small groups of four to five people, mixing races if possible. Have the small groups share their percentages with each other and consider the following prompts:
   • What are our highest and lowest percentages?
   • What are the reasons for discrepancies or similarities in the participants' percentages?

3. Explain to the entire group that this percentage is our racial consciousness. Refer to the Racial Consciousness Flow Chart (Figure 5.1) and discuss how this percentage identifies what "I know I know." The difference between our racial consciousness percentage and 100% is our racial unconsciousness, or what it is that "I don't know I don't know" in terms of how race impacts us.

4. Reiterate to the group that this condition deals with race personally, locally, and immediately, and have each participant complete the rest of the handout by addressing how
   • My race impacts my life emotionally . . .
   • My race impacts my life socially . . .

- My race impacts my life intellectually . . .
- My race impacts my life morally . . .

Remind participants that they need to address how their own race impacts their own lives—*not the race of others.* Have each person in the small groups choose one of these prompts to share with the others in their group.

5. Bring everyone back together and pose the following question for an open discussion:

> How does my own race impact me personally, locally, and immediately?

6. Have everyone keep the worksheet in their Courageous Conversation Journal.

First Condition of Courageous Conversations

Establish a racial context that is personal, local, and immediate.

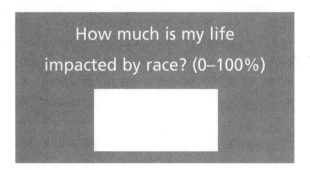

My race impacts my life

➢ Emotionally:

➢ Socially:

➢ Intellectually:

➢ Morally:

RACIAL AUTOBIOGRAPHY: CURTIS LINTON

I grew up in a suburb of Salt Lake City, Utah, with a 95% middle-class White population. We were not only racially homogenous but also culturally and religiously homogenous because most all of us were Mormon by faith and descended from Western European pioneers. It was a great place to grow up as there was significant honor attached to my heritage, and I was never culturally challenged or made to feel different. My first experiences with racial difference came with two large families living in my neighborhood—one of Latino descent and the other Polynesian.

Both families were poor and lived in quite humble circumstances. It was easy to associate their messy yards and ramshackle houses with their race. It was also easy to see them as representative of their race, and I believe that some of those earliest attitudes continue to influence me today. Every member of the Latino family was humble, kind, disciplined, and hard working, even though their huge family must have been hard to support. From my perspective, they almost lived a second-class existence, had a yard full of broken down cars, and mostly ate "Mexican food"—I assumed—because they could not afford anything more. Likewise, the Polynesian family also influenced my perceptions as they were mostly overweight, lived in very limited circumstances, were not academically ambitious, and seemed to be hobbled in their opportunity to excel in society, even though they were about as kind and contentedly happy as anyone I have ever known.

Seeing as I knew no other Latinos or Polynesians, it was easy to assume that every Latino and Polynesian must have been just like them. Of course, there were plenty of White families in my neighborhood who exhibited some of the same characteristics as these families of color, but I saw them as unique rather than as representative of our White race.

I remember from an early age thinking how horrible it was that institutions such as slavery and White supremacy once thrived in our society. But what I never saw was my own hand in these institutions. These were always bad things that happened to people of color long ago rather than circumstances to which White people subjected people of color. Consequently, I grew up thinking that I could just empathize with those who were victims of discrimination and thus extricate myself from the ongoing causes of racial discrimination.

Like any young child, I liked telling jokes. But I was never naturally funny so I would always retell the jokes that I heard somebody else share that caused a lot of laughs. This meant that most of the time, the jokes I told would either be sexually or ethnically related. I told a lot of Polack jokes when I was young, but I remember justifying them by thinking that *Polack* was a term that actually did not refer to anybody real because people from Poland were actually *Poles*.

I lost this justification, however, when I became an adolescent and started hearing—and sharing—blatantly racist jokes.

One joke I heard was extremely derogatory toward African Americans, but it got huge laughs from those who heard it. I laughed heartily myself but thought at the time that it was too tasteless to actually share. This reluctance lasted only until I was with a group of boys and everyone started sharing jokes. By this age, my Polack jokes were rather dated, and I was left searching desperately for something funny to tell. The only one that kept coming to mind was this offensive African American joke. Desperate to fit in with the rest of the boys, I finally shared it, and everyone laughed. For a rare moment, I was the funny guy, but I also felt very empty and ashamed inside for telling it. Nevertheless, I told this joke time and time again because it always got a good laugh. The price of those laughs, however, has been a lifetime of lingering shame about being so willing to profit at another's expense, even though I eventually grew beyond telling jokes.

As I progressed through high school and into college, I enjoyed seeing myself as slightly more intellectually and politically liberal than most of my peers. Commensurate with this was the desire to experience cultures other than my own. In a sense, I made myself out to be a modern social anthropologist. I would dabble in other cultures willingly, such as dating girls of a different color, listening to "World" music, taking road trips to Mexico, backpacking through Europe, and watching independent films that focused on societies different than my own. But like many budding White liberals, I was far more interested in cultures beyond my own shores rather than those within my own country. It was easy to romanticize the experience of cultures in South America, Africa, India, and elsewhere, but it was too grittily realistic to overtly engage myself in the cultures of color that existed right here in Salt Lake City. In my unconsciously distorted White eyes, Black and Brown cultures here in the United States were too closely associated with gangs, poverty, welfare, and conflict to hold the same appeal as some mystical culture in another land.

Much of this began to change when I moved to downtown Los Angeles to attend graduate school at the University of Southern California. For the first time in my life, I thought I was a minority. I lived in the neighborhood of Koreatown, where 60% of the population was Latino, 30% was Korean, and the rest was a mix of White and Black. Likewise, my church—which had almost always been predominantly White—was a very diverse mix of races and languages. Furthermore, my wife taught in a neighborhood elementary school where about 90% of her students were children of immigrant parents, spoke two languages, and lived—as I termed it then—a very "inner-city" existence.

Living in Koreatown was a cultural experience unlike any I had ever known, and I loved it. As I worked closely with people of different races in my wife's classroom and in our church, I truly grew to love and respect Latino, Asian, and Black cultures. I came to see their richness, values, and sincerity, and I became a voluntary advocate for their needs.

However, I was always there as a visitor and observer. I had the choice of living where I lived and interacting with whomever I pleased. I always knew that I was temporarily there and that their life wasn't exactly my life. Nevertheless, I never hesitated to offer a strong opinion about what should be done politically or otherwise for these "poor" people of color. As a typical White male, I continued to believe first and foremost in my understanding and interpretation of their existence. I knew that I had been blessed with a comfortable and privileged middle-class life, but I simply assumed that all they needed to do to attain what I had was to work hard and pursue opportunities.

Looking back now, I am astounded that I was so naïve to assume that the privileges afforded to White people are simply available to anyone for the taking. Likewise, it is almost comical to think that at first I thought of myself as a "minority" while living in Koreatown. I was counting myself as a minority only because Whites were outnumbered by people of color. What I did not want to take into account at first was the fact that I would always be in the majority because of my racial privilege. I had opportunities and access that few in my neighborhood shared. As I grew closer to people of color, I realized more clearly what I had and what they did not.

Eventually, I began to develop a growing sense of White guilt. I knew that what I had wasn't exactly available to just anyone. I decided at this time that what I needed to do was treat everyone equally—if I was going to lock my car doors when a Black man crossed the street, then I needed to lock my doors when a man of any race crossed the street. If I said hello to the White person in my building, then I needed to do the same to the Black, Brown, and Asian person as well. And if I sat next to my White friends at church, then I better sit next to some of my friends of color as well.

I later discovered that all of this was only a wall I built between me and my White guilt. By this time, of course, I no longer told any racist jokes, but I avoided them as much for the fact that I did not want to be seen as racist as for the reason that they were simply wrong to tell. I created a world for myself where I could continue in my White privilege but feel as though I was doing a service to all of the people of color who surrounded me just by treating them equally.

This all began to change when I started working with Glenn Singleton on a *Video Journal of Education* production. For the first time in my life, I actually sat down with a person of another race and talked about what race was like from that person's perspective, rather than assuming I already understood. It was eye opening, to say the least. I finally begin *seeing* people of color as equal rather than simply *treating* them as equal. Their intellect, opinions, ways of seeing the world, experiences, and understandings were every bit as valuable as my own. No longer could I rest within the comfort of my own existence simply because I was a member of the dominant group. From now on, I would be required to validate someone different from me every bit as much as I had always validated myself.

First Condition: Getting Personal

Probably the biggest growth I experienced was coming to recognize the power of White privilege. I had always thought that I was just good at school rather than recognizing the fact that my schools were designed from the ground up to teach me—a White suburban middle-class male. I had never before realized that I could probably have attended any school in the country and still had the same success—not because of my inherent skills but because of my perfect fit with the American public education system.

Likewise, I had to acknowledge that most of my success in life was not primarily due to any great and unique talent of mine. Rather, I benefited from a racial system that opened doors of opportunity for me to walk through and a White power structure that always assumed I would succeed. Faced with a lack of doubts, of course I succeeded. This was a hard reality to face, however, as I had always assumed that I was particularly gifted and talented (a lifetime of honors classes can do this to you).

What was at first hard to admit, however, later became a source of my own authentic living. When I began to acknowledge the reality of my privileged existence, I was then able to become much more honest about my own life and my place in this society. Rather than defending the myopic view of the American Dream—that anyone can get anything if they only work hard enough—and that I had accomplished this dream, I was able to thankfully acknowledge where I had received help along the way. Likewise, it became much easier for me to accept Glenn's experiences as reality rather than redefining his understandings so that they would better fit my own. To live authentically within myself and to be honest about my own accomplishments allowed me to listen to Glenn and to others who have not had my privilege with a more honest and accepting heart and mind. Just because their lives have been different than my own does not mean I need to be threatened by their difference. I am no less validated in my own existence just because their experience has not been like my own. Rather, in validating their existence, I find the opportunity to live more authentically and real in my own life.

As I grew in my racial understanding, I also had to deal with histories of racism, particular to my own culture. Up until the 1970s, the Mormon Church had not allowed Black men to participate in priesthood ordinances. These facts had always disturbed me—how could I reconcile a personal and strong religious belief with such blatant racism? What I finally came to conclude within myself is that the history of my church and culture is not honorable in regard to race, but change has occurred, and racial equality has been enshrined within the practice of my religion. I always felt that because of my strong beliefs in my religion, it would be wrong to abandon my church just because of its racial history—it would be like fully rejecting public education just because of its history of segregation and discrimination, especially considering the rapid growth in membership of people of color within my church. What I realized was that my responsibility within my culture was to be a strong and vocal advocate for the breaking down of racism found within those around me—racially, I am most effective by being honest about the history and proactive within the present.

Practice: The Foundation of Anti-Racist Leadership

What I focus on now—and it is always a challenge to maintain this focus—is racial equity rather than racial equality. Equality assumes that everyone should be like me and have what I have and be treated like me. But a world defined by middle-class White men is not the interesting world in which I want to live. Equity recognizes and values difference. It allows me to give to others what they are individually entitled to, whether it is respect, high expectations, opportunity, or dignity, regardless of their race. Authentic within myself, I can now treat others more authentically.

———————))))———————

6
The Second Condition

Keeping the Spotlight on Race

In My Heart

Why do you stare at me in the stores?
Is it because my skin is darker than yours?
Must you contaminate the American society
With your petty stereotypes?
Is it your hatred that blinds you,
Or is it your ignorance that feeds you?
I am from a culture of proud warriors and loving mothers.
But where I live now
They want to destroy our culture.
They can never stop what is kept in my heart.
But is it still here?
Am I looked down upon?
Well, don't look down on me unless you are picking me up.
Your hatred was made to tear me up.
It will never succeed.
In a time of freedom,
Racism is still here.

—Used with permission of Jamyan Brooks, Senior
Chapel Hill, North Carolina

Reflection

What thoughts and/or questions arose for you as you read this student's poem? How do the student's perspectives about race connect to your own *personal, local, and immediate* racial experience?

This poem illustrates the student's hyperawareness that others view him primarily as a racial being. As he comes "from a culture of proud warriors and loving mothers," he sees himself as more than Black. But he is exhausted by his reality: that non-Black members of American society see him in stereotypical ways that force him to fit within a preconceived mold. In this poem, this highly conscious student asks all of us to look more clearly at our racial prejudices and to grant him the equality, respect, and high expectations that he has thus far been denied.

ISOLATING RACE

The Second Condition of Courageous Conversation encourages us to

isolate race while acknowledging the broader scope of diversity and the variety of factors that contribute to a racialized problem.

This condition focuses on the critical need to address race explicitly and intentionally. In doing so, educators not only deepen their understanding of race but also develop skills to acknowledge and address those other diversity-related factors, such as economic status and gender, which often contribute to a racialized problem. Through the careful and isolated examination of race, educators not only discover new meaning in race but also more authentically recognize the intersection of race and other aspects of human diversity and culture.

Our experience suggests that when educators attempt to address too many phenomena coupled with race initially, they tend to converse about those other topics—say, poverty or family values—instead of race because those topics are easier to negotiate. It is extremely difficult to keep the conversation focused on race and not drift off into topics that are less emotional and about which people feel more knowledgeable. How common it is for the topic of race to surface during an examination of student achievement data, and someone says, "Well, what about poverty?" Then someone else might say, "And what about language?" Suddenly, the conversation loses focus around the challenge of race and is predictably redefined to any number of other diversity issues.

Furthermore, we have found that many prominent educational researchers and practitioners express solid understandings of other diversity topics but fail to explore or even recognize race as a viable factor affecting school culture and student achievement. Given our suggestion from the previous chapter—that race impacts 100% of our life experiences—how odd it is that popular educational research, theory, and practice virtually ignore and sometimes explicitly reject any notion that race matters in schooling processes and outcomes. Never do we suggest that race is the only factor for educators to consider as they struggle to improve schools. But, how can race at the very least not play a role in our cycle of inquiry regarding closing the racial achievement gap? The Second Condition of Courageous Conversation assists educators in avoiding the tendency to divert attention from race.

Redefining Race

Putting race on the table and keeping it there is a struggle because of the tendency to redefine institutional racial issues as internal factors that are more accessible and familiar to us or perhaps as challenges that are external to school and district operations. Specifically, educators often develop an understanding of the fact that Black and Brown students are not meeting standards by naming family, community, and the students themselves as the reasons for the problem rather than by examining how race influences school culture, the quality and delivery of instruction, and curricular choices. In essence, such a strategy encourages educators to blame students for what they bring to school, something over which educators ultimately have little personal control and, therefore, for which they can feel little responsibility. The following justifications for low student performance are drawn from interactions with educators grappling with the issue of racial achievement disparity, prior to their developing racial consciousness:

- Family

    No value for education

    A natural dislike for reading

    Parents don't read to their kids

    Parents are uneducated

- Poverty

    Parents are always working

    There is no money for books

They can't visit museums or travel

Kids have to work to support the family

- Community

    No value for education

    No respect for authority

    No good role models

    Kids feel too unsafe to focus on school

    Bad influences like drugs and gangs

- Language

    The students don't understand English well enough

    Since the parents can't speak English, they can't help their kids

    A lack of proper English proves a lack of intelligence

    I (the teacher) can't speak their language so I can't help them

- Mobility

    We (the school) are not responsible for their lack of learning since they just arrived here

    How can we help a student who is just going to move again?

    The student isn't stable enough to learn

Each of these excuses for the racial achievement gap carries the same message: It's not a school problem, it's the student's/the family's/the community's problem, and so on. Current and critical research, however, indicates that each one of these factors can be addressed effectively in a school environment (Haycock, 2003). Without question, these commonly mentioned factors can affect a student's learning, but data show that none of these excuses can prevent any group of students from achieving at high levels. What is also important to understand as it relates to the Second Condition, or isolating race, is that an educator's own personal racial perspectives, attitudes, and behaviors will impact how and what a student effectively learns and is able to do.

Race Is Pervasive

When we isolate race, we gain tremendous insight into just how pervasive a role race plays in our society. Whether blatant or subtle, raw or sophisticated, issues of race are foundational in much of public discourse, in media presentations, political campaigns, and public debate over economic development, urban renewal, new school construction boundaries, and textbook adoptions. And yet, race as a topic remains difficult to surface and even more challenging to examine in isolation from other social factors.

Consider your initial reaction to the following advertisement, which was published in a number of nationally circulated periodicals:

Naughty?   **Nice?**

This is by no means a complex illustration, and there is no right or wrong reaction; but what is quickly evident is that the ad at some level willingly plays on racial stereotypes. This is simply one tiny example of how pervasive race is embedded in society.

Reflection

As you look at this ad, what are the first thoughts that come to your mind? With whom or what do you associate the two cars? What do you see? What do you not see? What characteristics would you apply to the two cars?

This advertisement clearly communicates multiple messages. When asked to isolate race, however, we focus our examination on an understanding of the racial tone that underlies the messages. For many people, the Volkswagen advertisement immediately conjures up deep thoughts and sound connections to race. Consider as evidence the following popular responses educators have given to the advertisement over the past five years in Courageous Conversation seminars:

- Black is naughty while White is nice
- Black is bad and White is good
- White is boring
- Black is evil
- Black opposing White
- Black is rebellious while White is conservative
- Black and White don't go the same direction; they are oppositional
- Face-off

These age-old references to the American racial binary of Black and White seem to persist not only in media but also in literature, the arts, and our everyday euphemisms. Unfortunately for some, such images leave lasting personal scars and stimulate anger; others, who see racial messages as innocent or unintentional, may adopt a more defensive posture or altogether disregard them as insightful or impacting. Herein lies the apparent conflict that prompts the need for Courageous Conversations about race.

Defining Color

Even academically or intellectually speaking, race has a pervasive influence on our thinking schemas, as shown by the following edited dictionary definitions of *white* and *black:*

> White: 1 a: free from color; 2 a: being a member of a group or race characterized by reduced pigmentation and usu. specif. distinguished from persons belonging to groups marked by black, brown, yellow, or red skin coloration; b: of, relating to, characteristic of, or consisting of white people; c: marked by upright fairness; 3: free from spot or blemish: as a (1): free from moral impurity: innocent; c: not intended to cause harm; d: favorable, fortunate; 6 a: conservative or reactionary in political outlook and action

> Black: 1 a: of the color black; b (1): very dark in color <his face was ~ with rage>; (3): heavy, serious; 2 a: having dark skin, hair, and eyes: swarthy <the ~ Irish>; b (1) often cap: of or relating to any of various population groups having dark pigmentation of the skin; (2): of or relating to the Afro-American people or their culture; 4: dirty, soiled; 5a: characterized by the absence of light; 6 a: thoroughly sinister or evil: wicked; b: indicative of condemnation or discredit; 7: connected with or invoking the supernatural and esp. the devil; 8 a: very sad, gloomy, or calamitous; b: marked by the occurrence of disaster; 9: characterized by hostility or angry discontent: sullen; 12: characterized by grim, distorted, or grotesque satire

---

Reflection

When examining these definitions through the isolated lens of race, what do you see? In what ways do these definitions reflect societal views of and behaviors around race? What potential stereotypes do you see in the making or being fortified by these definitions?

Isolating race as we consider these definitions, we see that *white* is endowed with "upright fairness," "free from moral impurity," "favorable," and "fortunate," whereas *black* is considered to be "serious," "swarthy," "dirty," "wicked," "calamitous," and "angry discontent." Are these not some of the characteristics that many members of society attribute to White and Black people, respectively?

Racial Impact

The advertisement and the definitions clearly offer understandings about issues other than race, but race plays a significant role in interpreting their full meaning and, therefore, is worth careful consideration and examination. Rather than picturing cars, substitute the image of student achievement data disaggregated by race, and consider your personal response to the patterns you see. The data can lead educators into conversations about the multiple factors impacting achievement disparity, including teaching, learning, school culture, and family involvement. But the data also invite Courageous Conversations about the role race plays in student performance, discipline, and engagement.

When we isolate race, we expand our consciousness about the role race, racial identity development, and institutional racism play in our society. Clearly, the color of the paint on a car cannot cause different performance nor can cars be "naughty" or "nice." But it is not such a big leap to see how purposeful personification of the cars extends our thinking to determining who is appropriate for selling, buying, and driving them. Although we cannot determine the motives of the advertisers or the focus groups that helped select any given advertisement, we can get clear on what impact the image has on various racial groups' perspective, experiences, and behaviors.

Reflection

Based on your own personal racial confirmation, clarification, or discoveries thus far, answer the following questions using a lens or filter of race:

How does it feel to be characterized as naughty or nice or to be unidentified altogether?

Do these characterizations or omissions affect your level of engagement and achievement?

Who benefits/suffers from these existing racial representations?

UNPACKING RACE

Our Second Condition of Courageous Conversation—isolate race—prompts participants to bring race front and center in the conversation so that they may better examine and understand its impact. More specifically, at this point, educators "unpack race," hoping to understand the deeper meaning without distraction of other, albeit related issues.

When Glenn Singleton was in seventh grade, his family elected to place him in an independent, predominantly White, Jewish, suburban day school. As one of a handful of students of color in his middle school, Glenn was never allowed to "unpack" his racial identity, nor did his White teachers ever choose to acknowledge, much less "unpack," their racial reality. Consequently, Glenn was left struggling and searching throughout his time at Park School to explain what he was experiencing. He lacked any meaningful or constructive opportunities to talk about the primary cause for his unease: race.

The educators at Park School prided themselves on being race neutral and color-blind, which we view as the antithesis of the Second Condition because we all have racial perspectives that impact our daily racial interactions and experiences, whether we are conscious of them or not. Nevertheless, Glenn stood out as one of only four Black students in his class. He was hypervisible and thus a magnet for individual and institutional scrutiny. In his first year at Park School, a graduating Black senior he didn't know very well discreetly wrote in his yearbook:

> To Glenn, I wish you the best of luck in this crazy place. As we both know, because you are Black, you can only achieve as much as a White by being educated. Continue to strive hard and you will reach the goals that you have set. Just believe in yourself and what you can do and life will be that much easier to bear. Love, Wanda.

While Wanda's advice may have constituted some of the most important words written in Glenn's yearbook, it was not the advice he wanted. By the end of his first year at Park School, Glenn was already trying to gain the approval of his classmates and teachers, who seemed more interested in having him change how he spoke, what he ate, the music he appreciated, and the clothes he wore. Ironically, the Park School community professed itself to be color-blind, but they noticed that Glenn was different. Some classmates labeled where he came from as a ghetto and thus found it difficult to relate to his "culture." In order to "fit in," Glenn's only choice was to "pretend" that he, too, was White.

As any student would, Glenn responded to growing marginalization by assimilating to Park School's "normalized" White ways of being.

Again, as early as the end of his first year at Park, Glenn had begun the process of racial assimilation; many of his White friends and teachers eventually claimed to "not see him as Black." His "refined" choices in music, food, and clothing had transformed Glenn's racial identity but had not changed the fact that race had become a buried consciousness in his life.

To survive in this primarily White school, Glenn had to separate himself from his own community, which his classmates considered inferior. Such identity changes may have helped him fit in better, although he never fit in *totally* at Park because he was always pretending rather than being his authentic self. Racial assimilation also prevented Glenn from being fully a part of his family and community, which he previously had relied on for emotional, cultural, and spiritual sustenance.

Desegregated schools face the challenge of providing quality education for racially marginalized students while their staff members, for the most part, have not acquainted themselves with the experiences, perspectives, or understandings associated with being a person of color. Without "unpacking" race, White educators often attempt—whether intentionally or unintentionally—to make their colleagues of color as well as their students of color conform to the normalized conditions of White culture. By professing themselves to be color-blind, educators essentially indicate that no cultural differences exist between White people and people of color. Clearly, no one at Park School really believed that Glenn was White and Jewish. In fact, the administration prided itself on selecting a highly diverse student body. So why, then, were they quick to comment that "we don't see color" or "we don't think of you as Black," once Glenn began to comment on his racial experience and inquire about perceived cultural biases? For educators, students, and families of color, challenging White educators' mythical color blindness can lead to their further marginalization and often even stand in the way of their receiving critical resources, support, and advancement.

Reflection

Consider your own affiliations, such as your workplace, religious institution, social clubs, and recreational places that you frequent. What is the racial composition? If racial diversity exists, are tensions present due to race or racial differences? In what ways has this been addressed—or not addressed? If little racial diversity exists, why is this the case?

We believe that many educators fail to meet the needs of the growing number of students of color because this challenge is often labeled "diversity work" rather than effective pedagogy. Certainly, race is one of many categories of diversity, but making instruction accessible to students of color is not a matter of diversity: It is our responsibility to ensure quality education for all. Only when educators isolate race as a topic in their school improvement discussions are they certain to focus on issues that directly impact students of color and White students alike. Isolating race helps educators to understand race and simultaneously to develop real solutions to racial achievement disparities.

Implementation Exercise

Isolating Race

Time required: 45 minutes

Materials required: Courageous Conversation Journal for each participant and a copy of the handout that follows

1. Introduce the Second Condition of Courageous Conversations:

   Isolate race while acknowledging the broader scope of diversity and the variety of factors that contribute to a racialized problem.

   Ask the group why it is important to isolate race in the conversation rather than avoiding it altogether or addressing it in conjunction with other diversity issues such as poverty and gender.

2. Based on whether you are facilitating a group of district administrators, secondary teachers, or elementary teachers, pass out the appropriate handout.

3. Inform the participants that you are going to examine the racial makeup of the school or school system. By creating this racial demography map, you can begin isolating race and statistically examining how it impacts achievement.

4. Divide the participants into small groups of four to five people, mixing racial groups if at all possible. Assign each team one of the sections, such as Student Body or Community Participation, on the handout. At your next meeting, each team should submit a written report of findings to the facilitator and prepare to share with the entire group the following data:
   - Prior to collecting and examining any data, what did we believe to be the racial composition of the section that we were about to investigate? Why do we believe this composition exists/persists?
   - According to the data, what is the racial composition—White, Black, Latino, Asian, Native American, or multiracial—of each of the subgroups in the section you worked on?
   - What are the patterns you identified in your section in terms of the racial composition?

- What preliminary explanations have you identified that explain these patterns, including:
  – Participation and nonparticipation
  – Accessibility, opportunity, and inclusiveness
  – Prejudice and discrimination

- What are some initial ways that these discrepancies can be addressed?

5. At your next meeting, have each group report its findings.

6. After reporting, pose the following questions for an open discussion:
   - What racial beliefs are operational in our school or school system? How do the data we collected confirm or refute our racial beliefs?
   - In our school or school system, do we have a problem with racial inequity in terms of representation, participation, and/or achievement success?
   - Do we need to address these racial issues? If so, why and how?

Additional Exercises

1. Select several educators from a variety of departments or upper grade levels and have each identify a student of color. Have the teachers document how they see race impacting the students' schooling experience by selectively shadowing and conversing with these students during a full day. Have the educators report to the entire staff what they noticed and learned.

2. Guide grade-level or departmental teams in doing a racial audit of their curriculum, similar to the Volkswagen analysis. What racial messages and images are present in texts, bulletin boards, Web sites, teacher representation, school announcements, and so on? How do the images and messages correspond with the racial composition of the student body?

Second Condition of Courageous Conversations

*Isolate race while acknowledging the broader
scope of diversity and the variety of factors and
conditions that contribute to a racialized problem.*

Racial Makeup of Our School System

Identify the racial composition of every subgroup under each section of your school system. This can be done through quantitative analysis of data or qualitative observation.

➤ *District Administration*
  i. Superintendents and assistant superintendents
  ii. School board
  iii. Staff development department
  iv. Curriculum department

➤ *District Student Body*
  i. All district students
  ii. Graduation rates
  iii. Dropout rates
  iv. Disaggregated student achievement

➤ *District Personnel*
  i. Classified staff
  ii. Unclassified staff

➤ *Community Participation*
  i. District PTA
    1. PTA leadership
    2. PTA membership
  ii. School board attendance
  iii. Other district-community partnerships
    1. Police
    2. Colleges/universities
    3. Local businesses
    4. Others

Include the following racial identities as they pertain to your school system:

- Black
- White
- Latino
- Asian
- Southeast Asian
- South Asian
- Pacific Islander
- Middle Eastern
- Native American Indian
- Biracial
- Other racial identities or subgroups as needed

Racial Makeup of Our School

Identify the racial composition of every subgroup under each section of your secondary school. This can be done through quantitative analysis of data or qualitative observation.

➤ *School Student Body*
    i. All students
    ii. Attendance rates
    iii. Graduation/dropout rates
    iv. Retention rates
    v. Referrals and suspensions
    vi. Free and reduced-price lunch participants
    vii. Gifted and talented/advanced placement/honors
    viii. Special ed/remedial
    ix. Disaggregated student achievement

➤ *Community Participation*
    i. School PTA
      1. PTA leadership
      2. PTA membership
    ii. School meeting attendance
    iii. Parent-teacher conferences
    iv. Volunteers
    v. Other school-community partnerships
      1. Police
      2. Colleges/universities
      3. Local businesses
      4. Others

➤ *School Staff*
    i. Principals and assistant principals
    ii. School governing board
    iii. Counseling department
    iv. Teacher leadership teams
    v. School staff
      1. Classified
      2. Unclassified

➤ *Extracurricular Participation*
    i. Student government
    ii. Extracurricular activities (athletics, dances, drama, debate, academics, clubs, etc.)
      1. Advisers and coaches
      2. Student participants
    iii. Extracurricular spectator attendance (all events)
      1. Student attendees
      2. Staff attendees
      3. Community attendees
    iv. Before- and afterschool advisers and student participants
      1. Athletic programs
      2. Academic programs

Include the following racial identities as they pertain to your school, or other races or subgroups as needed:

- Black
- White
- Latino
- Native American Indian
- Asian
- Southest Asian
- South Asian
- Pacific Islander
- Middle Eastern
- Biracial
- Other racial identities or subgroups as needed

RACIAL AUTOBIOGRAPHY: GLENN SINGLETON

Before kindergarten, I don't remember having a construct for or consciousness around race. I grew up in an entirely Black community in the inner city of Baltimore, where the only initial images of Whiteness I saw were on television. At Hilton Elementary School, all certificated and classified adults were Black, and so interracial interaction was nonexistent. By fourth grade, I was attending YMCA camp for two weeks in the summer, where I recall being fascinated by the hair texture and different bodily odors of White campers. There was in my young mind a difference between White kids and Black kids, but I never gave it too much thought. My family loved Hilton Elementary School, so much so that when we moved out of the attendance zone, they continued registering me as a student there by using my grandparents' address.

Today, I realize how wonderful and important it was to my educational success that we would often see my teachers in the shopping centers, at social events, or at church on the weekends. As a student then, this form of omnipresent accountability brought distress to me when I was caught misbehaving in school. Most of my teachers were not shy about "airing the classroom laundry" to our parents, and our families truly welcomed the information and responded accordingly. Never did I question whether my teacher understood me, my family, or our Black culture as this was a shared experience. I believe that my K–4 teachers treated their students as if we were their own children, for better or for worse.

By fifth grade, Baltimore, like most U.S. urban centers, was required to desegregate public schools. The entire community was abuzz about the possibility of our having to be bussed away from Hilton Elementary and leave our highly qualified Black teachers behind. Fortunately for us, Hilton was an experimental site where some teachers rather than the students were forced to relocate. My fifth grade teacher, Fran Finnegan, became the first of many interracial relationships in which I would be involved. Mrs. Finnegan was said to be a wonderful suburban teacher, but in retrospect, she clearly lacked the cultural proficiency necessary to advance our gifted class. She said it did not matter to her what color we were, but unfortunately, our inquisitive minds could not share her perspective. She was really White in our eyes and subject not only to our curiosity but also to our childish malice. I guess the many years of family and community members returning from their workplaces having unfavorable experiences with "the (White) man"—who I later discovered could also be a White woman—had sunk in to our consciousness creating a sense of distrust of and dislike for our struggling White teacher.

As a class, we were quite aware of Mrs. Finnegan's racial foibles, and we also knew from experiences with Black teachers prior to fifth grade what it felt like to have a teacher who truly knew and liked us! To her credit, when most of the White teachers departed Hilton after little more than a semester, Mrs. Finnegan felt an unexplained need to hang around. But when the White teachers vacated, Mrs. Finnegan was forced to get to know the Black teachers, which I believe enabled her to begin figuring us out and improving the quality of her instruction. The days when we made Mrs. Finnegan break down in tears quickly dissipated into a new era of culturally responsive instruction. What a shock it was to hear my mother refer to good old Fran as "Sista Finnegan." In fact, she retired from Hilton and lives on as one of our family's most influential and memorable teachers.

Given our success at Hilton Elementary School, I often wonder why I was "strongly encouraged" by my mother to attend a private school for the middle and high school years. I recall feeling torn between the excitement of Park's well-resourced, extravagant campus and facility and a desire to walk to school with my neighborhood friends. The message I received explicitly from home and implicitly from the Park School community was "If it ain't White, it isn't Right." My best friend, Jimmy, and I were sent together, so I wasn't alone, except for the fact that Park School administrators never allowed us to be in the same classes. It seemed to me that Jimmy was responsible for diversifying one half of our class, and I the other. We would huddle for lunch each day and for class photos once a year. Jimmy's athletic prowess eventually earned him distinction as he could adapt his football and baseball skills to soccer and lacrosse, the only options available to Park students. I also played both sports but found little of my soul on the plush green athletic fields.

The state-of-the-art theater called out to me when I was forced into summer school before seventh grade. What a shock and a blow to my confidence to move from the ranks of gifted in the Black community to remedial among my soon-to-be White peers. While Park faculty "refreshed" the "slower learners" in summer school, the administrators opened the school's elitist doors each summer to inner-city teenage artists who staged Black musicals such as *The Wiz* and *Purlie* in Park's professional theater. Mingling among the summer arts students excited me so much that I later would be willing to find myself in the operettas of Gilbert and Sullivan. Once I arrived in the fall, the Black teenagers had all returned to their inner-city schools and taken the Black musicals, energy, and spirit with them. I was left with the theater and a long list of productions in which I would need to fit my Black body into a White role. Today, I am still known as the "Black Pirate King" from our eighth-grade production of *The Pirates of Penzance* by a school that adamantly insisted that they did not see color.

My new role as the king brought all kinds of lasting identity changes. Performing arts transformed me into a singing, dancing cowboy in *Oklahoma* and a racist White gang-leader in *West Side Story*. These were the major productions as I cannot recall the numerous short acts, in all of which I needed to discover a new White persona.

In the classroom, mastering the advanced curriculum mirrored the theatrical requirement that I think and act White. Park was quite impressed with my ability to imitate their culture so precisely in such a short time. I received the highest award for my contribution to life on campus. My award in my family and neighborhood was a feeling of alienation and internalized White supremacy creating long-lasting self-hate.

By senior year, my family was convinced that I would be the first to attend college, but beginning a Black college tradition at Morehouse, Morgan, or Howard was out of the question as my counselor felt an Ivy League university such as Penn, Brown, or Cornell would bring greater prominence to Park School and, in their minds, my family. I left Park deeply connected to the institution, my education, and my faculty and friends. I was indeed proficient in Whiteness and ready for the next level.

At Penn, I made the choice, based on my experience at Park, to embrace the White community and neglect all things Black. In the White dormitory, I befriended White students and eventually pledged a "very White" fraternity, Sigma Chi. How deep was my investment in Whiteness by this stage? So much so that I found nothing wrong with shouting "All Honor to His Name" as my overtly racist White fraternity pledge master read the names of the known White supremacist founders. My initiation was just short of a Ku Klux Klan rally complete with white hooded robes, fire-lit torches, and a cross burning— defined as the blazing symbol of the fraternity. Given that we never studied such a heinous American past at Park School, I must say that I was dangerously naïve. There are so many painful memories related to Sigma Chi that I have buried; I am now convinced it was the wrong choice for me, and a poor reflection on the state of higher education in our country. Later, as an administrator at the University of Pennsylvania, I quietly advocated for the removal of the Greek system. Quietly because the president of the Board of Trustees and many other big givers were also Sigma Chi "brothers."

In my first job as an advertiser in New York City, I began to get a slow and painful wake-up call from my slumber in Whiteness. My boss, Fred Dubin, recognized my talent and potential and wanted to see me promoted to media buyer on a prestigious account. Our client, however, did not share my boss's vision for my future. Although I was told that I was not promoted because of my age, Fred allowed me to listen in on a conference call as the client revealed that my color, not my age, was the concern. Of course, the client couched his racism in terms of economics, and specifically that he feared the "marketplace" might not respect my color. In truth, he did not believe in my proven ability to succeed in spite of the racism my color had evoked in others since arriving at Park School a decade earlier. I left advertising soon after this incident but was still in denial about my ability to achieve Whiteness. In retrospect, I believe I returned to Penn to be an admissions director not only because I missed working in education, but also because I knew how to be White at the university, and I was well respected for my assimilation efforts.

Traveling to New England to recruit for the University of Pennsylvania served as a second wake-up call. Not only did the largely White high school educators and Penn alumni disrespect me racially, but I was often not considered to be the "real" Ivy League admissions director. Many had trouble with a Black man having such power. As a university administrator, I got to see my alma mater in a completely different way. I watched talented students of color come to Penn and not fit in culturally. I could truly see the forced process of assimilation that had been my own daily diet as a student there and now as an administrator.

Five years later when Penn moved me to California to direct the West Coast admissions office, I initially believed the hype surrounding the wonderful diversity and interracial solidarity in California. I guess I was amazed to see how close together the different races lived, worked, and played. I also learned quickly that it was not "politically correct" to talk about race in the Golden State. Although the East was incredibly segregated by comparison, I felt safer being Black in Philly, Baltimore, and New York City. In California, I could never quite figure out how people felt about me racially, whereas the racial writing was, both literally and figuratively, on the wall back East.

Since my move to the West, I can name thousands of times in which race has dramatically impacted the outcome of a situation. From attending Stanford, to purchasing my first house, to buying cars, to being seated in restaurants, to walking down my fancy neighborhood streets and having some kid, teenager, or adult call me a "Nigger." With each of these demoralizing experiences . . . those situations I once believed would no longer happen once I earned my degrees and entered the middle class. Some friends are still quick to suggest to me that I am "playing the race card." Today, I just get quiet when these occasions arise. In my mind, I know that if I were truly playing the mythical race card from a deck of 52 cards, I would have played all of my cards by the end of seventh grade!

—————————— \\\\ ——————————

The Third Condition

Engaging Multiple Racial Perspectives

We are trapped in our history and our history is trapped in us!

—James Baldwin

As Baldwin so eloquently writes, it seems impossible for any of us to fully separate our current reality from our history of experiences. Even if we *could* do so, why would we, given that there is so much to learn from what has happened in our individual and collective pasts, especially with regard to race, race relations, and racism? We can uncover critical perspectives and develop deeper interracial relationships as we examine our interrelated histories, which continue to nourish the foundation of our daily racial interactions.

The Third Condition of Courageous Conversation prompts participants to

normalize social construction of knowledge, thus engaging multiple racial points of view in order to surface critical perspective.

To *normalize social construction of knowledge* is to acknowledge the process through which racial meaning is inherited, interpreted, and passed on from one generation to the next. Each of us creates meaning around our current racial reality based on how we have experienced and understood our near and distant pasts. The Third Condition enables educators to develop will, skill, and capacity for listening to and engaging with conflicting racial perspectives and experiences. In their discussions around race, educators formally recognize and respect that people offer a broad continuum of willingness and ability to examine and understand racial matters.

Where and how people have grown up creates the lens through which they see the world racially. This is known as the *social construction of knowledge* about race. If everyone involved in a Courageous Conversation brings somewhat of a unique social construction of racial knowledge, then there will necessarily be *multiple racial points of view* to consider. Because we view this as a normal phenomenon of our interracial existence—especially in education—the Third Condition of Courageous Conversation invites participants to normalize social construction and multiple racial points of view to surface conflicting or critical perspectives.

SOCIAL CONSTRUCTION OF KNOWLEDGE

We see things not as they are, but rather as we are!

—Pastor Douglas Fitch, Glide Memorial Church

Tremendous complexities exist around race as a socially and politically constructed phenomenon because race both *exists* and *does not exist* in the United States specifically and more generally throughout the Western world. In spite of the specific racial meanings that we have learned to associate with skin and eye color or hair texture, all human beings are scientifically of one species. Only socially and politically do we exist in the variety of racial groups we have learned to recognize. With respect to race, how, where, and with whom we live, work, and play forms our personal and collective racial contexts and is at the heart of how we interpret race in our lives and define race in the lives of others.

Racial issues are not about physical skin color but rather stem from the meaning and value people assign to skin color. Remarkable variance exists in how different racial groups determine, define, and describe their own collective racial experience as well as the experiences of "the racial other." Clearly, then, it is important to recognize that definitions of race and shared racial experiences in the United States of America are derived from national, state, and local community contexts. Through developing a greater understanding of these contexts, we can better understand the thoughts, beliefs, and feelings that people of each "racial group" bring with them into Courageous Conversation.

In Chapter 9, a description of the Fifth Condition of Courageous Conversation provides opportunity to explore briefly how history has shaped current racial realities. What we hope to indicate in the Third Condition is just how much historical perspective about race is passed down from one generation to the next, thus shaping the way people view contemporary racial images and their interracial interactions.

Reflection

Can you think of a time when someone you knew did something that you viewed to be racially unjust or even racist, but the person engaged in the action saw it differently? Describe the differing racial contexts that you believe influenced your and the other person's contrasting points of view.

Internalization and Transfer of Racism

As people of color are continuously subjected to racist acts, an eventual internalization and transfer of racism often occurs. This is a process in which people of color begin to believe all that they hear about their own racial image, potential, and power. When people of color internalize negative racial messages, they may lose hope, thus buying into notions of second-class or subservient citizenship. Eventually, this conditioning or racism undermines their confidence and ability to function successfully in the White-dominant culture. According to Weissglass (2001),

> The patterns of internalizing and transferring racism (insults, criticism, slurs, and violence) are rooted in genocide, slavery, subjugation, conquest, and exploitation. When people are hurt and not allowed to heal through emotional release, they are pulled to re-enact the hurt on someone else. Since People of Color have rarely been able to act out their hurt on Whites, they tend to act it out on family members and other people of Color. These behavior patterns tend to get passed on from generation to generation. (p. 50)

Similarly, White people can develop skills to not see and acknowledge the impact of race in their lives or the pervasiveness of institutionalized racism. This is called "structured color blindness" and is found within a White belief that people of color are less successful because they try less, or worse, because they are inferior to White people. Internalizing such beliefs of White supremacy is quite harmful to White educators and the White children they teach.

SURFACING CRITICAL PERSPECTIVES

Multiple points of view about race, racial identity development, and racism serve to sustain interracial dialogue because critical perspective surfaces. But the various racial points of view can also bring the dialogue to an abrupt conclusion. The Third Condition of Courageous Conversation suggests that it is normal for different racial groups to offer different racial points of view as determined and defined by their shared racial experiences. Even more confusing, however, is the fact that people of the same racial group may also diverge in their point of view in spite of having a shared racial context.

Recall for a moment Glenn Singleton's racial autobiography. Clearly, Glenn's view of White racial culture changed dramatically as he left an all-Black school, in which the meaning of Whiteness was limited to books and media, and transferred to a predominantly White school. Glenn's changing viewpoint affected not only his attitude but also his behavior, both in White contexts and in his own Black community. In this relatively short period of time, race—as a social and political construct—did not change in Baltimore, but what race meant to Glenn, and perhaps to those who knew him, certainly changed dramatically.

By normalizing the presence of multiple racial points of view, we avoid a situation in which one way of understanding race—typically a dominant one—invalidates other points of view and thus invalidates their racial expressions and experiences as well. Although it may not be done maliciously or even intentionally, it is nonetheless not uncommon for White educators to discount, disparage, or deny the racial views of educators of color. Perhaps only because the dominant culture does not witness or experience a situation or circumstance in the same way as people of color, there may be a gentle insistence that all people see it the "White way." To sustain a Courageous Conversation, educators must avoid forcing their own individual and collective racial point of view onto others, which often means enforcing a dominant White racial understanding of schooling as normal and correct.

Reflection

Think of an interracial situation or conversation that was dominated by a White racial point of view. What was the prevailing tone? Was the process inclusive or not? What was the outcome, and was it satisfactory to all participants?

Counterstory

When multiple points of view are embraced, educators are better able to understand racial conflict and become aware of racial bias. Essentially, they uncover the *counterstory*, a critical perspective that reveals and explains the impact of racism. Only through surfacing an understanding of how racism is experienced by those most keenly aware and conscious of it can educators arrive at a critical racial perspective about student learning and their work in schools.

In our experience, as White educators normalize multiple points of view, they come to a much deeper understanding of the cumulative effect of racism for people of color. Rather than feeling personally challenged, put off, or offended by this process, they often come to feel greater personal and professional empathy and responsibility. As educators of color witness this transformation of their White colleagues and discover their true lack of racist intent or malice, they are less likely to be guarded and suspicious in their commentary and interactions.

This mutual redefinition and resulting belief in the possibility of effective interracial relations invites the necessary exploration toward a critical perspective of how students of color experience school.

Validating Multiple Points of View

By normalizing social construction of knowledge and thus engaging multiple racial points of view, participants in Courageous Conversation surface critical perspectives that open the door to new ways of looking at the challenge of effectively educating all students. Often, what is most difficult—and the essence of this Fourth Condition—is listening to the racial views of people of color as intently as White ideas about race and allowing people of color the same variation in their views that is acceptable among White people.

As an American culture, we often recognize, embrace, and promote people of color whose racial ideology is aligned with more conservative White ideologies. Often, these people of color express a point of view that exists outside the majority viewpoint among people of color. The appointment of Clarence Thomas to the U.S. Supreme Court is illustrative of this phenomenon. His appointment provided a way to racially diversify the Supreme Court without diversifying its racial ideology. This same phenomenon can exist in schools where largely White staffs are more sympathetic to the voices of educators, students, and parents of color when they impart an understanding about the impact of race on schooling that is closely aligned to the dominant White point of view.

Keep in mind that the Third Condition of Courageous Conversation does not require participants to agree, while the Fourth Agreement ensures that we will not reach closure. The Third Condition merely encourages educators to entertain diverging points of view as a way of engaging with race in a deeply critical way.

Reflection

Consider the following racially "loaded" topics:

- Affirmative action in college admissions
- The O. J. Simpson trial verdict
- Illegal immigration and or insuring civil rights for undocumented citizens

First, isolate race (the Second Condition) and try to give voice to at least two conflicting points of view for each topic. Next, determine the factors that have shaped your own social construction of knowledge on these issues. What seems to be the dominant viewpoint among your family members, friends, colleagues, and social circles? How closely do their racial ideologies align with your own opinion?

As participants engage in Courageous Conversation, the First Condition (focusing on the personal, local, and immediate) and the Second Condition (isolating race) serve as the foundation on which the multiple points of view and the critical perspective (the Third Condition) can rest. Once these are engaged—and, in a sense, discovering or reaffirming that race impacts each of us all the time—the Third Condition of Courageous Conversation invites educators to speak their truth about their varied racial experiences. Rather than bringing conversation to a silent halt, these conflicting viewpoints serve as the doorway to sustained dialogue and as an opportunity to surface critical perspective about race, racial identity, and institutional racism.

Implementation Exercise

Engaging Multiple Racial Points of View

Time required: 45 minutes

Materials required: Courageous Conversation Journal for each participant and a copy of the poem below

1. Explain and explore the Third Condition of Courageous Conversation:

   Normalize social construction of knowledge, thus engaging multiple racial points of view in order to surface critical perspective.

   Based on your reading, describe for the group the following terms:

   - Normalize
   - Social construction of knowledge
   - Multiple racial points of view
   - Critical perspective

2. Ask the group how the application of this condition can create a safe environment for people to share their honest opinions and feelings about race and racism.

3. Conduct a listening exercise. Divide participants into groups according to their race (racial affinity groups), and have them read the poem "I Dream" by Pablo Vega, which is on the worksheet.

4. Invite each educator to provide an individual response the following question:

   What is Pablo saying about the impact of race on his life both inside and outside of school?

   Have members of each racial affinity group share their responses with others in their same group, and create a unified interpretation of the poem that highlights the shared meaning and understanding arrived at by all or most of the group members.

5. Bring all of the participants back together, and have each affinity group present its interpretation of the poem.

6. Invite the participants to examine each racial affinity group's interpretation of the poem summarizing the multiple racial viewpoints and surfacing the critical racial perspective, or the *counterstory,* and revealing ideas of which most people in the room were not aware.

- What were the similarities, and what were the differences in racial viewpoints?
- What social constructions were apparent in each group's interpretation?
- What value to the group's understanding came from hearing multiple racial points of view regarding Pablo's experience described in "I Dream"?
- How can these multiple viewpoints be more fully honored in all conversations?

7. Have each participant reflect on this conversation in his or her Courageous Conversation Journal.

I Dream

I am from a clash of Color,
From an idea of love, modeled for others' perception.
I see me as I am, but am hidden from others' views.
I am who I am, but a living contradiction to my peers.
I see life as a blessing, a gift granted to me.
Why should my tint describe me? Why should my culture degrade me?
Why should the ignorance of another conjure my presence?
Too many times I've been disappointed by the looks,
By the sneers and misconceptions of the people who don't get me,
Who don't understand why it hurts.

I dream of a place of glory and freedom,
Of losing the weight of oppression on my back.
I dream of the enlightenment of people,
Of the opening of their eyes.
I dream for acceptance,
And for the blessing of feeling special just once.
One moment of glory . . . for the true virtue in my life.
For the glimmer of freedom, and a rise in real pride.

—Used with permission of Pablo Vega
Chapel Hill High School, North Carolina

Reflection

What is Pablo saying about the impact of race on his life both inside and outside of school?

RACIAL AUTOBIOGRAPHY: ANN

At San Altos High School where I teach as a biracial Japanese American, an annual spring event known as "Fractured Follies" features teachers as entertainment and brings in lots of money for leukemia research. Last year during the morning announcements, a very popular and talented teacher involved in the show was doing a promotional bit that made me very uncomfortable. Speaking in a thick "Boris Badenov" Russian accent and butchering the English language, he cracked up everyone in my second period class and, I assume, the school. When the comedy bit continued the next day, I said to my class, "I wonder how the Russian students feel every time Mr. L speaks in a fake Russian accent? Do you think they feel uncomfortable? Do you think everyone turns around to look at the lone Russian kid in the class? Do you think he's feeling horribly embarrassed, but is chuckling weakly alongside his classmates because he wants to appear to be 'OK with it'?"

After a brief period of uncomfortable silence, a few students tried to defend Mr. L. I explained to my students that I knew how that Russian kid in the classroom felt. I smiled weakly when other kids pulled up their eyes and said, "Ching Chong Chinaman" or mimicked my mother's accent. I wondered whether or not I was being too sensitive. After all, Mr. L is popular and has a reputation for being sensitive and caring. We had recently been through school- and districtwide tolerance training, particularly as it related to gay and bisexual issues, and I knew that many students were sensitive to these issues. I suggested that had Mr. L spoken in a lisping, effeminate parody of a homosexual male, he would have been told to discontinue the act. I also said that the same might be true had he been speaking in a heavy Spanish accent or in the voice of an inner-city African-American rapper.

The act—which seemed to offend only me—was allowed to continue every day until the day of the show. Although it provided me an opportunity to give my students another perspective, I wasn't brave enough to bring it up to the administration or even to the teacher in question. This year, I intend to gently explain to the teacher why I don't think the comedy bit is funny. The reason I found no humor in this has much to do with my personal history. I feel for that one kid in the classroom who—try as he or she might to blend in—is constantly betrayed by an accent, a darker shade of skin, or differently shaped eyes.

I was born in 1956 in Norman, Oklahoma, to a White American father and a Japanese mother. My father grew up in a racist Southern Baptist culture from which he fled at the age of 17 to join first the merchant marines and then the U.S. Army. My mother grew up in Tokyo as the eldest child of a Christian family whose progressive patriarch insisted on a university education for his daughter.

Despite my grandfather's liberal and pacifist politics, he arranged for my mother to be married into a military officer's family. She spent about eight months in this unhappy union before being "released" from the marriage shortly before the end of World War II.

My parents' lives intersected at the University of Oklahoma where one was an Asian Studies major on the G.I. Bill and the other was a foreign student working on a master's degree in education.

There has never been a time when I haven't been aware of my culture and my race. My conscious memory begins from around the age of two and a half when my Japanese grandparents were living with us in Monterey, California. While my father was gone to Korea for a year, we spoke Japanese, ate Japanese food, and socialized with other Japanese families. Within that world, it was OK to be Japanese, but outside of that world, it was embarrassing to be different. I remember cringing in public if my mother spoke Japanese to me, and I begged her to speak English. Of course, the same thing happened in reverse when we lived in Japan, and I cringed in embarrassment when my brother's loud English drew attention to us in public places and gave us away.

Blatant racism has been rare in my life. When my family moved to the Baltimore area, my father made several telephone calls looking for a rental home. One of the houses seemed perfect, and the landlady was very eager to rent to us until she took a look at our biracial family. Suddenly, the house was not available. My father was furious.

I also remember my parents talking about how my Oklahoma grandparents refused to speak to my father for months when he announced his intention to marry my Japanese mother. It is hard for me to reconcile that image with the one of my loving grandparents who—once they accepted the idea—became my mother's greatest ally. I remember my grandfather proudly telling of his verbal exchange with the counter girl at a cafeteria where my parents and grandparents were having lunch one Sunday in Oklahoma City:

Girl: You see that couple over there? Can you believe he's marrying a Jap? With all the American girls around, why do you suppose he'd want to marry her?

My grandfather: That girl is going to be my daughter-in-law, and he's marrying her because he loves her!

My pivotal events related to race and culture have mostly been about an awareness of being outside of the majority group in both countries. I'm not half of one culture and half of another. Because I was raised in both Japan and the United States in two cultures and speaking two languages, there isn't a point at which one part of me ends and the other begins. Snapshots in my scrapbook of racial perspective would have to include the following experiences:

Age 6, Fort Ord, California. The whole family gathers around the TV set to watch a Chinese American girl play the piano. She's not Japanese, but she's as close as we can get to being on television in the sixties. I relive this moment about 30 years later when my daughter is so excited about Trini, the Asian Power

Ranger, who happens to be yellow. I realize it's because she rarely sees anyone on television who looks like her. A year later, my daughter yells at the television when she sees that Trini has been replaced by a different non-White female Power Ranger. She learns early on that the "American network television tent" is not big enough to house more than a few token non-White characters.

Age 7, Tanuma, Japan. We are visiting my uncle's family, which is living here for a few years while he pays his dues as a doctor at a hospital in the boon-docks. I accompany my grandmother to the store followed by a parade of children, which gets longer and longer as the children call to their friends to come see the *gaijin* (foreigner). The climax occurs when we are surrounded by yelling children, I am hiding horrified behind my grandmother, and she is yelling at them to go away.

Age 10, Houston, Texas. We are visiting with my American grandparents on our way to a year-long stay in Baltimore. The neighborhood kids are all coming over to see the girl from Japan and to ask her to "say something in Chinese."

Age 10, Edmonton Elementary School, Catonsville, Maryland. My brother and I are the only Asian kids in the school. Even though our last name is American, my hair is brown, and my eyes are hazel, kids keep asking me how I learned to speak English so well. When my mother substitutes as the teacher in a class down the hall, kids slow down by her classroom because they've never seen a "Chinese lady" in person.

First day of school, Zama American Middle School, Zama, Japan. A good quarter of the class looks like me. I am not alone. In fact, it is soon apparent that the cool kids are all half-Japanese—Japanese and Black, Japanese and White, Japanese and Mexican. There are half-Japanese football players, cheer-leaders, student council officers, and even half-Japanese hoods. I love this place but find that it exists only in Hawaii and on U.S. military bases in Asia.

First day of high school, Salinas, California. Back to racial reality. I notice that my White friends try to pair me up only with Asian guys, which at North Salinas High School is a very limited pool. The unspoken message here is "stick to your own kind."

College at an international university, Tokyo, Japan. Just like middle school, except now it's half-Japanese and half the rest of the world. At least in school, I'm in the majority. I and others like me appeal to Japanese men because our partial American-ness makes us exotic, but not too different.

First year of teaching, Chualar, California. The school is embroiled in political and racial turmoil. In comments off the record to a local reporter, the president of the local League of United Latin American Citizens expresses his disbelief and disgust that the school hired a Japanese over a Latino. The reporter, who is a friend of mine, relays the racist comments to me.

Culturally, my daughter is much more American than I am, but she looks much more Asian than I do since she is three fourths Japanese. As I have watched my daughter develop her own racial awareness, I have been surprised and bewildered that too many of her experiences are like mine, despite the passage of time. Her racial autobiography would no doubt include the day at the Montessori preschool when her little friend pulled up her eyes and said, "Ching Chong Chinaman," or the day in fifth grade as she stood in the lunch line when a Latino student came up to her and spat out, "Hey, Chinese girl!" Later on, she said to me, "Mom, it was like it was a really bad thing to be Chinese."

The Fourth Condition

Keeping Us All at the Table

We Need to Really Talk

I am overwhelmed.
Don't make me wash the colors, the heritage, the languages—
I don't want to.
We need to really talk . . .
as though no one is judging
but everyone is listening.
It's easy to forget that life is complex enough that love and hate,
acceptance and fear grow in one.
Don't just like me, ask me, make me question,
make me uncertain and in this time of doubt,
let's do something.
Forget stereotypes,
lose our words to internal thoughts.
I am not saying we're going to move the world,
but we can provoke a shift in our minds,
moving away from ignorance, discrimination,
and the belief that
we understand without experiencing.

—Used with permission of Janaka Lagoo, sophomore
Chapel Hill, North Carolina

As so eloquently stated by this African American sophomore in Chapel Hill, North Carolina, a significant challenge to addressing race interracially in the United States is our ability to actually just talk about it. Mainstream American culture reinforces a message that race is something we simply don't talk about, especially if our group includes members of different races. But absent open and honest dialogue between people of different races, there is little hope that racial aggressions, misunderstandings, and tensions will lessen. This is especially true in our schools, where the culture of silence surrounding race serves only to perpetuate racism and to exacerbate the racial achievement gaps that exist among students.

Our numerous experiences participating in both successful and unsuccessful interracial dialogue have enabled us to consider exactly what sends a well-intentioned conversation into dangerous territory. Typically, Courageous Conversation begins with participants examining race in their own individual lives. Making race personal, local, and immediate is what we refer to as the First Condition. Often, our struggle is to help participants stay focused on the impact of race in their own lives, given the "hot-button" nature of the subject and the reality of how race intersects so many other issues.

The Second Condition of Courageous Conversation fortifies our focus by instructing us to isolate race. While we might want to examine how race affects someone's economic or gender status, we first need to discover what race is and how it impacts our lives. The Second Condition guides us toward recognizing that although race is always a factor in life experiences, people have different levels of consciousness of this omnipresent racial impact, based on their upbringing, the current racial context in which they live, and how they identify racially.

The Third Condition of Courageous Conversation sets the stage for ushering in multiple racial points of view and critical racial perspective. It is here that participants search for their own personal meaning regarding any racialized situation and recognize that others will do the same. Because diversity of racial opinion can breed contention among participants, we often notice the potential for conflict for the first time at this point of the conversation. Acknowledging that different points of view are both normal and necessary to surface critical perspective, or the *counter-story* about race, enables participants to survive the storm of conflicting racial viewpoints. Critical perspective will indeed sustain the conversation and advance it toward a deeper level of racial inquiry; but conflicting racial opinion also heightens discomfort and challenges educators' commitment to stay engaged.

For this reason, the Fourth Condition of Courageous Conversation specifically focuses participants on the dialogue process as a way of ensuring greater safety and sustained, deeper introspection. The Fourth Condition provides an opportunity to examine intentionally and consciously who is engaging, how they are engaging, and from where on the Courageous Conversation Compass they are entering and moving about in the dialogue. The Fourth Condition of Courageous Conversation asks participants to

> *monitor the parameters of the conversation by being explicit and intentional about the number of participants, prompts for discussion, and time allotted for listening, speaking, and reflecting. Use the Courageous Conversation Compass to gauge where you and other participants are in terms of your emotional, intellectual, moral, and social proximity and connection to a given racial topic.*

Paying attention to the formal elements of conversation fosters greater safety for all involved. With maximum safety comes an increased willingness on the part of all educators to step courageously out of their comfort zones and take the risk of speaking their truths.

Reflection

What do you believe to be some of the necessary parameters for effective conversations about race to occur?

INTERRACIAL DIALOGUE

Why is interracial dialogue so difficult? To begin with, we are socialized to understand and comment on race differently based on our own racial affiliation. Of course, it's not true that *all* White people will respond one way while *all* people of color respond another way, but some racial patterns in the interracial dialogue have emerged in our research and practice. For example, many White Americans have been raised to believe that it is racist to notice race—that it is virtuous to be color-blind, so to speak. Thus, talking about race is viewed by many White educators as inappropriate, particularly while in mixed racial company. Conversely, people of color need to notice race in this country as a variety of racial situations are still damaging to their mind, body, and soul—indeed may be fatal if ignored.

Just 40 years ago, segregation of White people and people of color was indeed legal in the United States. Although racial desegregation is the law of the land and achieving racial equality is an avowed goal, not a day goes by when people of color are not publicly labeled as some form of burden to this country's progress. Descriptions such as *alien, violent, lazy, immoral, illegitimate, at-risk, low-performing,* and *disadvantaged* must be overcome by hard-working, patriotic people of color every day. Thus, it is virtually impossible for people of color to not notice color or to ignore White people who seem to have difficulty with the existence of non-White people. Consequently, people of color tend to bring more experience and a resulting greater racial consciousness to the conversation. As co-author Glenn Singleton says, "As people of color, we talk about race all the time to ourselves and anyone else who will listen!"

Racialized Communication

Another reason why the interracial conversation is so difficult is that people enter it having very different communication styles and desired outcomes. For many people of color, a productive conversation about race is, in and of itself, healing, whereas for many White people, the conversation is often viewed as threatening, especially when it appears to have no concrete result. Understanding these and other predictable and patterned racial experiences helps educators engaged in Courageous Conversation to anticipate and identify their own behavior as well as the behavior of conversation partners.

Distrust exists on both sides of the interracial conversation. For example, many educators of color believe that White educators don't want to talk about race and have a hard time listening to and accepting as valid the racial perspectives of people of color. Keeping this in mind allows participants in Courageous Conversation to monitor for these problematic circumstances. Lisa Delpit has done a significant amount of research identifying these difficulties in interracial dialogue. In her article, "The Silenced Dialogue," Delpit (1995b) shares the thoughts of a Black educator teaching in a multiracial urban elementary school regarding her interactions with many of the White teachers with whom she works:

> When you're talking to White people they still want it to be their way. You can try to talk to them and give them examples, but they're so headstrong, they think they know what's best for *everybody,* for *everybody's* children. They won't listen; White folks are going to do what they want to do *anyway.*

What Delpit captures here is the frustration of a teacher of color who wants to have a conversation about race but feels as though she can't do so effectively, as shown in her concluding statement, "It's really hard. [Whites] just don't listen well. No, they listen, but they don't *hear.*"

This teacher's challenge could have been examined by focusing on the Fourth Condition of Courageous Conversation, which alerts White teachers, in this case, to talk less, listen carefully, and reflect more on what is being said. The Fourth Condition might have helped reduce the Black teacher's frustration by providing upfront insights surrounding how and why White people tend to struggle with conversations about race. According to Linda Chambers, a retired African American principal at Johnston H. Cooper Elementary in Vallejo, California, "Race is a very taboo subject. It's like it's there and it's in your face, especially if you're an educator of color; but White educators don't typically think about race, they don't talk about race" (Singleton, 2002). As we implement Courageous Conversation in various settings, we have found that difficulties in discussing race stubbornly persist among educators despite the public and political efforts to address racial achievement disparities.

White Talk Versus Color Commentary

Historically and still to some degree today, racial discourse in the United States is governed by the cultural parameters of the dominant White population. Consequently, when discussing race and racial issues, White people tend to engage from a place of certain authority, even though they have quite often been remiss in conducting their own racial introspection. In contrast, people of color initially tend to communicate in the interracial forum in a more cautious and tempered manner. Having observed countless interracial dyads and larger teams of educators attempting to conduct meaningful discourse about racial matters, we have observed predictable patterns in conversation. As a result, we have identified eight characteristics that describe the nature of the communication in Courageous Conversations. We have labeled these patterns *White Talk* and *Color Commentary,* each of which is described below:

White Talk	*Color Commentary*
• Verbal	• Nonverbal
• Impersonal	• Personal
• Intellectual	• Emotional
• Task oriented	• Process oriented

Although the eight characteristics emerge in predictable and patterned ways in interracial dialogue in which race is the topic, we are not suggesting that *all* White people or *all* people of color will follow the pattern of White Talk or Color Commentary based solely on their racial affiliation.

Rather, these patterns are characteristic of how people of racial groupings *typically* rather than stereotypically respond when faced with racial subject matter in interracial discourse.

Initially, some people feel that these characteristics represent stereotypes—that only a few White people or people of color succumb to the characteristics of White Talk and Color Commentary. We argue that they go well beyond stereotype to represent *patterns* of racial discourse based on monitoring thousands of interracial conversations about race over the past 10 years among both male and female educators of various ages, economic backgrounds, and geographic locations throughout the United States.

Probing deeper into the conflict inherent in the very ways we talk about race, the Fourth Condition of Courageous Conversation suggests that we create a balance between White Talk and Color Commentary. Our experience tells us that without careful monitoring and intervention, all four characteristics of White Talk will be dominant in the dialogue simply because more White educators are present in our schools and thus involved in the Courageous Conversation. When the discussion is predictably and significantly unbalanced, the fewer people for whom Color Commentary is natural and normal will feel they have not had the opportunity or the encouragement to participate. By examining and better understanding these eight characteristics, educators have the opportunity to bring balance and sustenance to Courageous Conversations about race.

Reflection

Think of an interracial conversation about race in which you have been involved. Can the overall conversation be characterized more by the features of White Talk or Color Commentary? Which of the characteristics best defines your own personal contributions to the dialogue?

Identifying and remaining conscious about how we differentially communicate and exercise control in conversations based on our racial identity is critical to interracial understanding and progress. Table 8.1 provides further examples of White Talk and Color Commentary

---

Reflection

Describe your own typical communication style using the terms of White Talk or Color Commentary. How and to what degree does your typical communication style change when you are in an interracial professional setting such as a staff meeting, parent conference, or classroom situation and race is the presenting topic?

Table 8.1 Understanding White Talk and Color Commentary

White Talk	Color Commentary
Verbal: Characterized by loud, authoritative, and interrupted speech. Value is placed on expressing oneself and controlling the conversation.	**Nonverbal:** Characterized by silent respect for as well as disconnect from the one talking and/or positional/cultural authority. Communication takes place through body motions and other nonverbal expression.
Example: Who speaks first, longest, and most often	Example: Folded arms, silence, sighs, rolling of the eyes, refusal to offer direct eye contact
Impersonal: Typically spoken in third person. Prone to explaining opinion through use of other people's stories or experiences.	**Personal:** Typically spoken in first person. Great value placed upon sharing one's own story and experiences.
Example: "My best friend who is Black . . . I am married to a person of color who thinks that . . . I grew up around Asians and they said . . ."	Example: "The police pulled me over because I am Black . . . As a Chicano, I don't trust White people . . . We believe that 'such-such a place' has a problem with people of color."
Intellectual: Dialogue is abstract and disconnected from immediate and local reality. More interested in quantitative analysis of one's thinking.	**Emotional:** Dialogue is centered on an immediate and local racial reality. More interested in qualitative analysis and feelings.
Example: "Statistics say . . . Does the data really suggest that it is because of race? I once read that . . . [So-and-so] said . . . Can you give me a citation that supports that? What university did he attend? He studied with . . ."	Example: "I don't feel as though you like or respect me as a Black teacher . . . I feel alone here as the only teacher of color . . . I get so angry when they speak for me, misinterpret and misrepresent me . . . I don't trust . . . I don't feel safe."
Task oriented: Organized around the need "to do" something and to find solutions. An impatient focus on locating tools and strategies to address racial issues. Views the racial challenge as a technical problem in which the solutions exist and simply need to be unearthed. Sees introspective conversation as a waste of time.	**Process oriented:** Organized around the need "to be" respected, validated, and affirmed. Developing trust in others occurs through the examination of racial attitudes and beliefs in public. Racial challenges are viewed as adaptive problems that require us to deal with our inner thought processes and to explore our biases to create undiscovered solutions.
Example: "When are we going to get to the actions? I'm tired of talking . . . What does talking about race have to do with the achievement gap? Give me a strategy."	Example: "How do you feel about this Black student? How do you believe your students of color feel about you as a teacher? How do Latino faculty feel about working in a predominantly White school?"

Of course, not all White people engage in White Talk, and not all people of color engage in Color Commentary. In fact, to survive and advance in educational contexts usually governed by White people, people of color typically learn and practice White Talk because it is the language of power and influence. Likewise, some White people have developed Color Commentary characteristics as a way of being more effective and accepted in their conversations with people of color.

Balancing Power in Communication

Consider this common illustration of how White Talk and Color Commentary can collide, resulting in a nonproductive exchange.

> A White teacher prepares to be in conference with a Latino family. As the parents sit down, the time-conscious teacher dives right into a list of what the student has and has not accomplished according to the grade-level standards. With achievement data in hand to support her assessment, the teacher continues by explaining what types of support she is trained to provide and what assistance might not be possible, given her time with respect to the large number of children in the classroom. The teacher then politely suggests to the parents what they need to do for their child at home to ensure success.
>
> Now finished, the teacher has talked only about the "to do's" and the data. Breathless, angry, and flustered, the parents unsuccessfully fight back intense emotion as they challenge the teacher with one question: "Do you like my child, and is her spirit safe while in your care?" After saying this, they begin to express to the teacher how special they believe their child is and how important it is that their child feel appreciated by the teacher. Not prepared to converse at this level, the teacher grows flustered and launches into a defense of her practice. In the end, both the parents and teacher fail to engage in meaningful dialogue about the student's experience.

This interracial conversation lacked an effective balance in communication styles between the participants. The White teacher's conversation manner was extremely verbal, impersonal, intellectual, and task oriented. Predictably, the parents were nonverbal as they fearfully absorbed and processed the assessment of their child. Without question, the teacher must inform parents of what their child needs "to do" to achieve academic success. But educators should do this in a way that balances White Talk and Color Commentary when attempting to communicate cross-racially. Effective interracial conversations require time for trust building through first-person sharing and examination. Only when we have established ourselves personally, locally, and immediately can we engage in safer interracial dialogue. Monitoring our communication characteristics and balancing the White Talk and Color Commentary in the conversation will ensure fuller participation.

Reflection

Have you ever been in an interracial conversation that was unbalanced in terms of communication style? How did it feel? In terms of White Talk and Color Commentary, how might you have helped bring greater balance to that conversation?

Educators are challenged in interracial dialogue by the fact that power is usually located in White Talk. Consider once again the commentary of Lisa Delpit (1995b) on this culture of power, where power is data and power is impersonal:

> Either by virtue of their position, their numbers, or their access to that particular code of power of calling upon research to validate one's position, the White educators [have] the authority to establish what [is] to be considered "truth" regardless of the opinions of the people of color, and the latter [are] well aware of that fact. (p. 26)

Given this consolidation of racial power through communication style, Delpit (1995a) clearly identifies how and why the authority to focus efforts primarily on accomplishing the tasks of school restructuring easily overshadows the need for educators to examine emotional issues related to personal relationships and overall culture and climate of the institution.

Educators have much "to do," but schools also need "to be" developed as places where people of all races are valued, appreciated, and heard. Schooling as a process is difficult enough without depersonalizing the experience and leaving educators, students, and their families emotionally disconnected. Regarding the role that racial power plays in interracial communication, Delpit (1995a) further explains,

The worldviews of those with privileged positions are taken as the only reality, while the worldviews of those less powerful are dismissed as inconsequential. Indeed, in the educational institutions of this country, the possibilities for poor people and for people of color to define themselves, to determine the self each should be, involve a power that lies outside of the self. It is others who determine how they should act, how they are to be judged. When one "we" gets to determine standards for all "wes," then some "wes" are in trouble! (p. xv)

Empowering Communication

It is particularly challenging for administrators of color to lead their primarily White staff in conversing openly and honestly about race. Andy Garcia, principal at Christopher Elementary in the Oak Grove School District in San Jose, California, explains,

I think it's hard for someone who is not of color to understand that there is a difference being a person of color coming into a building where you don't see staff of color there. It's a little bit more intimidating to give your voice, to give your point of view, to give your understanding. (Singleton, 2002)

Despite the conflicting racial communication styles and the imbalance of racial power in the institution, Courageous Conversation is a surmountable hurdle for all administrators, including administrators of color. The Oak Grove School District leadership team has participated in Courageous Conversation for several years. As part of the district's practice with the Fourth Condition of Courageous Conversation, Manny Barbara, a White superintendent in the Oak Grove School District, established an advisory panel of African American and Latino administrators, known as ALLIED (African Americans and Latinos In Equity Development), who meet together to share their perspectives, develop insights, and explore ways to effectively engage their White colleagues, staff members, and families in Courageous Conversation.

The support of ALLIED administrators demonstrates the Oak Grove School District's commitment to developing leadership of color to engage and sustain multiple points of view and critical perspective. Courageous Conversation is an essential foundation for districts that want to examine the inequitable ways power is traditionally determined and distributed. Andy Garcia continues,

Through the process of learning I've seen my fellow administrators who are not of color begin to say things that have really fascinated me. Things like, wow, I'm not feeling comfortable with these conversations. And I thought, wow, these are the conversations that we have to deal with every day. All of a sudden these guys are saying they're not feeling comfortable in these conversations. To a certain extent, that's strength because suddenly they're not feeling comfortable. All of a sudden I'm able to share because of the power of [ALLIED], because of the support of my superintendent. I'm able to really share my struggle and what it's like. That's been very empowering. (Singleton, 2002)

Reflection

In your experience, what takes place when you engage in interracial discussions about race or racism with other educators? In what ways have the conversations been successful or unsuccessful?

CREATING SAFETY

Despite the discomfort that many educators experience when discussing race, an environment can be created that provides safety for educators of all races to effectively participate in Courageous Conversation. Working together as an adult learning community, educators can lay the essential foundation for honest and open conversations about race sustained by their shared commitment to meet the needs of all children.

Good intentions and hard work are not sufficient for eliminating racism in schools. Neither will excellent curriculum and pedagogy in and of themselves be enough to eradicate the achievement gap. We need communities where it is safe enough for the invisible to be made visible, where Whites can listen to people of color talk about how they and their ancestors have experienced racism, and where people of color can listen to Whites talk about how they saw racial prejudice in operation and how it affected them. Listening to one another's stories and emotions helps people identify what needs to change within their institutions, their colleagues, and themselves. Being listened to helps us heal. (Weissglass, 2001)

The Fourth Condition of Courageous Conversation guides us in the development of strategies and tools that challenge the culture of silence surrounding racial matters. Specifically, we break the silence that prohibits educators from exploring deep-seated, unexamined attitudes and beliefs about student learning as well as teacher ability. Many educators of color feel it is unsafe or futile to give voice to their inner thoughts regarding the impact of race on teaching and learning. This phenomenon illustrates Lisa Delpit's (1995b) "silenced dialogue" in which learning does not occur among educators because a high level of racial tension and division exists.

In typical discussions, White educators fill the room with ideas for improving the achievement of students of color, but their ideas often are not welcomed or supported by their colleagues of color. This is because such ideas reflect the distance between the White educators' racial experience and that of their colleagues, students, and families of color. As Lena Williams suggests in *It's the Little Things* (2002), White educators may also resort to silence in fear that their comments will be misconstrued as evidence of racist thinking.

The result of these converging phenomena is what we refer to as the culture of silence, making race "a nondiscussable," as described by Roland Barth (2004):

> Nondiscussables are subjects sufficiently important that they are talked about frequently but are so laden with anxiety and fearfulness that these conversations take place only in the parking lot, the rest rooms, the playground, the car pool, or the dinner table at home. Fear abounds that open discussion of these incendiary issues—at a faculty meeting, for example—will cause meltdown. . . . Schools are full of these land mines from which trip wires emanate. We walk about carefully, trying not to detonate them. Yet by giving these nondiscussables this incredible power over us, by avoiding them at all cost, we . . . condemn ourselves to live with all the debilitating tensions that surround race. (p. 8)

Dr. Neil G. Pedersen, a White superintendent, and Dr. Nettie Collins-Hart, a Black assistant superintendent, both in Chapel Hill-Carrboro City Schools in North Carolina, worked to develop the skills necessary to move past the "culture of silence" toward effective interracial conversations about how race impacts student achievement throughout their school system. According to Dr. Collins-Hart,

> We really had to begin to look at the things we hadn't talked about and race, in a very sensitive and direct way, was the one thing we

hadn't dealt with. . . . I think at first the biggest challenge for me personally was getting used to the idea that we were actually going to talk candidly about race. But the next hurdle was developing some skills to talk about it, such as having the same basis of vocabulary and having a similar understanding of race, because it is not something people do naturally, and in interracial groups particularly. (Singleton, 2002)

This conversation was equally uncomfortable for Superintendent Pedersen; not only is he the image of our White-dominated education system, but also he previously embraced the culture that implicitly encouraged silence around issues of race, racial identity development, and institutional racism. He says,

It is uncomfortable being the superintendent of a district and to talk about the issue of institutional racism knowing that you are the leader of that organization and what that may say about you personally. That makes me uncomfortable because I have to reflect on what role I have in perpetuating policies and practices that need to be changed. (Singleton, 2002)

To counteract their inhibitions and fear of discussing race, Drs. Pedersen and Collins-Hart worked to formally and informally establish and monitor the parameters surrounding their discourse, and doing so ultimately assisted them in engaging in Courageous Conversation.

Context and Conditions

The backdrop for the Courageous Conversation matters, especially if the school system has a history of division among educators of color and White educators. This context, representing how the community has experienced racial matters in the past, has tremendous impact on educators' ability and willingness to engage in the conversation.

Some thought and effort on the part of educators are required to determine how, when, and where the subject of race is presented. For example, examining how race impacts schooling after a long day of testing or as the final agenda item at a faculty meeting does not usually facilitate Courageous Conversation. We have found in our work that springing the topic of race on unsuspecting educators typically does not provide the kind of safe environment required for deep and personal inquiry. Let educators know up front what to expect and when to expect it, and then work to guarantee that the timing and the environment are conducive to effective dialogue. Certainly, giving advance notice allows some people to find excuses for not being present. On the other hand, a well-planned and well-timed Courageous Conversation is always designed to promote maximum participation and to carry on beyond a single scheduled meeting.

For school leaders, however, the subject of race may arise unexpectedly. In these cases, leaders should determine whether a response, action, or solution is required in the moment. In many cases, the situation affords leaders at least a few hours to collect their personal thoughts and gather racially diverse viewpoints. When lacking a culture in which racial issues are confronted spontaneously, educators should recognize that spontaneously jumping into interracial conversations about race with other educators, students, parents, or even friends can be explosive and quite unproductive. We continue to hear from educators how much they appreciate leaders who take time to thoroughly examine the school or district's current racial context, climate, and culture as a way of ensuring that more effective dialogue can take place.

Establishing the proper parameters includes reestablishing commitment to the Four Agreements of Courageous Conversation. We have found it effective to post the agreements, conditions, and compass in the spaces where educators practice Courageous Conversation with each other. Leaders should refer to these guidelines at various stages of the interaction, especially when educators stray from the topic, limit participation of some members of the community, or completely withdraw from the dialogue at a moment of heightened discomfort.

By beginning to establish parameters for a safer, albeit uncomfortable conversation about race five years ago, educators throughout the Chapel Hill school system today use a common vocabulary as a way of developing common and deeper understandings about the impact of race on student achievement. Not only did the silence in the superintendent's office need to be broken, but other administrators, equity coaches, and eventually school-based equity teams in each building soon replaced silence with Courageous Conversation. Many of the tools and exercises that Chapel Hill found effective in shifting the racial culture and climate of their district are found in the chapters of this book.

According to Dr. Collins-Hart,

It really gave us the shared courage to look at issues through the race lens. It equipped us with the skills for looking at schools through a racial lens without attacking or being attacked, but still being critical and honest while reflecting upon race. (Singleton, 2002)

With this safety net in place to catch them, participants began the real work of closing their school system's racial achievement gap.

As guided by the Fourth Condition of Courageous Conversations, Chapel Hill-Carrboro City Schools ventured into the difficulty of sharing power with all stakeholders and intentionally creating formal and informal space for previously marginalized voices of color to influence policy design and instructional practice. According to Dr. Pedersen,

> The work that we have done has really provided an environment in which people can have conversations that simply don't take place on a day-to-day basis. And our success is measured to some extent by the degree to which those conversations now take place outside of the formal workshops. (Singleton, 2002)

Furthermore, the very nature of the conversations has changed dramatically over time. Dr. Pedersen continues,

> We are able to be more direct with each other and more honest with each other rather than being circumspect. It helps us get to the point, and it also helps us to not miss the point. We are not talking around things, and I am able to understand what [educators of color] are saying more accurately than I would have. (Singleton, 2002)

Parameters

The Fourth Condition of Courageous Conversation draws our attention to the complexity of White Talk and Color Commentary and the need for parameters in the conversation. By creating parameters, we create established guidelines for exactly what participants speak about, how long they speak and listen, and who is and is not speaking or listening. In essence, parameters help participants to pay attention to the voices, time, subject or themes, and communication styles present in the conversation. Monitoring the parameters means focusing on how time in the conversation is allocated equitably and how nontraditional ways of communicating are encouraged and valued. As we have observed time and time again, conversations about race are rarely successful when they occur haphazardly or in a highly unstructured fashion. Courageous Conversation initially requires tremendous preparation until the culture of the school embraces such dialogue. Then, as witnessed in Chapel Hill as well as other districts, these conversations soon happen as a natural and normal part of the school's interactions.

Reflection

What are some of the necessary parameters that you believe may have allowed the leadership in Chapel Hill to have successful Courageous Conversation? To what degree do these same parameters already exist in your system?

People

We have discovered that the very way in which educators are seated or grouped dramatically impacts the quality of the conversation about race. This conversation is best discussed in heterogeneous groups that are just large enough to offer multiple points of view and diverse enough to prevent cultural domination in terms of a preferred communication style.

In large high schools, facilitators of Courageous Conversation have found value in mixing up the academic departments. In elementary schools, upper grade-level teachers have been grouped with primary grade-level teachers. Initially, small groups might spend a little less time addressing the topic and more time reflecting on the quality of conversation so that members can be aware not only of the content contributions but also of the process evolution. When educators are more practiced in Courageous Conversation, they can talk for longer periods and will naturally monitor the process, thus adjusting the parameters accordingly as they go along.

Whenever possible, the most important consideration is that each dialogue group be multiracial; but keep in mind that just because a group looks racially diverse does not mean that multiple racial perspectives will surface. Thus, leaders should take care to avoid the propensity to isolate people of color in mostly White groups, as this makes it difficult for critical perspective to surface. Ideally, a group should consist of both White people and people of color in relatively equal numbers. We recognize that many school systems have yet to attract and maintain a sizable number of educators of color, but an effort to bring voices from nonteaching roles in the school community into each conversation and to always acknowledge missing voices usually provides a sufficiently divergent perspective to carry the group forward.

The size of these groups should ideally be slightly larger than the three to four participants that research typically suggests (Marzano, Pickering, & Pollock, 2001). Creating two-person groups makes for more manageable and inviting dialogue, but this may leave White educators to generalize

---

the experience and perspective of one person of color over an entire racial group. Considering that people of color are constantly and continuously interacting with White people, there is less of a chance that one interracial conversation will have the same impact on an educator of color's perception of White culture.

It is important to distinguish between *racial stereotypes* and *racial patterns*. A stereotype exists when a relatively isolated characteristic is assumed to be representative of the entire group. In contrast, a racial pattern reveals a characteristic or experience that many or most members of a racial group have been documented to actually share. When several dyads merge together after some initial conversation, participants' newly formed, larger group is more likely to be able to differentiate between a racial stereotype and a racial pattern.

Explicit and Focused Prompts

Organizing the dialogue around specific, racialized prompts enables educators to delve in deeper and more effectively uncover a critical racial perspective. When trying to develop understanding about the intersection of race and schooling, educators must not hide behind protective, politically charged, and vague language such as *diversity, culture, multiculturalism,* or *differences.* Being explicit means using the words *race, racism, racial discrimination, racial prejudice,* and *institutionalized racism.* In addition, it is important to use the racial terms that speak to color, such as *Black, Brown,* and *White,* except where the color term is generally viewed as offensive or unacceptable among the identified groups, which is the case of *Yellow* and *Red.* When protective terms such as *African American* and *European American* are used, the conversation is more likely to stray away from race. The next chapter, which introduces the Fifth Condition of Courageous Conversation, provides greater insight into these critical distinctions and explains how the interchangeable use of labels related to race, ethnicity, and nationality can lead to heightened confusion and escalating tensions.

When educators are called to examine racially disaggregated student achievement data, it is helpful to use prompts that explicitly drive their thinking and response to race. For example, if the goal is to better understand why Black and Brown students are not excelling in reading, the questions should be, How does this particular reading program support the improved achievement of Black and Brown students? It is insufficient to say "all students" when the data points to an achievement pattern of a particular racial group.

Table 8.2   Using Explicit Language Substitutes

Traditional Conversation	Courageous Conversation
Our school is becoming more and more diverse each year.	We are noticing an annual increase in our student of color populations.
It is not their culture to disagree with the teacher.	Brown families, more than Black and White families, are likely to view the teacher as a knowledgeable, authority figure.
The data show that some children did not meet proficiency.	The data show that Southeast Asian students are failing.
The teaching population is not reflective of our student population.	All of our teachers are White while 90% of our students are Black and Brown.

The long history of circumventing the conversation on race is interconnected to the use of "low impact" language to address a "high impact" phenomenon. Because of this, traditional conversations about diversity have not eradicated disparities in racial achievement. Consequently, educators need to create a climate that supports the development of honest dialogue about race wherein educators can say what they mean and mean what they say. Table 8.2 shows examples of explicit language substitutes in which more traditional low-impact language is replaced with high-impact language that supports Courageous Conversation.

Time

Courageous Conversation requires a high level of thinking and an equally high level of emotional investment. For this reason, a Courageous Conversation about race that substantially influences the way in which school leaders examine educational philosophies, policies, structures, and practices requires a significant amount of time. Rather than rushing through the dialogue, effective leaders allow everyone to share their feelings, which often means continuing the discussion in the next meeting. Allocating sufficient time enables all participants to feel listened to and validated. The Courageous Conversation safeguard for negotiating this precious commodity of time—of which nobody ever has enough—is to recall the Fourth Agreement: *Expect and accept non-closure.*

It is also important to notice who does and does not occupy the time allotted to talking. Leaders may determine a signal that alerts educators when their contributions might be preventing others from having an opportunity to speak. Although highly structured conversations that specify how long and how often one may speak can stifle some participants, some limited structure invites greater participation by those educators who are reticent or more reserved. Being specific at the outset of the conversation about the amount of time allotted for speaking, listening, and reflecting allows all participants to feel included and respected.

Reflection

Reflect on a previous interracial conversation about race. Describe the context and parameters that you believed contributed to its success or lack of success:

- Backdrop
- Topic/prompts
- People
- Time and space

THE COURAGEOUS CONVERSATION COMPASS

Linda Darling-Hammond (1997) writes, "In order to create a cohesive community and a consensus on how to proceed, school people must have the occasion to engage in democratic discourse about the real stuff of teaching and learning" (p. 336). Democratic discourse means providing time and space in the Courageous Conversation for every educator's perspective and experience to be listened to and affirmed. When this occurs, then everyone at the table feels validated and respected. With personal validation comes a greater willingness to honor the opinions and views of others, no matter how different they may be.

For this reason, we have developed the Courageous Conversation Compass as a personal navigational tool that guides educators through these conversations about race. It helps participants to know where they are personally as well as to understand the place from which others' contributions come; the result is an expansion and deepening of beliefs and opinions for all participants.

On this compass, we have identified four primary ways that people process racial information, events, or issues: moral, intellectual, emotional, and social. These are the four points or cardinal directions of our compass. Those positioned in the *moral* quadrant develop a deep-seated

Figure 8.1   The Courageous Conversation Compass

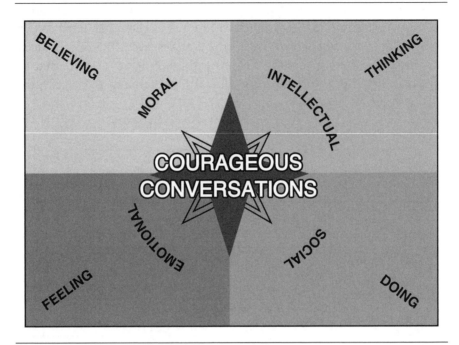

belief related to the racial information or event. This belief has to do with the "rightness" or "wrongness" of any given issue. One's justifications for a moral viewpoint are often located in the "gut," and articulating them verbally may not be possible. On an *intellectual* level, the primary response to a racial issue or information is characterized by a personal disconnect from the subject or a steadfast search for additional information or data. The intellectual response is often verbal and based in one's *thinking*. In the *emotional* arena, educators respond to information through *feelings* in the sense that a racial issue strikes them at a physical level causing an internal sensation such as anger, sadness, joy, or embarrassment. Finally, a view positioned in the *social* zone of the compass reveals one's connection and response to racial information through *doing*, as defined by specific behaviors and actions. In a sense, moral responses reside in the soul, intellectual in the mind, emotional in the heart, and social in our hands and feet.

The Courageous Conversation Compass resembles a Chinese compass, which has five coordinates: east, west, north, south, and center. On our compass, the four cardinal points are moral, intellectual, social, and emotional while the fifth point is where the coordinates symbolically converge in effective and productive interracial dialogue about race: Courageous Conversation.

Reflection

For the purposes of understanding and personalizing the Courageous Conversation Compass, consider the following issues:

- Affirmative action
- Bilingual education
- O. J. Simpson trial
- Indian gaming

As you say each of the aforementioned phrases, where do you locate yourself in terms of your initial response? As you ponder the issue for a longer period of time, where do you travel to on the compass?

As we wrote this book, we pushed ourselves to examine numerous racial matters from the multiple positions on the compass and various intersections such as the moral/emotional border. To address the racial inequities in schooling, we believe educators must first recognize the existence of the foundational issue of race as experienced through the four cardinal positions of engagement. This recognition permits educators to move beyond misunderstanding and differing viewpoints toward a much deeper understanding of their own and each other's racial viewpoints.

As participants develop greater will, skill, knowledge, and capacity for Courageous Conversation, they will find themselves centered on the compass, with a deeper understanding of all four positions. Typically, discussions about race end unfavorably because people struggle to locate themselves or understand the many places others are positioned around a particular racial issue. For example, a White person may speak from an intellectual place when arguing against affirmative action whereas a Brown person may try to convey emotionally how such a policy provided a much needed opportunity to attend college. Without understanding how the other is positioned, participants in this dialogue would walk away frustrated, believing the other had little respect for or understanding of their perspective. When educators attempt to discuss race without considering all four positions and without recognizing the goal of getting centered on the compass for any given racial issue, the result is typically unfavorable.

By using the Courageous Conversation Compass, educators can transform predictable land mines of interracial dialogue about race into fertile grounds for understanding and healing. Guided by the compass, a White teacher can recognize the limits of the typical presentation of data from the social and intellectual position. Also, the compass enables Black parents to recognize how their entrance to the conversation and response from an emotional or a moral position can create a challenge for the teacher to truly understand the reasons for their child's achievement decline. By working together, teacher and parents can center their Courageous Conversation on the compass and discover each other as essential partners in improving student learning.

The Compass: Our ProMISE for Racial Healing

This process of "getting centered" using the Courageous Conversation Compass is what we refer to as our *ProMISE for Racial Healing.* ProMISE stands for

a ***Pro****active* journey towards examining and understanding the ***M****oral,* ***I****ntellectual,* ***S****ocial, and* ***E****motional* foundations required ***for Racial Healing*** to occur.

This process brings balance, openness, honesty, and understanding to interracial dialogue about race. The very best Courageous Conversation, which occurs in the center of the compass where all four positions converge, is the most authentic and fulfilling. Like the pivot point on a navigational compass, the center of the Courageous Conversation Compass is the position from which educators can understand and articulate four distinct viewpoints of a racial issue. In moving toward the center on any given issue, a person's location on the compass, and thus awareness of the topic, will change. By exploring their own racial ideas and those of others, participants achieve a deeper understanding of race and racialized problems like achievement disparity. Doing this, educators also develop an acceptance of and respect for each other's positions, even when they differ.

As an example of how to use the compass to guide interracial discourse, consider the following scenario.

A White history teacher strongly believes that all students, regardless of their racial identity, should meet the same requirements for enrollment in honors or advanced placement classes. In exploring the teacher's opinion, it is clear that his *belief* in equal opportunity drives his perspective. Hence, the arrow is pointing toward the moral position on the compass.

To more critically examine the issue, the aforementioned teacher suggests to his colleagues that they use the compass to examine each other's viewpoints. First, they consider the social quadrant by talking with teachers of color about their own experiences in advanced level coursework and the impact enrollment trends in such courses had on their performance. Next, the educators explore the intellectual position by studying the disaggregated data, which specifically show how many students of color are enrolled in these courses and what their achievement record has been when compared to White students. Finally, to investigate the emotional position, they listen to students of color share what it feels like to be denied access to higher level coursework or perhaps to be the only student of color in the entire class.

After engaging with the compass to this degree, the White teacher who prompted the Courageous Conversation has developed in the following ways: He has broader perspective about why access to honors classes may need to be expanded, a deeper understanding of racial injustice, and clear knowledge of the experiences of students who have been denied access to or have felt isolated in the courses.

The compass illustrates our belief that when engaging in Courageous Conversation, the viewpoint of participants typically moves and shifts. Participants find themselves tuned in to some positions and oblivious to others. But, as they move about the compass, they experience continuous growth in their racial awareness.

Reflection

Reflect on your own conversations with colleagues and students who are racially different than you. In what ways have your discussions been limited due to a difference of point of view? How could your familiarity with the Courageous Conversation Compass help you to clarify your own position and better understand the positioning of others?

Talking about race interracially is clearly difficult and can even be scary or frightening. We believe this is why people so often resort to silence. Silence among educators when it comes to addressing racial achievement disparities only results in wider gaps and diminished engagement in the process of schooling by students of color and their families. Paying attention to the Fourth Condition of Courageous Conversation is the best assurance that safety and authenticity will be maximized. We imagine a time when educators will not need to establish parameters simply to have an everyday conversation about race. But until such a time, the carefully determined parameters and the Courageous Conversation Compass will help participants to better understand their various racial positions and how they can begin to navigate toward the common center at which all students, as W. E. B. Dubois suggested in 1949, will have the "Freedom to Learn."

Personal Activity: Part 1

Interracial Dyad

Here is a transcript of an actual conversation on race that took place in one of our Courageous Conversation seminars. The moderator used a process of constructivist listening to guide three people through an exercise called *15-Minute Race.* Participants use specific prompts and parameters to investigate their own racial perspective in contrast to their partner's. The participants included one White female educator and one Black male educator, respectively Person A and Person B, and one White female observer. Person A and Person B responded to prompts given by the facilitator. The observer's directive was to listen and, at the conclusion of the conversation, help A and B recognize their differing styles of conversation known as White Talk and Color Commentary.

Study this Courageous Conversation closely, and identify the process that takes place by following the directions at the top of each column:

- Underline any prompts, parameters, or directions that you find.
- Identify and describe all examples of White Talk or Color Commentary.
- After studying this conversation, engage in the prompts that follow.

Figure 8.2   15-Minute Race

Participant [Describe actions of participants]	Dialogue [Underline prompts, parameters, and directions]	White Talk Versus Color Commentary [Describe the White Talk or Color Commentary]
Moderator:	This process is called constructivist listening and is made up of pairs of one White person and one person of color. We are going to give timing and prompts. When A is speaking I'll say, "A, you have so many minutes to talk on . . ." and I will give you the prompt. When A is speaking, B is completely silent. This isn't a conversation in a normal way. B completely listens. Then I'll give B a prompt and a time, and A completely listens. There is no exchange. This is called constructivist listening, and it is designed with a purpose. So A, you are going to have one minute to share the first words that come to mind when you think about race. A, one minute, go.	

Participant [Describe actions of participants]	Dialogue [Underline prompts, parameters, and directions]	White Talk Versus Color Commentary [Describe the White Talk or Color Commentary]
Person A: (White woman)	The communities people live in, how communities deal with difference. I think about school, how school deals with differences. I think about color, did I say that? I do think about people's color, and how that makes people see them. That's about all I can think of.	
Moderator:	Stop. B, you have one minute to say to your partner how you define racism. B, one minute, go.	
Person B: (Black man)	The institutionalized practices of a particular racial group to disenfranchise, discriminate against, or in various other ways marginalize another racial group based solely upon that person's race. And, I'd have to add that there is a certain power component to racism. You can have the subordinate disenfranchise and marginalize the dominant group, but it's not racism. It's something else, because that power component's missing.	
Moderator:	Stop. Take 30 seconds for silent reflection. Think about what A said, think about what B said . . . A, you get to start again. This time you'll have two minutes, and you are going to share with your partner one experience you have had with racism and how you responded. Two minutes, go.	
Person A: (White woman)	Well, fortunately—or unfortunately—I haven't had too many. We were kind of talking about one eating with somebody who's another ethnicity at lunch. But that is not so much my experience. But I would say for me, ah, two Black women were having a conversation about their children, and I was . . . it was at the end of a meeting, and it was kind of naturally, we were standing there, and definitely I was not included in this conversation. And it was made really clear by body language that they wanted to have the conversation without me. It was kind of a freeze-out kind of a thing. So, I can't think of many experiences which tell me much, you know, about this whole conversation for us.	

(Continued)

Figure 8.2 (Continued)

Participant [Describe actions of participants]	Dialogue [Underline prompts, parameters, and directions]	White Talk Versus Color Commentary [Describe the White Talk or Color Commentary]
	I haven't always lived, I mean, I have lived in a lot of different places and been in a lot of different areas and still I can't think of any.	
Person B: (Black man) *Interjecting outside of the prompt while time is still available.*	Well, I think the definition that I gave doesn't allow for that. I'm talking about race and power. If we are all African American in this closed group, it doesn't work. Could you have discrimination based on something else or marginalization within the community, oh certainly! We can go on for a while about that. But, it's the dyad. You have two different ethnic groups, and one is the "dominant" one in society. That's what is kind of driving that.	
Moderator:	B, you have the same prompt, one experience you have had with racism and how you handled it. Also two minutes, go.	
Person B: (Black man)	All right, oh, it's a bad one. It's really kind of small, it's minor, it's petty, but that is the definition of them. I went to a department store at the Sun Crest Mall. I guess I wanted to buy some shirts and—I mean, you've heard the stories—well, there's someone following you around to see if you're going to steal anything. Well, I could not get someone to help me.	
Person A: (White woman) *Interjecting*	Oh, you had the opposite experience of me.	
Person B: (Black man)	Yes, I had to literally confront a salesperson to help me on finding sizes, and she was very reluctant to help me.	
Person A: (White woman) *Interjecting*	Do you think she thought you weren't going to buy something? You have no idea.	
Person B: (Black man)	The impression that I got was that she really couldn' t be bothered. On the other hand, last Christmas in the same department store, I was looking for some jewelry for my wife. I' m walking down the display case and the salesperson-who happened to be	

Fourth Condition: Keeping Us *All* at the Table

Participant [Describe actions of participants]	Dialogue [Underline prompts, parameters, and directions]	White Talk Versus Color Commentary [Describe the White Talk or Color Commentary]
	British—wouldn't even greet me. These two guys come in from the street, they walk up to the display case, and she's greeting them.	
Person A: (White woman) *Interjecting*	Different race?	
Person B: (Black man)	Yeah, OK.	
Person A: (White woman) *Interjecting*	So then what do you do? What do you say?	
Person B: (Black man)	Ah, two things: Do you want to fight over it and confront the person? Or, you can say, "OK, fine, this is how you are. I will do something else."	
Person A: (White woman) *Interjecting*	(Referring to earlier discussion): So, when we talked about those micro-aggressions?	
Person B: (Black man)	Yeah.	
Person A: (White woman) *Interjecting*	That is definitely . . .	
Person B: (Black man)	You can always point to one or two of them every day. I mean . . .	
Person A: (White woman) *Interjecting*	Every day, seriously?	
Person B: (Black man)	Every couple of days.	
Moderator:	Stop. I want you to think about the observation. I want you to think about how hard it is to stay just a listener. I want you to reflect on what A said and what B said, and on how hard it is to be the listener. 30 seconds . . .	

(Continued)

143

Figure 8.2 (Continued)

Participant [Describe actions of participants]	Dialogue [Underline prompts, parameters, and directions]	White Talk Versis Color Commentary [Describe the White Talk or Color Commentary]
	B, you are going to start this time and you are going to have two minutes to share one feeling you have about dealing with racism. One feeling, two minutes. B, go.	
Person B: (Black man)	I expect it. At some point every couple of days, I expect to have some sort of a thing where I am, you know, kind of shaking my head saying, "Well, what was that all about?" And again, every so often my wife and I will be leaving some place and I'll look at her and say, "What was that?" And she'll look at me and say, "I don't know." Or she'll say sometimes, "You know what it was." You expect it; you deal with it as best as you possibly can. Also, it's kind of hard to figure out—at least for me—is this person just being really, really rude? Or is it that they are rude to everybody? Or is it that they are just rude to me? And, if it is just me, it's a very short step to go from that to, "Oh, it's because of race." I don't know, it slows down how I react to it. I am kind of looking for ways to say, "Well, if it is based on race, do I have to do something, respond in some way?" I don't know.	
Observer: (White woman) *Interjecting*	How often is it that the thoughts come to you, "Is it just that this person is rude and ignorant, or is it just me?"	
Person B: (Black man)	Well, whenever it happens.	
Observer: (White woman) *Interjecting*	Every time?	
Person A: (White woman) *Answering for the Black man*	Every time.	
Person B: (Black man)	That is the first thing.	

Participant [Describe actions of participants]	Dialogue [Underline prompts, parameters, and directions]	White Talk Versus Color Commentary [Describe the White Talk or Color Commentary]
Moderator:	Stop. B, stop. A, you have the same prompt. You have two minutes. Share one feeling you have about dealing with racism. A, go.	
Person A: (White woman)	I don't expect it. When you said that, it makes me sad because I just assume that they are rude or a jerk, you know. I mean, I never, I don't expect it at all, even if the person is another race than me. I don't expect that it has anything to do with it. You know, I just think they have had a bad day. I don't personalize it. And I can't think of a time that I have even gone back over it and thought, "Gee, what was that about?" You know, I assume more that it's maybe my age, or that I'm a woman, or, I don't know what. But I never go there, never, really. I really don't. Not with me personally, my own personal experience. Sometimes with students I do. Sometimes with students I definitely feel like that they're looking at me as the White teacher, you know? And they don't see me as a person. Especially near the beginning of the year. But, usually that disappears fairly quickly for me. I think for them I'd have to ask them. But, you know what I mean? I can't assume that just ever completely disappears because we are just such a power, you know, in the classroom. But, yeah, when it says, if we're talking about keeping it personal and I'm not getting into the racism of the world, um, I don't expect it at all. I don't get into the car and think, "OK, what's going to happen today?"	
Moderator:	Thirty seconds to silently reflect. What did A say? What did B say? All right, observers, we are going to ask you to share what you heard.	
Observer: (White woman)	The person that was not of color mentioned her experiences as far as racism which was directed at her because she was not of color. I thought it was interesting, she was not of color, but she had a circumstance that she felt uncomfortable in because it was two Black women that excluded her from a conversation. And the person of color said	

(Continued)

Figure 8.2 (Continued)

Participant [Describe actions of participants]	Dialogue [Underline prompts, parameters, and directions]	White Talk Versus Color Commentary [Describe the White Talk or Color Commentary]
	that he expected racism to happen every day. And the person not of color never expected it, never. You know, it wasn't that they got in the car and expected it to happen that day. I had a hard time with my own personal experiences popping up in my head, and I wanted to talk.	
Moderator: *Commenting to entire group*	Now, one of the things that's clear is that A and B are engaged, OK. And you all are going off on your conversations now. You had a systematic input into the conversation, which we don't typically suggest is so structured and rigid since it is really hard. But, what we do suggest is that you monitor the real parameters or conditions of the conversation. That is to say that you don't just walk out into U.S. society and find people just breaking out into effective racial conversation. You know, it just doesn't happen for us yet, OK? Maybe one day we will see that, but it's not now.	

Personal Activity: Part 2

Interracial Dyad

The purpose of the preceding dialogue was to listen, build trust, and believe the stories that another person shared, even if that person's experience was different from one's own. This conversation stands as an example of what typically happens in interracial dialogue around race. It was hard for the White woman to stick to the rules of the conversation and not interrupt; the protocol reinforces the necessity of having strong guidance during the dialogue. This is why there is such a need for the established time allotments, designations for speaking and listening, and closely monitored prompts. Without these, the conversation typically becomes imbalanced.

Nevertheless, notice how powerful the structure became in this conversation. Despite the interjections and the rule breaking, the structure was strong enough to allow both the Black man and the White woman to speak honestly about their respective feelings, experiences, and insights. Effective dialogue took place, and each educator gained a heightened understanding of the other's experiences.

To reflect on this conversation, answer the following questions:

Parameters

What does the moderator do to ensure effective dialogue?

What parameters exist to guarantee equity in the conversation?

In what ways could this conversation be better managed and run?

White Talk Versus Color Commentary

Give examples of White Talk and Color Commentary that occur in this dialogue.

Where was the power in the conversation?

What could be done to create a better balance between the White Talk and the Color Commentary?

What did you learn about your own communication style as a result of this dialogue?

Implementation Exercise: Part 1

Interracial Dyad

Time required: 45 minutes

Materials required: Courageous Conversation Journal for each participant and a copy of the worksheet that follows

1. Present the Fourth Condition of Courageous Conversations:

   Monitor the parameters of the conversation by being explicit and intentional about the number of participants, prompts for discussion, and time allotted for listening, speaking, and reflecting. Use the Courageous Conversation Compass to gauge where you and other participants are in terms of your emotional, intellectual, moral, and social proximity and connection to a given racial topic.

2. Introduce the concept of White Talk versus Color Commentary. Explain that this does not mean that all White people use White Talk and all people of color use Color Commentary. Rather, we need to recognize both as styles of communication that can create difficulty if they are not understood and are imbalanced.

3. Describe the following contrasting traits:

White Talk	*Color Commentary*
• Verbal	• Nonverbal
• Impersonal	• Personal
• Intellectual	• Emotional
• Task oriented	• Process oriented

4. Divide the participants into interracial groups of three to five people and have them fill out the chart on the worksheet by identifying traits that characterize White Talk and Color Commentary. Have the entire group discuss these traits.

5. Create as many interracial pairings or dyads among your group as possible. Those who are not paired can observe the interracial pairings.

6. Identify two or three racial issues that relate to your school or school system. Give the participants one of these at a time as prompts for discussion.

7. Instruct the participants that they will have two minutes to discuss each prompt. Rather than questioning each other's opinion, have the listeners explain where they heard examples of White Talk and Color Commentary.

8. If desired, the observer can trade places with one member of the dyad for the next prompt, as long as the dyad remains interracial.

9. Bring the group back together and debrief the experience. In what ways did the observers hear White Talk and/or Color Commentary? Who primarily used each style of conversation? Was their use balanced in the dialogue?

10. Have each participant reflect on this conversation in their Courageous Conversation Journal.

White Talk Versus Color Commentary

Fourth Condition of Courageous Conversations: Part 1

Monitor the parameters of the conversation by being explicit and intentional about the number of participants, prompts for discussion, and time allotted for listening, speaking, and reflecting. Use the Courageous Conversation Compass to gauge where you and other participants are in terms of your emotional, intellectual, moral, and social proximity and connection to a given racial topic.

Practice: The Foundation of Anti-Racist Leadership

White Talk	Color Commentary
Verbal Traits: Example:	**Nonverbal** Traits: Example:
Impersonal Traits: Example:	**Personal** Traits: Example:
Intellectual Traits: Example:	**Emotional** Traits: Example:
Task oriented Traits: Example:	**Process oriented** Traits: Example:

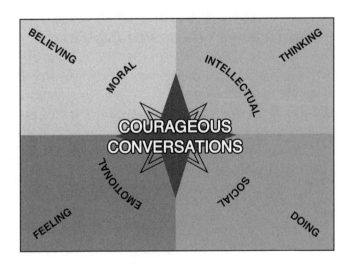

Implementation Exercise: Part 2

The ProMISE of Racial Healing

Time required: 45 minutes

Materials required: Courageous Conversation Journal for each participant and the worksheet that follows

1. Before introducing the Courageous Conversation Compass and the ProMISE for Racial Healing, pass out the accompanying sheet to each member of your group.

2. Have each participant describe in writing his or her basic opinion in the following areas: affirmative action, race riots, immigration laws, and welfare.

3. Present the concept of the Courageous Conversation Compass to the group, and explain what ProMISE means:

    A ***Pro**active* journey towards examining and understanding the ***M**oral,* ***I**ntellectual,* ***S**ocial, and* ***E**motional* foundations required ***for Racial Healing*** to occur.

4. Have participants identify whether their four opinions point toward moral, intellectual, social, or emotional. Label them accordingly.

5. Instruct the participants to mingle with one another and listen to at least three others whose opinions represent a different point on the compass for each of the subjects. For example, someone who has an intellectual opinion concerning affirmative action should talk to three others who have social, emotional, and moral opinions on affirmative action.

    It is important to note, however, that there should be no discussion after hearing another's opinion—this is meant only as an exercise in hearing different points of view.

6. Bring the group back together and reflect on the experience. Could you find people who were positioned differently on the compass? In what ways was it difficult just to listen to the multiple perspectives without commenting?

7. Have each person personally reflect on the differing opinions for each of the four subjects and keep this exercise in his or her Courageous Conversation Journal.

The ProMISE of Racial Healing

Fourth Condition of Courageous Conversations: Part 2

Monitor the parameters of the conversation by being explicit and intentional about the number of participants, prompts for discussion, and time allotted for listening, speaking, and reflecting. Use the Courageous Conversation Compass to gauge where you and other participants are in terms of your emotional, intellectual, moral, and social proximity and connection to a given racial topic.

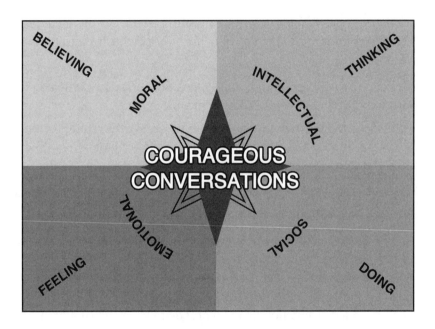

Describe your basic opinion in regard to

Affirmative action:

Reflection:

Race riots:

Reflection:

Immigration laws:

Reflection:

Welfare:

Reflection:

RACIAL AUTOBIOGRAPHY: SUPRIYA

As a recent immigrant from India along with my brother and his wife, I am an outsider looking in. My seven-year-old niece, Naeha, was born in the United States and is being raised here. Naeha once told me that her class consisted of a lot of "Americans" and some "Indians" like herself. Try as I might to persuade her otherwise, she never once referred to herself as an American.

Back in India, museums charge extra for foreign visitors. My brother, who is a naturalized U.S. citizen, never has to pay extra. No one questions whether he is Indian. Try as we might to assimilate—melt even—in this country, we will always be outsiders on account of how we look. Immigrants from Europe never have to face this problem. They have the "look," and no one ever questions if they are an American. The "look" that I possessed became even more danger-ous for a brief period of time after September 11, 2001, as people would honk when I drove by and call me unprintable names.

My first personal encounter with racism shook my foundations. I was teaching freshman chemistry labs at San Jose State University, where at the end of the semester, students anonymously evaluate their instructor in a paragraph. One of my students bemoaned the fact that he had to learn chemistry from a "brown fob" (fresh off the boat) with a "thick accent." "What is our country coming to?" he pondered in his evaluation. Indeed. I have often wondered where we are "coming" and "going" with all the pent-up anger.

A few years later, I had to travel to a U.S. consulate in Mexico to obtain a multiple entry visa that would enable me to travel outside the United States whenever I chose. My attorney prepared all the paperwork and said that I was a shoo-in. "It should take you only a couple of minutes at the counter," she said. At the embassy, I engaged in a casual conversation with a German immigrant who was seeking the same visa that I was, except that he had no paperwork. Of course, he got the visa whereas I did not. When I asked the immigration officer to kindly explain, he said, "There are too many people like you" already in the country. "We don't need more," he said.

My first year of teaching at Mar Vista was a nightmare. I did not have a full teaching credential, and I was asked to teach an advanced class at the last moment. I survived that year due in main part to an assistant principal who was Asian and brand new to her job as well. She came by and visited my class often, always encouraging me and totally helpful. I will never forget the dedi-cation she brought to her job and the hard work that became her trademark. She only survived for one year as an assistant principal. I often wondered what made her quit. When I happened to ask one of the teachers at school recently why she left, she replied, "You know, the only reason she was made an [assis-tant principal] was because she was an Asian female—we knew she would not make it."

Fourth Condition: Keeping Us *All* at the Table

Most of the time, racism permeates at a very subtle level throughout the social fabric in the United States. Sometimes, a trigger can get it going at dangerous levels. The Rodney King beating, O. J. Simpson trial, and 9/11 are some of the recent triggers we have seen. At school, students of different races do not intermingle, and the same cliques are seen in the staff cafeteria. As an outsider looking in, I am appalled at the lack of social interaction or even basic understanding of other races in the United States. If this trend continues, we will have a lot of young people disenfranchised like my niece and feeling that they do not belong, a frightening thought for any country.

The Fifth
Condition

What Do You Mean By "Race"?

Race is an artificial barrier that defines us. Race makes me feel proud but it also makes me feel cautious. I try to go through my day without focusing on it, but I am constantly aware of it. If I am in a place where no one looks like me, I am self-conscious. When I am surrounded by diversity, I feel comfortable. Race makes me feel good when I think of my ancestry, but it makes me feel bad when I think of division. It is the package that we come in, but it does affect our interactions with others. Race plays a big part and we have to get beyond those barriers.

—Jackie Thompson, professional staff developer,
Davis School District, Farmington, Utah

What is race? To this Black educator, race is very real. To others, race might be abstract, a label, a box to check, a history, an ethnicity, a memory, a nonentity, a judgment. Despite how differently people may view race, the truth is that race is quite real. Certainly, race is a constant reality for Jackie Thompson, a professional staff developer in the Davis School District in a suburb of Salt Lake City. Whereas Jackie is Black, most of the staff in her school system are White—and at the same time, the student of color population is doubling every few years. One of Jackie's responsibilities is to train teachers in REACH, which stands for Respect

Ethnic and Cultural Heritage. The purpose of this program is to help the primarily White educators in her system begin to understand the cultural differences that exist between them and their students of color. Her work begins with helping the largely White staff understand race.

First and foremost, race in the United States is the social and political meaning that we individually and collectively affix to the color of our skin and other visible physical traits. Although technically race means little more than this, it is arguably the reason for more national unrest, misunderstanding, and terror than any other aspect of our diversity. Because race is so tightly linked to our personal and collective identity, an insufficient understanding of race stirs predictable emotions. Feelings connected to race are strong and polarizing; they trigger denial for some and life-defining acceptance for others.

To reach some shared understanding of what is race, the Fifth Condition of Courageous Conversation guides participants to

> *establish agreement around a contemporary working definition of race that clearly differentiates it from ethnicity and nationality.*

Scientifically, race is nothing more than the color of our skin, texture of our hair, and shape, color, and dimension of physical features such as eyes and lips. So much social and political meaning has been attached to these physical determinations of race, however, that the simplicity has given way to a complex phenomenon in this country over the past four centuries.

Reflection

What is your own working definition of race? Do you feel that your definition is sufficient? In what ways do you differentiate race from ethnicity and nationality?

A BRIEF HISTORY OF RACE

Racial differences are a social construct rather than a biological reality; science has found far more genetic differences within individuals of the same so-called race than among those of different races (Adelman, 2003). The very term *race* is problematic, as described by Henze et al. (2002): "It has been used to describe physical differences of populations which are then erroneously associated with mental capacities and the ability to achieve a high level of civilization" (p. 8). Furthermore, in addressing the socially constructed realities manifested by race, "it is precisely because racial discrimination has been real, even though race is not, that we have to continue to monitor inequities by examining data across racial and ethnic categories" (p. 8).

Both social and natural scientists will undoubtedly continue to debate the true meaning of race in universities, governments, and corporations around the world. In the meantime, what does not seem to change is the fact that race is lived in patterned and predictable ways, regardless of how we may intellectually construct it. It is precisely this notion of how we live race, rather than what race means, that deepens the conversation about race for educators. Examining and understanding how race is lived differently by White people and by people of color today in the United States of America is what the Fifth Condition of Courageous Conversations refers to as the "working definition of race."

To establish a working definition of race, we first need to briefly explore the historical and contemporary evolution of race. We also must investigate how and why people tend to collectively redefine race by using descriptions based on ethnicity and nationality rather than skin color. Developing a clearer understanding of race allows for more effective dialogue about race and the racial achievement gap.

Race in American Society

Speaking about the history of race in the United States and the way racial determination has been justified scientifically, Evelynn Hammonds, a historian of science, once wrote,

> If we just take African Americans as an example, there is not a single body part that hasn't been subjected to [scientific] analysis. You'll find articles in the medical literature about the Negro ear, and the Negro nose, and the Negro leg, and the Negro heart, and the Negro eye, and the Negro foot, and it's every single body part. They're constantly looking for some organ that might be so fundamentally different in size and character that you can say this is something specific to the Negro versus Whites and other groups. Scientists are a part of their social context. Their ideas about what race is are not simply scientific ones, are not simply driven by the data that they are working with. They are also informed by the societies in which they live. (quoted in Adelman, 2003)

The history of race in the United States is both long and complex, and it is not our goal to retell it, even though we firmly believe that exploring non-White historical perspectives can support the development of critical thought about the impact of race on schooling. Instead, we will simply highlight a few key and well-documented moments that shape the arc of the American collective racial reality.

American Racial Binary

It begins with the arrival of Northern and Western European settlers in the 1600s, a period marked by the extermination of indigenous peoples and the enslavement of Africans. Each of these occurrences establishes in this country the racial hierarchy of Whites over people of color, or the American racial binary of White to Black.

In this emerging racial caste system, immigrants from Eastern and Southern Europe suffered initial domination at the hands of the established nobility class of those who owned property, not only land but also slaves. Whether they worked out their term of indentured servitude or relinquished their language, religion, or customs, White-skinned ethnic newcomers were encouraged, if not pressured economically, to "melt" into what was already forming as the dominant White American race.

For most immigrants from Asia and present-day Middle Eastern countries, it became clear by the late 1800s that the meaningful American racial classifications were White and Black. Whiteness or Blackness determined whether or not people received the full rights of citizenship. This blatant social, political, and economic racial hierarchy prompted most of these groups—Chinese, Japanese, Arabs, and Armenians, to name a few—to strive for the White label and accompanying status. Some even asked that their request for Whiteness be adjudicated by the highest courts in the land.

Thomas Jefferson gave tremendous support to the emerging Black and White racial caste system by advocating the development of a U.S. Census. His beliefs regarding Black inferiority and White superiority are clearly stated in his seminal work, *Notes on the State of Virginia* (1781). Jefferson also characterized the racial ambiguity for groups existing between Black and White on the continuum, which he referred to as mulatto. In his writings, he posits that mulattos could—with care—eventually become White. In Jefferson's influential eyes, however, Black people lacked the intelligence and other genetic properties ever to be White.

Although today his beliefs seem radical and even offensive to many people, Jefferson's thoughts of scientific racial determination, also called *eugenics*, resurface every so often in popular films like D. W. Griffith's *Birth of a Nation* in 1915 and recently in Richard Herrnstein and Charles Murray's (1994) best-selling book, *The Bell Curve: Intelligence and Class*

Structure in American Life. As we have participated in Courageous Conversations about race, we have discovered these Jeffersonian ideas about race are still deeply embedded in the attitudes and practices of a surprising number of educators today.

This division of White and Black continued into the 20th century. The return home of World War II veterans created greater permanence in the alien status of Asian groups and other people of color while providing government-sponsored privileges for White Americans. The rapid influx of Latino immigrants, which also characterized the 20th century, boosted White Americans' fear that they would miss out on limited resources. Political efforts in the late 1990s and early 2000s in California and Florida to promote English-only legislation, restrict drivers' licenses to legal citizens, and even make public education and health care unavailable to "nondocumented" people all may be reflective of this ongoing fear of "non-White" immigrants.

Although these "scientifically reasoned" ideologies have been categorically disproved, whispered beliefs about superiority and inferiority based on race have in many ways led schools to unconsciously support institutional policies and cultures that tend to favor White students over non-White students. Such policies continue to support a racial achievement gap today.

When the United States swelled with pride and confidence as a young industrial nation, the image of wealth, success, and power was unfailingly White by design. Contrasting with images of hope, wealth, and prosperity or rags-to-riches fables was the poverty and despair experienced by many non-White people as a result of social bigotry and government-supported racism, for example, Jim Crow segregation and "fair" housing laws. White Americans—now a culture into which the once-hated Eastern and Southern European ethnics have "melted"—assumed that their refined culture and wealth was, according to Evelynn Hammonds, a "pre-ordained natural order" (quoted in Adelman, 2003). This contemporary perspective was grounded in White society's preexisting beliefs in social Darwinism, the idea that only the fittest and most talented race deserves to survive in society, accumulate riches, and gain power. Hammonds continues,

> Those that [believed in] White racial superiority wanted to confirm what they saw, which is to say that the proper place of the Negro, or in other regions of the country the Native American or the Chinese, was at the bottom of the social and political hierarchy. And if you can say that they are fundamentally biologically different, then it's natural for them to be at the bottom of our social hierarchy.

Racial purification was one of the primary aims of the 20th-century eugenics movement. Consequently, practitioners of the movement focused on propagating a White race that was more physically fit, intelligent, and capable than people of other races. The inverse of this objective was to orchestrate a well-planned genocide of the weak and infirm—the "colored" of society. To this aim, eugenicists proposed a number of unthinkable measures, including lifelong segregation, sterilization, restrictive marriage, eugenic education, forced breeding, and even euthanasia. Despite their extreme nature, these proposals were actually adopted both inside and outside of the United States, eventually giving justification to the 20th century's greatest horror, the Holocaust. According to Joseph Graves, "The Nazi propaganda machine pointed out that their eugenic policies were entirely consistent with and in fact derived from ideas of American race scientists" (Adelman, 2003).

The triumph of Black athlete Jesse Owens at the 1936 Berlin Olympics in Nazi Germany began a slow shift in racial beliefs toward the more prevalent thoughts of today. These games were supposed to serve as concrete proof of White supremacy and legitimize the global domination of Hitler's Aryan nation. Yet, Jesse Owens won four gold medals in competition against White athletes. The United States and much of the Western world were faced with a quandary: How could a society that believed in White racial dominance come to terms with the Black athlete's success? Ever since, the belief in Black physical dominance and athletic superiority has persisted, although in some circles, Black people are still thought to lack the same mental capacity and other more common White civilized traits; evidence of the power of this belief is shown in the fact that the number of coaches of color is significantly smaller than the number of professional athletes of color. At the time of victory, Dean Cromwell, Owens's coach, said the Negro athlete excelled because he was "closer to the primitive. It was not so long ago that his ability to sprint and jump was a life and death matter to him in the jungle" (quoted in Adelman, 2003). Such beliefs indicate how tightly held views about racial supremacy can be.

Today, belief in the athletic dominance of Black people and their lack of so-called civilized traits persists within White culture—and unfortunately, within our schools. Comments like "We can't teach those kids," "It's not our fault they don't learn," and even "You are a role model for your race" communicate the persisting White cultural belief that people of color are inherently inferior.

It is naïve to assume that such an influential movement as eugenics has no lasting impact, both among the White community in terms of lingering beliefs and among communities of color, which bear the brunt of such degrading and debilitating "scientific reasoning." This "lack of opportunities to heal from hurt," as Weissglass (2001, p. 50) says, is a primary reason that racism persists today. Weissglass continues,

> It is obvious to most people that it is hurtful to be the target of racism (or any form of bias). It is less obvious that any oppressive attitude is harmful to the individual who holds it. Oppressive attitudes limit one's potential, actions, relationships, and emotional health. (p. 50)

Beliefs in racial superiority inhibit not only the person of color who is the victim but the holder of that belief as well.

White Flight

Despite the history of enslavement, extermination, internment, colonization, and annexation of people of color; despite the racist foundations of this country; despite eugenics; and despite the Supreme Court rulings on schooling, some argue that the most dramatic racial impact on education continues to stem from the government's housing policies of the 1940s. Specifically, the G.I. Bill and the Federal Housing Authority (FHA) provided the conditions that led to suburban expansion, urban renewal, "White flight," ghettoization, and the so-called inner-city problems that exist today.

As military personnel returned from World War II, the U.S. government aimed to support some veterans in achieving the American dream of home ownership. Consequently, the government spent billions of dollars to stimulate suburban housing developments and to make available low-interest mortgage loans. For the first time in history, men and women who had served their country could purchase a new home with a down payment as little as 10% of the selling price and a low-interest mortgage loan for the remaining 90%. To guarantee that its investment in property would appreciate in value over the life of the loan, the U.S. government instituted a system of determining investment growth potential. Government-determined *red-lining* became the way in which real estate developers and mortgage lenders identified communities. Still grounded in beliefs about racial supremacy and inferiority, property value seemed to be based as much on race as it was on the physical structure or size of land.

In the sophisticated system of color coding, communities where high concentrations of Black people lived were red-lined, whereas areas that were integrated or becoming more Black or mixed neighborhoods were, respectively yellow- or green-lined, and areas that were all White were blue-lined. This federal assessment encouraged bankers to expedite loans to those who could bring racial value to an area while it also encouraged developers to place "White Only" clauses in community association bylaws and charters.

Today, as postindustrial cities undergo urban renewal, once red-lined neighborhoods where Black and Brown families find themselves in alarming numbers are now being re-gentrified for White ownership. Poor families of color increasingly have nowhere to move except into the remaining housing projects that the government financed for people of color as an alternative to the White suburban expansion.

Not only did White people actualize White flight from their once loved suburbs back into a re-gentrified city or to an ever-farther away suburb, but they took with them their property values. This, in turn, affected the resources available for municipal services such as schools and law enforcement. Many Americans seemed to think the new residents of color willingly allowed the neighborhood to deteriorate after they moved in. However, what might be more accurate is that our entire society, including the government, contributed to the devaluation and eventual demise of communities of color by assigning and perpetuating a cultural belief that greater value is attached to Whiteness.

Reflection

Reflect on your own family's history in this country. How has your family been involved actively or passively in the U.S. racial binary, eugenics, and/or White flight phenomenon? Where do you see lingering evidence of these historical events in modern U.S. race relations? How might these events affect the schooling of children of color and White children in this country today?

History of Race in Education

Racial inequity in American education—and frustration with it—has a long history dating back to the founding of the nation. While the Declaration of Independence holds that "all men are created equal," the historian James Horton has said,

> We are a society based on principles literally to die for, principles that are so wonderful that it brings tears to your eyes. But we are a society that so often allows itself to ignore those principles. We live in a kind of heightened state of anxiety because we know we are not what we could be or what we say we are. (quoted in Adelman, 2003)

This perpetual anxiety about schools has resulted in extensive efforts to criticize, change, and use public education as a means to some other political end.

As it stands, the American public school system has never quite lived up to expectations. As Linda Darling-Hammond (1997) states, "Through decades of separate and unequal schooling that continue to the present, the right to learn in ways that develop both competence and community has been a myth rather than a reality" (p. 7).

This myth of effective education began with the creation of public schools, originally intended only for the White people and the well-to-do. During the first half of the 19th century, it was a crime in the southern states to teach an enslaved person how to read, and school funding for the rich and the poor in the northern states was purposely unequal.

As the Industrial Revolution came into full gear after the Civil War and segregation was officially instituted, public education came to be seen as a factory system to create the nation's workers. There was always a constant divide, however, between the rich and poor, the White and Black. According to Darling-Hammond (1997),

> Large impersonal factory-model schools with rigid tracking systems were created to teach rudimentary skills and unwavering compliance to the children of the poor. The more affluent and advantaged were taught in small elite private and public schools or carefully insulated special tracks within comprehensive schools, where they were offered a stimulating curriculum, personalized attention, high-quality teaching, and a wealth of intellectual resources. (p. 7)

There was never any intention to create equitable institutions of education, and thus, non-White schools were so chronically underfunded and inadequately supported that they could never rise above mediocrity.

The Color Line

Aside from the sociopolitical struggles around racial determination of citizenship and American ethnicity, the public education of all school-age children and the manner in which the history of the United States would be taught have required generations of legal action and public advocacy. Initially, legislators barred non-White children from schools, but the underground education process and the work of missionaries provided well-established schooling for Black children by the time of Emancipation. As the schooling of Black children moved into the public sector, segregation was the norm. This was officially upheld in 1896 by the U.S. Supreme

Court decision, *Plessy v. Ferguson,* which legalized separate schooling for White children and children of color in the United States.

In 1903, W. E. B. DuBois, among the first African Americans to receive a PhD from Harvard, described the problem of the color line wherein he illustrated the "relations of the darker to the lighter races of men" (1996, p. 15) DuBois and other prominent scholars recognized that despite efforts to educate non-White children in this country, ideas and practices connected to race would create a lasting achievement gap.

It took more than 50 years for the Supreme Court to acknowledge, in 1954, that the unleveled social playing field for White people provided educational advantage as well. The *Brown v. Topeka Board of Education* decision also led to scrutiny of other racially segregated institutions and is widely viewed as the turning point in American civil rights. Although *Brown* made racially segregated schooling illegal in the United States, the implementation of this decision "with all deliberate speed" led to some desegregation efforts that are in and of themselves cause for the persisting racial achievement disparity that exist today.

It is not our intention to debate the merits and effectiveness the Court's decision and laws. Nor can we offer the detailed historical perspective surrounding the many other events that have brought permanence to our racial challenges in the United States. We are primarily interested in assisting educators in having a conversation about race as it relates to schooling today. At the same time, we suggest that educators take the necessary time to deepen their understanding of how the history of race is inextricably linked to modern education. Some may want to pause here and review some primary source documents and historical artifacts. Remember to search for multiple racial perspectives, as the Third Condition suggests, as this will help flesh out some critical understandings. In your research, undoubtedly you will come across issues such as IQ (standardized) testing, bussing, redistricting, academic tracking, and special education, to name only a few. Each of these topics has not only a historical foundation but also racial implications for contemporary schooling.

Reflection

In your own school or school system, what evidence suggests that the history of race still impacts institutional philosophy, policies, programs, and/or practices? Does your system still experience academic tracking, course and activities enrollment, intelligence/aptitude testing, and remedial education, which stratify students, unintentionally perhaps, by race? How are these unintended racial outcomes being addressed?

A WORKING DEFINITION OF RACE

Race continues to create confusing and often polarizing relationships among and between people of all racial groups. For example, on a school's faculty, race—as a sociopolitical phenomenon—can be embraced by a few who wish to exploit it, upheld by some who have come to accept its reality, denied by others who don't understand it, and avoided by those who are shamed by it. It is clear, however, that few people of color have been able to or allowed to fully transcend a deficit racial identity imposed by society. Even Oprah Winfrey—one of the wealthiest and best-known women in the world—has talked about being followed by suspicious sales clerks in stores, when she was not recognized, simply because she is Black. Second, we struggle to find White Americans who have not benefited, to some degree, by having White skin. At the least, they have not had to think about race, much less worry about being mistreated because of it.

Defining Racial Identity

As a way of defining race and racial identity, we choose to initially examine the racial experience and commentary of someone who figures prominently in the public's eye: Tiger Woods. At 30 years of age, Tiger has become a phenomenal professional golfer and thus a recognizable name and image to many Americans. Having won dozens of tournaments, including four Masters, two PGA Championships, two U.S. Opens, and one British Open, in 2001, Tiger Woods became the first ever to hold all four professional major golfing championships at the same time.

Not only is Tiger an extraordinary golfer, it can easily be said that he is also the greatest Black golfer to ever live. Because of this public description, Woods is said to have broken the color barrier in a sport which, until recently, has been largely White. For this, he is compared to the likes of Willie Mays, Henry Aaron, Althea Gibson, Arthur Ashe, and other sporting firsts. But is Woods Black? Or is he African Thai American? Could he be *Cablasian*—a term he used to define himself when answering the persistent public questions about his racial identity? What race is Tiger Woods, and who gets to decide?

Tiger Woods represents a classic case of racial complexity and confusion for people living in the United States. Ethnically, he represents multiple cultures due to the honored traditions and backgrounds of his parents, and publicly, he acknowledges this fact. But Tiger, for a variety of reasons, struggles to accept the Black visual or racial identity that society frequently uses to describe him. In his own statement regarding his identity, Tiger Woods (1997) writes,

I am the product of two great cultures—one African American and the other Asian.

On my father's side, I am African American. On my mother's side, I am Thai. Truthfully, I feel very fortunate, and *equally proud,* to be both African American and Asian!

The critical and fundamental point is that ethnic background and or composition should NOT make a difference. It does NOT make a difference to me. The bottom line is that I am an American . . . and proud of it!

Without question, Tiger Woods has the right to be proud of his multi-ethnic heritage, and he also has the choice to claim his own racial identity. And despite his intention to control claims about his race, much of society will box him in with other Black people due to his obvious appearance, while they attempt to recognize and understand his more subtle ethnicities. In truth and in accordance with how race is lived in the United States of America, Tiger Woods can claim to be part Asian and part African American, but most will continue to see him as "just Black."

In 1997, when Tiger won his first PGA Master's Tournament, he was widely heralded and embraced as the first "Black man" ever to win that competition and don the "green Master's jacket," the traditional symbol of the tournament winner.

Because Tiger saw himself as just a golfer and not a "Black" golfer, he appeared unprepared for this "breaking the color-barrier" experience in what was virtually a White-only sport. The onslaught of praise, empathy, rejoicing, anger, and even racial slurs that resulted from Tiger's triumph illustrates what is meant by the working definition of race in the United States. Unfortunately, heated public discourse did not center on Tiger as a golfer or Tiger as a young man born to an African American father and Thai mother. Tiger was called the first Black man to win the Master's. In accepting this distinction, Tiger was from then on to be celebrated, owned, defended, and even chastised by a Black community. Equally fascinating were the reactions from appropriation to guilt and disgust that circulated throughout White America. Certainly, the lack of public response from Asian communities only adds additional layers to an already complex tapestry known as the American racial experience.

Reflection

How does the story of Tiger Woods reinforce and/or challenge your current beliefs about racial identity development?

Tiger's story reveals the power of race. Race outweighs or *trumps* other identities because it is the way in which American society initially identifies and defines people living both here and abroad. How we individually and personally view ourselves may have little to do with how our race is determined by society collectively. With all due respect to Tiger Woods' rich ethnicity, the fact remains that he is viewed as Black and many of the children and adults he inspires—and attracts to golf—are Black. Recently, Tiger himself indicated that he relates personally with other great Black athletes, such as Michael Jordan. Furthermore, his charitable work is focused around helping children of color enjoy golf. For someone who began his career having little public regard for the meaning of race, Tiger has illustrated just how powerful and overwhelming race in the United States can be.

Three C's of Identity

The Fifth Condition of Courageous Conversation encourages us to establish and use a working definition for race. Racial labeling in the United States has traditionally confounded and confused the Three C's of Identity: Corner, Culture, and Color. Although intense debate still occurs in our society about the meaning and functionality of one's nationality, ethnicity, and race, it is essential that we agree on a workable definition of each of these three characteristics. The criteria we offer focus us on how each of these phenomena is lived by people in the United States.

Corner

Both Glenn Singleton and Curtis Linton share the same U.S. origin or nationality. *Corner* designates citizenship, either by birth or naturalization, as specified on a government-issued passport. A person must be able to locate his or her nationality on a globe and name it as such.

Culture

The word *American* reflects another factor, our ethnicity. While both Curtis and Glenn are U.S. citizens, their racial biographies illustrate that their *culture* or ethnicity varies considerably and significantly. Glenn's culture is African American or, as he prefers, Black American; it includes Black English, Black Baptist and Methodist religions, jazz, soul, rap and R&B music, and soul food. Curtis's cultural affiliation is White American; it includes White English, the Mormon religion, White rock and roll, and the food and lifestyle of the American West.

Our culture describes how we live on a daily basis in terms of our language, ancestry, religion, food, dress, musical tastes, traditions, values, political and social affiliations, recreation, and so on. When hyphenated descriptions are used to describe ethnicity, the hyphen represents the balance between the two cultures or perhaps an emerging third culture or cultural hybrid. For example, a student of Mexican ancestry who was born in the United States, speaks English in public but Spanish with relatives, and occasionally partakes in celebrations recognizing the traditions of Mexico most definitely exists in a culture best described as between American and Mexican and thus is ethnically Mexican American. However, a Black student whose ancestors are a family of former Ghanaians, captured and enslaved in the United States in the 1600s, today has an experience and perspective that is different than that of contemporary White Americans and or Ghanaians. Thus, ethnically speaking, he is African American or Black American. The former describes a student who is actively bridging cultures whereas the latter illustrates a third culture or cultural hybrid that offers its own history, language, music, religion, food, fashion, and values.

Color

The final C of identity denotes *color* characteristics, or race. According to these terms, Glenn is Black, and Curtis is White. For the most part, race is the meaning affixed to the melanin content found in the skin, hair, and eyes. Those who are rich in melanin are said to be "of color," whereas those who have the least amount of visible melanin are defined as White.

Reflection

Identify your own personal three C's of Corner, Culture, and Color. Can you identify the three C's of your closest friends? To what degree do your friends represent national, ethnic, and/or racial diversity?

The Fifth Condition of Courageous Conversation helps us to avoid the tendency to use identity terms interchangeably. For example, to isolate race—which the Second Condition encourages Courageous Conversation participants to do—one must recognize and understand exactly what race is and how it is lived. Too often in the United States, we blend the three C's of our nationality, ethnicity, and race, even though when we reference any of these three, race is typically the operative in our minds and actions. This is why the Courageous Conversation strategy posits that race typically trumps ethnicity and nationality in our interactions.

Racializing Culture

Another way of viewing the interplay of the three C's is to recognize that we racialize our culture and corner. For example, specific color images are conjured up when we say *all-American, rap, country,* and *NASCAR,* even though no racial terms are specifically fixed to these ethnic traditions. Similarly, some people may decide "who belongs in this country" and "who doesn't" by the way they look, without ever actually considering the person's actual country of birth, naturalization, or current legal citizenship.

The Fifth Condition of Courageous Conversation encourages participants to deepen the discourse by being intentional and explicit about their own racial identity. When examining race, aside from the notion of racial culture, ethnicity and nationality are of less importance. Specifically, Latinos who have dark skin will have similar experiences even when they don't share Spanish language skills or come from the same country. Their common experience is racial despite their ethnic and nationality differences. Even more interesting is how our society will predictably look on these darker Latinos with expectations that they have limited English skills and, if in California or Texas, are of Mexican ancestry; if in Florida, are Cuban; or if in New York, are Puerto Rican. For these reasons, ethnicity and nationality need to be clearly differentiated so that race can gain our focus.

Ethnic Versus Racial Experiences

In the discussion of race and ethnicity, race as it relates to color begins to affect and even overshadow ethnicity. For example, music and food originate in a place or with an ethnic group and are not inherently racial, yet we may make references to Black music or Asian food. Ultimately, ethnic markers become racialized in the United States except when they reference the behaviors, attitudes, beliefs, and traditions of White American culture. For example, it is likely and acceptable to hear a group of White people say, "Let's visit a Black church and have some soul (i.e., Black) food," but they wouldn't say, "Let's visit a White church and then have some White food." *White* is the ethnic description often left out of the conversation, even though White American is the dominating ethnicity in the United States. Why is it that when the phrase *"all-American boy"* conjures up an image of a *White* boy, *White* is not a part of the description and yet a part of our collective expectation? Does *country western* mean White music and if so, why is it offensive to many if we refer to it as such?

This process of racializing ethnic experience also happens with individuals. Sandra Cisneros is considered a Brown or Hispanic author, Gwendolyn Brooks and Maya Angelou are seen as Black authors, and

Amy Tan is an Asian author. But F. Scott Fitzgerald and John Grisham are identified simply as American authors—not White authors. This is how race enters the conversation discreetly when referencing Whiteness and boldly when referencing color.

Reflection

Have you ever engaged in or observed a conversation in which you noticed race trumping ethnicity or nationality? If so, describe the circumstances which made this occur? In what ways did this race trumping complicate or simplify the conversation?

Assimilation Versus Acculturation

A person's ethnicity is indeed fluid, and these changes occur through the process of assimilation or acculturation. Through assimilation, people are required to sacrifice their primary culture or relinquish their ethnic traits in exchange for new and different traits. For example, although they hear Spanish spoken at home, Brown students may lose their fluency because of pressures from educators and perhaps parents to speak English only.

Through acculturation, people integrate their primary ethnic characteristics into the new culture they are adopting. For example, our adopted "Tex-Mex" food fuses the cuisines of Mexico and the American Southwest. The process of acculturation can also enable students to hold on to their own cultural traditions while sampling or even immersing in a different school culture. Specifically, Chinese American students can enjoy a hamburger in the school cafeteria, eat Chinese American food in a predominantly White suburban mall food court, and still crave authentic Chinese food prepared at home using spices, produce, and seafood purchased at the Chinese grocery. These blended cultures stem primarily from desired acculturation but can also be born out of a purposeful but unsuccessful resistance to assimilation. In the face of dominant White culture, many people of color fail in their attempts to maintain their own ethnic culture, while others wish to assimilate into Whiteness but feel unwelcome due to their identifiable non-White racial characteristics.

Defined by Race

Distinguishing between ethnicity and nationality helps us to understand the labels we place on others and that others place on us. As stated previously, race denotes the social meaning affixed to skin color, whereas ethnicity defines cultural markers, such as language, religion, and food; nationality describes only country of origin or naturalization and is a matter of official and legal documentation. The working definition of race, however, recognizes that these three identifiers do not operate with equal force and familiarity in U.S. society. As a result of our racialized culture, people's color tends to define much of their culture, as well as determine whether they should gain full access to the benefits of U.S. citizenship.

When Curtis Linton enters the room, he is seen as a White male first and Mormon later, should he choose to reveal this latter part of his ethnicity. If he publicly identifies as Mormon, few would question the validity of his affiliation to the Church of Jesus Christ of Latter Day Saints because it is seen traditionally as a White institution in the United States, even though its racial membership is more diverse around the world.

When Glenn Singleton enters a room, he is viewed as a Black man. When he speaks, some will question his Blackness because he has spent much of his educational and professional life in and around White culture. That is to say that his references and phraseology are familiar to White people. The fact that Glenn attends a Black Methodist church, appreciates Black music, and favors soul food is not questioned. But, if he were to say he was Mormon, many would experience dissonance and perhaps have trouble believing him. This is because Mormonism has traditionally not been viewed as a part of the Black American experience.

When it comes to nationality, however, neither Glenn nor Curtis is questioned on U.S. citizenship because racially, they both fit the look of an American citizen even though Curtis appears "all American." Their U.S.-born Latino and Asian American friends, however, are often required to prove their national identity. They may not be asked to show their passports, but they are commonly asked where they are from. This is one way in which race is lived in the United States.

Unfortunately, the conversation about ethnicity is often short-circuited because race enters so quickly into the dialogue. People may believe that they are talking about ethnicity when they address differences, but in fact, they are talking about race. Educators purport to be looking at student achievement data disaggregated by ethnicity when they are actually examining data more closely linked to the race of their students. By separating race from nationality and ethnicity, we can better practice Courageous Conversations that focus on race.

Reflection

Answer the following statements:

Racially speaking . . .

the "me" I see is _____.

the "me" you see is _____.

the "me" I think you see is _____.

Is each of these responses the same? How are they different? How do some of your closest colleagues and/or older students answer these questions? Do you or they experience struggle or conflict as they complete the sentences? What do you believe to be the reason for this dissonance?

Implementation Exercise

Three C's of Identity

Time required: 45 minutes

Materials required: Courageous Conversation Journal for each participant and the worksheet that follows

1. Present the Fifth Condition of Courageous Conversation:

   Establish agreement around a contemporary working definition for race that is clearly differentiated from that of ethnicity and nationality.

2. Introduce and differentiate between the Three C's of Identity:

   - *Corner*: Nationality
   - *Culture*: Ethnicity
   - *Color:* Race

3. Describe the intersection of race, ethnicity, and nationality, as shown in the following diagram. Explain that the star symbolizes the working definition of race or a clear understanding of one's racial identity or racial culture.

4. Have each participant define and identify his or her own personal *Corner, Culture,* and *Color* on the worksheet. Emphasize the need to differentiate among the Three C's. Remind participants that race is not the same as ethnicity or nationality.

5. Divide participants into small interracial groups of three to four people. Have each person share with the group their Three C's.

6. After this discussion, have each participant create his or her own working definition of race, one that represents a clear understanding of racial identity or racial culture.

7. Address the following prompts within the small groups:

   What is the identity with which you feel most comfortable?

   How does your Corner identity differ from your Culture identity?

What connections exist between your Culture and Color identities?

Of the three identities, which do you believe others see in you?

Do you feel comfortable explaining how you derived your working definition of race?

8. Share small-group observations with the larger group, and have participants reflect in their journals.

Three C's of Identity

Fifth Condition of Courageous Conversations

Establish agreement around a contemporary working definition of race that is clearly differentiated from that of ethnicity and nationality.

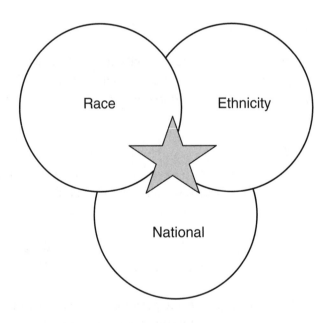

➢ *Corner*

My nationality is . . .

_____

_____

_____

➢ *Culture*

My ethnicity is . . .

_____

_____

_____

➢ *Color*

My race is . . .

_____

_____

_____

⭐ *My working definition of race is . . .*

_____

_____

_____

RACIAL AUTOBIOGRAPHY: KATHERYN

As a young biracial Chicagoan born to a White father of Italian ancestry and a Hispanic mother, I certainly "stuck out" in our south-side Irish Catholic neighborhood. I remember being singled out any time there was trouble—a stolen bicycle, a vandalized home, a schoolyard fight—as the responsible party. I responded to these false accusations by being the *best* kid on the block— the *perfect* kid: always doing my chores on time, applying myself in school, having perfect manners, and doing favors for all my neighbors. This was my out—to be so perfect that no one could accuse me of anything.

As a youngster, racism was all around me. I would hear racial slurs and really ugly racial jokes, usually aimed at African Americans or Hispanics, used frequently by my neighbors. Later, I would see these same people at Mass as many of them were leaders in our church: ushers, Eucharistic ministers, members of the Holy Name Society. It was such a contradiction for me! I knew that what these people were doing was wrong. How could they be leaders in our church? How could Christians act in this manner?

When I began elementary school, I became the target of constant bullying by a group of classmates. All were of Irish ancestry and would hurl verbal assaults at me throughout the school day because I looked different from them. Their favorite names to call me were *nigger* and *blackie*. The most painful episodes always happened at lunchtime because the nuns (our teachers) did not have lunch with us. Parent volunteers were supposed to be watching us during lunch, and I know that many of the parents witnessed the way I was being treated and simply looked the other way.

One day, there were not enough parent volunteers so the principal asked some of the eighth-grade girls to supervise our second-grade lunch period. One of the girls assigned to my classroom instantly told my teacher, Sister Virginia, what was happening to me. Sister Virginia acted immediately. She gathered all of us together and threatened the bullies with severe consequences if the harassment did not stop. After that, they left me alone.

I vividly remember Sister Virginia asking me why I did not tell her about the bullying and name calling. I told her that she had told us not to be tattletales, and I did not want to disappoint her. I also told her that I was "turning the other cheek" just as Jesus did (a complete misunderstanding of scripture, I know, but understandable for a seven-year-old). At that point, Sister Virginia turned her back to me. I remember thinking at the time that she was too mad to even look at me, but I now know that she turned her back to prevent me from seeing her cry.

During the 1970s in Chicago, one of the most controversial political events was the city's attempt to desegregate schools. Because I attended Catholic school, I was not in jeopardy of being bused. However, my childhood home was directly across the street from Johnson School, a local public school that was greatly affected by the busing mandate. After much heated debate, the city council decided to begin voluntary busing of students. This meant that most White students would stay at their home school but that Black students who wished to attend a different school could do so.

As a result, Stevenson School received several busloads of young Black students every day. This angered many of the people in my neighborhood, who formed daily picket lines to meet the buses. Every morning and afternoon, local film crews gathered on our front lawn to cover the chaos. People shouted horrible things to the students as they got on and off the buses and carried signs with nasty things printed on them. Film of our tiny bungalow always made the nightly news. These problems continued for quite some time.

In middle school, one of our teachers gave us a journalism assignment. We were to choose a controversial topic and then interview someone in authority and write a newspaper article about the interview. I chose the topic of busing and asked a classmate's father, who was the assistant principal at Johnson School, if I could interview him. I remember having to call his secretary to arrange the meeting and being very proud as I entered his office in my best clothes with pen and writing pad in hand. Once we began the interview, however, my spirits quickly plummeted. This man—a highly educated member of our community and someone I saw at church every Sunday—told me exactly how much he hated the busing and African Americans in general. He went so far as to call the students "animals" that couldn't be taught to behave. I remember making up some quotes for the article because I was too embarrassed to have my teacher read what the man actually said.

Throughout high school and college, I had many boyfriends who would not take me to their home or never saw me again after introducing me to their parents. I remember the parents of my prom date commenting on my beautiful tan—I didn't have the heart to tell them that I hadn't been in the sun at all, and it was just my normal skin color. Later when I met my future husband and he asked me to meet his parents, I was very nervous. He was also nervous and prepared his parents beforehand by telling them that the girl he was in love with was Hispanic. At our first meeting, they also seemed nervous, but we all survived the experience unscathed.

Once I married into the family, it became very clear that—although my in-laws cared for me a great deal—I would never measure up to their White daughter-in-law. No matter how hard I tried to win their favor or how many perfect grandchildren I produced, I was never as good as their other daughter-in-law. Even though my sister-in-law and I had children at the same time, my mother-in-law made it very clear that while she loved our children, she really favored the blond grandchildren that my sister-in-law had given her. She would repeatedly state in front of me and the kids how much she loved little "tow-headed kids" (my kids have dark brown hair just like their mother). Whenever my sister-in-law and I are arguing about anything, my mother-in-law will always take her side. My mother-in-law's bias and my husband's inability to stand up to her have been a source of great distress over the course of our 18-year marriage.

The Sixth Condition

Let's Talk About Whiteness

> *The virtual invisibility that Whiteness affords those of us who have it is like psychological money in the bank, the proceeds of which we cash in everyday while others are in a perpetual state of overdraft.*
>
> —Tim Wise (2000)

Conversations about race often prove difficult, and shining light on White as a color, culture, and consciousness is the most challenging aspect of these interactions. Not only does White define the dominant race, but also it represents the standard by which our racial awareness, experiences, and perspectives are judged.

At the foundation of all race relations in the United States of America is the presence of White people sharing a somewhat common level of understanding—or misunderstanding—about their own racial roles and experiences. Also at this racial core, White people are prominent in interpreting the experience and perspective of the racial "other" through their White lens. In other words, the way in which the dominant racial group collectively determines what is and is not *White, Black,* or *Asian,* for example, determines how each of us will be included and excluded in conversations. Equally significant is that many White educators, as Tim Wise suggests in the preceding quote, fail to recognize that White is a race, much less that Whiteness represents a culture and consciousness that is shared by White people.

The Sixth Condition provides guidance as educators venture into this deepest and most essential dimension of and challenge to racial dialogue:

> *Examine the presence and role of Whiteness, its impact on the conversation, and the problem being addressed.*

In this chapter, we will shine the light on racial dominance to uncover how Whiteness challenges the performance of students of color while shaping and reinforcing the racial perspective of White children. Initially, we must explore White as a color, culture, and consciousness. Second, we will revisit the previous five conditions, only this time with the explicit purpose of understanding how they are each impacted by Whiteness. Finally, we will examine how White racial identity is formed and developed as well as explore how White cultural identity influences teaching and learning.

WHITE IS A COLOR

> *I was faced with a reality I had never anticipated. I began to realize that despite my activism, despite my good intentions, despite how "down" I perceived myself to be with the cause of justice, I was still part of the problem. I was actively receiving the perks of Whiteness, and collaborating with the system of White supremacy, whether I liked it or not.*

> —Tim Wise (2002, p. 227)

These feelings captured the racial predicament of Tim Wise, a White social justice activist from Nashville, Tennessee, as he faced for the first time the uncomfortable reality that—even though he fought for racial justice—he still partook daily in the benefits of being White. Despite his good intentions to be anti-racist, what Wise discovered was that his existence was made much more pleasant and less complicated because he was White. Without ever choosing it, he had received racial privilege his entire life. Wise (2002) continues, "It wasn't just the privileges and advantages that I remembered, but the silences as well; the times I had sat back and said nothing despite knowing that I was surrounded by racial injustice—injustice that was operating to my benefit" (p. 232).

When examining racial privilege in our system of education, the experience of White students is just as informative as that of students of color. Consider Tim Wise's (2002) experience in school: Even though he admits he was not a very serious student, the system still encouraged his eventual success. Wise now recognizes that, from the earliest days of kindergarten, his peers of color were not offered the same wonderful opportunity, high expectations, or encouragement to excel. As Wise finally realized, the privileges he received were primarily due to the color of his skin: White. Educators cannot truly understand the challenges faced by students of color—challenges that result in lowered achievement—until we all develop a deeper understanding of what it means to be White.

WHITE PRIVILEGE

We often hear people referred to as being privileged, which usually is a comment pertaining to the individual's financial or economic status. To be privileged, indeed, means to be of elevated economic means. To have a privileged background means that one's family had material wealth. In Courageous Conversation, however, privilege takes on a different meaning: it refers to the amount of melanin in a person's skin, hair, and eyes. Ironically, the more melanin a person has, the less *privilege* or racial advantage he or she receives.

For those who have not examined their lives through the lens of race, the mere suggestion that they are privileged might evoke strong emotions, particularly if they see themselves as hard-working or from challenged economic circumstances. It may be difficult to grasp the fact that White privilege has little to do with a person's economic status. It refers to the advantages that White people receive simply by virtue of their appearance and, to a lesser degree, the privilege lighter-skinned people of color garner as compared to darker members of the same or different non-White racial groups.

Consider the following thoughts about White privilege by Wellesley College professor Peggy McIntosh (1989):

> I think Whites are carefully taught not to recognize White privilege, as males are taught not to recognize male privilege. So I have begun in an untutored way to ask what it is like to have White privilege. I have come to see White privilege as an invisible package of unearned assets that I can count on cashing in each day, but about which I was "meant" to remain oblivious. White privilege is like an invisible weightless knapsack of special provisions, maps, passports, codebooks, visas, clothes, tools, and blank checks.

Describing White privilege makes one newly accountable. As we in women's studies work to reveal male privilege and ask men to give up some of their power, so one who writes about having white privilege must ask, "Having described it, what will I do to lessen or end it?"

After I realized the extent to which men work from a base of unacknowledged privilege, I understood that much of their oppressiveness was unconscious. Then I remembered the frequent charges from women of color that White women whom they encounter are oppressive. I began to understand why we are justly seen as oppressive, even when we don't see ourselves that way. I began to count the ways in which I enjoy unearned skin privilege and have been conditioned into oblivion about its existence. (p. 10)

Source: Copyright © 1988 by Peggy McIntosh. Reprinted with permission of the author. mmcintosh@wellesley.edu.

Reflection

What is your reaction to the concept of White privilege? If you are White, does this challenge your self-identification in society? If you are a person of color, how do you cope with the daily injustices triggered by White privilege?

Educators must acknowledge White skin privilege and work to develop a deeper understanding of this reality in order to fully examine the cultural implications of Whiteness in schools. By completing the following exercise, entitled *Understanding White Privilege: The Color-Line*, educators can develop a clearer understanding of the ways in which skin color, and specifically Whiteness, impacts their daily experiences.

Although the directions call for you to conduct the exercise with a large group such as a faculty or staff, we suggest you first complete the exercise on your own and then do it again with a friend of a race different than your own. Once you have finished reading *Courageous Conversations* and guided your colleagues through some understanding of the Four Agreements and Six Conditions, you may then choose to guide your colleagues through the color-line exercise.

Implementation Exercise

Understanding White Privilege: The Color-Line Exercise

This exercise is based on the work of Peggy McIntosh (1989). Her article, "White Privilege," is autobiographical wherein she compared her circumstances only to those of a small group of African-American women in her building and in her line of work. She did not claim that her examples of privilege applied to all White people in all times and places relative to all people of color. Many people have found, however, that McIntosh's observations on her life have some bearing on their own experiences. The point of this exercise is to think about racial privilege as a corollary of racial discrimination and to see whether and how any of the points on McIntosh's list apply to you.

Time required: 60 minutes

Materials required: Courageous Conversation Journal for each participant and Table 10.1

Review the Four Agreements and first Five Conditions of Courageous Conversations.

Prepare the group by introducing the Sixth Condition:

> *Examine the presence and role of Whiteness, its impact on the conversation, and the problem being addressed.*

1. Invite participants to make personal sense of Whiteness. Offer them an explanation of White as a color. If the color-line exercise is to be effective, you must be working with a racially diverse group.

2. Have each participant complete the color-line exercise in Table 10.1, adapted from the work of Peggy McIntosh (1989), using the scale it provides.

3. Have participants total their scores and then line up in an arc, with the lowest scores to the right and the highest scores to the left.

4. With the group arranged in this arc, pose the probing statements in the box.

Probing Statements

- Would all women step forward?
  What you see is how race impacts women.

- Would all women with an advanced degree step forward?
  What you see is how race impacts women with higher-level education.

- Would men with an advanced degree step forward to join the women with advanced degrees?
  What you see is how race impacts people with advanced degrees.

- Would all White people step forward?
  What you see is White privilege and the color line.

- With each statement, have appropriate members take a step forward into the center of the arc.
- Once the group has noted the response, have those who stepped forward return to their original places.

5. Following the series of probing statements, allow the entire group some time to process the exercise together in the arc.

6. Finally, have the participants return to their tables, where they will continue conversations in smaller multiracial groups. Recognize that the color-line visuals may be upsetting and even shocking to some participants.

7. You may wish to have each educator complete the White privilege instrument with a friend of a different race and report on this at your next meeting.

   Recognize that some White participants may not know anyone of a different race whom they consider a friend. These educators might reflect on why their friendships only include people of the same race.

8. Now read to the group the following excerpt:

   In his book, *The Souls of Black Folk*, published in 1903, Black Harvard graduate Dr. W. E. B. DuBois (1996) wrote the following:

   > The problem of the twentieth century is the problem of the color line, the relation of the darker to the lighter races of men in Asia, Africa, America and the Islands of the Sea. . . . Curious it was, too, how this deeper question [of the color line] ever forced itself to the surface despite effort and disclaimer.

   - Where is our color line between the lighter and darker races?

Table 10.1   Understanding White Privilege: The Color-Line Exercise

Respond to each question using one of the following scores:

    5   if the statement is mostly true for you

    3   if the statement is sometimes true for you

    0   if the statement is seldom true for you

Because of my race or color . . .	*My response*	*Friend's response*
If I wish, I can arrange to be in the company of people of my race most of the time.		
If I should need to move, I can be pretty sure of renting or purchasing housing in an area which I can afford and in which I would want to live.		
I can be pretty sure that my neighbors in such a location will be neutral or pleasant to me.		
I can go shopping alone most of the time, pretty well assured that I will not be followed or harassed.		
I can turn on the television or open to the front page of the newspaper and see people of my race widely represented.		
When I am told about our national heritage or about "civilization," I am shown that people of my color made it what it is.		
I can be sure that my children will be given curricular materials that testify to the existence of their race.		
I can go into supermarkets and find the staple foods that fit with my cultural traditions; I can go into a music shop and count on finding the music of my race represented; I can go into any hairdresser's shop and find someone who can cut my hair.		
Whether I use checks, credit cards, or cash, I can count on my skin color not to work against the appearance of financial reliability.		
I can arrange to protect my children most of the time from people who might not like them.		
I can swear, or dress in secondhand clothes, or not answer letters, without having people attribute these choices to the bad morals, the poverty, or the illiteracy of my race.		
I can speak in public to a powerful male group without putting my race on trial.		
I can do well in a challenging situation without being called a credit to my race.		

(Continued)

Table 10.1 (Continued)

Because of my race or color . . .	*My response*	*Friend's response*
I am never asked to speak for all the people of my racial group.		
I can remain oblivious to the language and customs of persons of color who constitute the world's majority without feeling, in my culture, any penalty for such oblivion.		
I can criticize our government and talk about how much I fear its policies and behavior without being seen as a cultural outsider.		
I can be pretty sure that if I ask to talk to "the person in charge," I will be facing a person of my race.		
If a traffic cop pulls me over, or if the IRS audits my tax return, I can be sure I haven't been singled out because of my race.		
I can easily buy posters, postcards, picture books, greeting cards, and children's magazines featuring the people of my race.		
I can go home from most meetings of the organizations I belong to feeling somewhat tied in, rather than isolated, out of place, outnumbered, unheard, held at a distance, feared, or hated.		
I can take a job with an affirmative action employer without having co-workers on the job suspect that I got it because of race.		
I can choose public accommodations without fearing that people of my race cannot get in or will be mistreated in the places I have chosen.		
I can be sure that if I need legal or medical help, my race will not work against me.		
If my day, week, or year is going badly, I need not ask of each negative episode or situation whether it has racial overtones.		
I can choose blemish cover or bandages in "flesh" color and have them more or less match my skin.		
TOTAL SCORE		

WHITE IS A CULTURE

Although shocking and disturbing to many of us, White privilege is often a difficult phenomenon for White people to acknowledge and own. Sometimes, a sophisticated level of understanding occurs, but White educators feel challenged in mustering the will and finding the skill to confront their privilege or the corresponding oppression experienced by people of color.

Even Peggy McIntosh (1988), the White scholar who worked to make the concept of White privilege accessible to White people, says,

> I repeatedly forgot each of the realizations on this list until I wrote it down. For me, White privilege has turned out to be an elusive and fugitive subject. The pressure to avoid it is great, for in facing it I must give up the myth of meritocracy. If these things are true, this is not such a free country; one's life is not what one makes it; many doors open for certain people through no virtues of their own. (p. 9)

Entitlement

Beyond skin color privilege exists a racial culture that is defined by the behaviors of White people, who often function unaware that they live a privileged existence. When White people are unconscious of their privilege, these skin color benefits are viewed as entitlements. Therefore, when people of color question these privileges, they are viewed as aggressive and seen as encroaching on the lifestyle that White people believe to be their legitimate right.

Furthermore, when people of color—not having these benefits or advantages—are unable to reach the same life goals as White people, they are viewed by the privileged race as weak, unskilled, unintelligent, and even lazy. In a protected enclave of Whiteness, be it a suburban neighborhood or a faculty meeting room, White people are buffered from encroachments on their privilege. Sharing perspective about what is hard work and what are the appropriate ways to behave within protected environments of unacknowledged privilege, White people define the right way to do school and live a productive life. This forthrightness in determining the "right" way to do things could also be seen as determining for people of color the "White" way to function in life and specifically in school.

Understanding White Culture

Even though much of a school's decision making occurs on an intellectual level in White majority enclaves, White people tend to understand little about what it means to be White. Conversely, because deriving material success in our schools and society most often involves negotiating White culture, people of color can define multiple characteristics of White culture with relative ease.

When teachers venture into their classrooms, most teach their own personal culture first and the subject matter or standards second. Similarly, when educators assess student performance, much of the process and content of the assessment has more to do with the teacher's culture than the student's culture. To what degree, then, do students need to be proficient in White culture to achieve in schools where most teachers are White females?

Likewise, what happens when the culture of our Black and Brown male students does not correspond to the White female teachers' culture in the classroom? Can effective teaching and learning take place when there is cultural conflict in the classroom and throughout the school? Racial conflict among educators and between educators and students cannot be resolved when White educators are unaware of their racial culture and people of color feel unsafe to reveal the characteristics of Whiteness.

Defining White Culture

From the work of Elise Trumbull, Carrie Rothstein-Fisch, Patricia M. Greenfield, and Blanca Quiroz (2000), we have learned that *White culture* is characterized by individualism, whereas *cultures of color* are more often characterized by collectivism. In their research entitled *Bridging Cultures,* they studied the classroom and home behaviors of Latino and Southeast Asian American students in Southern California and compared them to behaviors of White students. These two differing sets of characteristics impact the actions and interactions of both groups. Understanding these differences is critical if White people and people of color are to engage in more effective dialogue. The cultural differences based on race are detailed in Table 10.2.

From a cultural standpoint, examining the presence and role of Whiteness is the most critical condition for innovating and differentiating instruction in such a way that all students achieve in a rigorous curriculum. This same examination, however, often triggers defensiveness in White people, particularly those challenged to embrace the concept of White privilege.

Table 10.2 Cultural Differences

White Individualism (Representative of prevailing U.S. culture)	Color Group Collectivism (Representative of many immigrant cultures)
• Fostering independence and individual achievement	• Fostering interdependence and group success
• Promoting self-expression, individual thinking, and personal choice	• Promoting adherence to norms, respect for authority/elders, and group consensus
• Associated with egalitarian relationships and flexibility in roles (e.g., upward mobility)	• Associated with stable, hierarchical roles (dependent on gender, family background, age)
• Understanding the physical world as knowable apart from its meaning for human life	• Understanding the physical world in the context of its meaning for human life
• Associated with private property, individual ownership	• Associated with shared property, group ownership

Nonetheless, as certain as we are about the existence of Black culture, indigenous culture, and Latino culture, White culture must also exist, simply by virtue of the number of White people in American schools and society. It is White culture that primarily establishes the standards for all intraracial and interracial group interactions. Thus, White culture dictates to some degree how, when, and where other racial groups determine, develop, and honor their own cultures.

Reflection

How have you observed White individualism and/or color group collectivism in your personal life? Your professional life? In the school system where you work? Can you describe a personal or professional situation in which there was balance between White individualism and color group collectivism?

WHITE CONSCIOUSNESS

Given their position in terms of racial privilege and cultural dominance and power, White educators are apt to develop a certain way of thinking or a consciousness about specific educational and societal challenges that is often not aligned with the perspectives of educators of color. Many White people do not consider how their lives are impacted by their own Whiteness. Conversely, people of color feel, consciously or not, that they often must determine and declare what is the proper White behavior and operating White perspective in any given situation.

For example, many people of color feel the need to be cautious in mixed racial groups to not offend or disturb White people's disconnect from their own racial behaviors. When more than two people of color gather together, it reminds White people that race, in fact, exists. As the number of people of color in a room or on a committee increases, many caring White educators' greatest fear surfaces—that of being labeled a racist. People of color are required to be aware of White icons, fashions, and follies to participate appropriately in interracial professional and social interactions. Furthermore, White people tend to dominate conversation by setting the tone for how everyone must talk and which words should be used. All of these "White ways" must be recognized, internalized, and then silently acted on by people of color.

People of color must become proficient in balancing their primary culture with White culture, or they run the risk of either being marginalized from the powerful racial mainstream or being consumed by it, which is also known as "acting White."

The aforementioned White cultural characteristics, such as individualism, blur into the consciousness of Whiteness, which becomes not only a way of behaving but also a way of thinking. Throughout our Courageous Conversation research and practice, four distinct and yet overlapping ideals emerge as defining elements of White consciousness: universal perspective, individualism, avoidance, and decontextualization.

We acknowledge that these characteristics could be linked to other diversity phenomena apart from race. What we are suggesting, however, is that White privilege and entitlement lead people to develop perspectives and reach intellectual conclusions that are racially unique and at times create conflict for people of color.

Universal Perspective

The notion of a universal perspective begs the question, "Doesn't everybody experience life the way that White people have experienced it?" In his article "White Is a Color!" Glenn Singleton (1997) coined the term *Whiteism* and defined it as (1) not recognizing White as a dominating color nor the unearned power and privileges associated with having white skin and (2) having a sense of (White) entitlement but lacking awareness of the experiences and perspectives of non-White-skinned people.

Because White people are rarely forced to acknowledge the reality of their skin color privilege, there is little or no collective recognition or empathy for the struggle experienced by people of color who, by definition, lack these privileges. Thus, when the notion of racial privilege and the corresponding oppression is brought to the attention of White people, they often struggle to see it as real or valid. Consequently, White people embrace the cultural conclusion that people of color use race as an excuse for their individual failures and shortcomings. Because White people so often see personal effort as the only source of success in life, they believe that people of color use a "race card" to avoid hard work. Although it is true that hard work will lead to better results for all students, given the racial imbalances discussed earlier, effort and rewards do not always align for people of color, simply because they do not receive White privilege.

Individualism

Individualism claims that "I earned this," making the "effort equals reward" perspective a deeply embedded ideology within White culture. Because of this, White people often fail to make the connection between themselves and the many other White people in any given situation who reinforce the White cultural values and thus ensure maintenance of the systemic delivery of White privilege.

For example, when White teachers make references to White icons, events or places that White people visit, and issues that draw the interest of largely White audiences, White children are more likely to make the critical connections because of their White cultural upbringing. The school day consists of multiple opportunities for students to connect with or disconnect from the teacher. Depending on the educator's attention to this intercultural relationship based in race, his or her students will succeed or fail.

To assert that White people are individualistic disregards to some degree this backdrop of White racial bonding. White people depend on the overwhelming presence of other White people in positions of power and influence to maintain a system of racial advantage. At the same time, many White educators believe that gains in school, as in their own lives, come from individual effort and accomplishment.

Peggy McIntosh (1988) speaks to the White cultural disposition surrounding individualism in the following way:

My schooling gave me no training in seeing myself as an oppressor, as an unfairly advantaged person, or as a participant in a damaged culture. I was taught to see myself as an individual whose moral state depended on her individual moral will. My schooling followed the pattern my colleague Elizabeth Minnich has pointed out: Whites are taught to think of their lives as morally neutral, normative, and average, and also ideal, so that when we work to benefit others, this is seen as work which will allow "them" to be more like "us." (p. 4)

For these reasons, schools and classrooms are organized in many ways around the idea of individual effort; this includes the way we test, call on children for responses one at a time, and provide individualized work spaces and personal supplies. Although group work has become more acceptable, students often strive to differentiate themselves, their own personal effort, and their individual high level of understanding from that of the group.

Beverly Daniel Tatum (1997) titled her book, *"Why Are All the Black Kids Sitting Together in the Cafeteria?"* partly to attract the attention of White educators who struggle to understand why students of color behave the way they do. We have heard many White educators express curiosity and concern about students of color congregating in racial affinity groups. This is evidence of White individualism as it represents an unspoken belief that members of a given racial group do not need one another for fellowship, safety, or survival.

Tatum could just have easily named her book, *"Why Are All the White Kids Sitting Together in the Cafeteria?"* or in the classroom, on the swim team, or in the National Honor Society. But this concept would be foreign and even insulting to White people who choose not to notice their own need for White racial collectivity. It is ironic, however, that the cultural demand for racial dominance coexists with a White cultural belief in individualism. This incongruence is often troubling for people of color.

Avoidance

"This isn't my problem" represents the attitude of avoidance. Many White people have developed and embraced sophisticated ways to avoid thinking and conversing about their own positions of racial privilege and power. In his book, *Uprooting Racism*, Paul Kivel (2002) explores stages of avoidance, which begins with denying the entire notion of racial dominance and progresses to counterattack/competing victimization—a claim that society is out to persecute White men.

Recent conversations about "reverse racism," which traveled as far as the U.S. Supreme Court in 2003, show the power of White people to defend their perceived entitlement and racial dominance. Since the 1970s, the Court has not acknowledged the escalating images of Whiteness at the highest levels of government and industry in relation to the dramatic demographic shifts in favor of people of color. Again, McIntosh's comments (1988) add insight:

> In proportion as my racial group was being made confident, comfortable, and oblivious, other groups were likely being made unconfident, uncomfortable, and alienated. Whiteness protected me from many kinds of hostility, distress, and violence, which I was being subtly trained to visit in turn upon people of color. For this reason, the word "privilege" now seems to me misleading. . . .
>
> I want, then, to distinguish between earned strength and unearned power. (p. 12)

Decontextualization

Decontextualization is evidenced in the oft-heard question, How does this particular situation have anything to do with race? Given that so many White people have trouble seeing themselves as part of a dominating racial group endowed with privilege and power, they also tend not to see how this context of Whiteness has connections to events and outcomes at home and abroad. The moment-to-moment impact and influence that White thinking has on the lives of people of color create a web of racial cause and effect that is invisible to many White people. Because of this virtual invisibility, White people tend to focus on only one part of the event and forgo analysis of a larger historical racial dimension or its present impact and future implications.

For example, as White educators wonder why Black and Brown boys are disproportionately prone to fighting in school, they criticize Black and Brown culture and question why violence is taught in homes of color. Missing from their inquiry and analysis, however, is how these boys might be affected by growing up in a White-governed country, which threatens young men of color at will, distrusts their ability to succeed and follow laws, and allows daily racial stress to mount in neighborhoods, schools, and classrooms. In her book, *It's the Little Things* (2000), Lena Williams writes, "My actions . . . are the results of the cumulative effect of a lifetime of racial slights and injustices suffered because of my color" (p. 10). Because the privilege of Whiteness is to not suffer these micro-aggressions, the White consciousness does not incorporate race as a topic into their reasoning and analysis of local, state, national, and world events.

Reflection

What personal connections can you make to the universal perspective, individualism, avoidance, and decontextualization of White consciousness? As a White person, how do these characteristics of consciousness impact your relations with others? As a person of color, how do you handle White people who unconsciously exhibit these characteristics?

WHITENESS AS EXAMINED IN THE FIVE CONDITIONS

When conversing about race, we ultimately must speak to Whiteness. Our most significant interaction revolves around our ability to inquire into Whiteness at all three levels: color, culture, and consciousness. To summarize our discussion on race, we will now review the first Five Conditions of Courageous Conversation through the lens of Whiteness. By merely substituting *White, Whiteness,* and *Whiteism* for all references to race, we will arrive at the deeper examination and understanding that the Sixth Condition offers.

Remember that according to the definition of Courageous Conversation, the first two conditions are about *engaging,* the second two conditions are about *sustaining,* and the last two conditions are about *deepening* our interracial dialogue and understanding. The most difficult and most discomforting of the conditions is the Sixth Condition—examining the presence and role of Whiteness. Personalizing (First Condition) Whiteness (Sixth Condition) is the essential progression that enables educators to attain a workable understanding of how race impacts schooling in general and, specifically, the achievement of all students.

Whiteness in the First Condition

To examine Whiteness within the First Condition is to *establish a White racial context that is personal, local, and immediate.* Traditionally, White Americans have failed to view White as a race. Consider once again the exercise that asks, "How much does race impact my life?"

Race in my life?
0–100%

Typically, when White people consider this question for the first time, they do not count their time spent with other White people as having racial impact. Consequently, they often see race as being synonymous with color, but colors other than White. To view the First Condition through Whiteness is to ask the degree to which White, Whiteness, and Whiteism impact my life. With this phrasing, it is virtually impossible to leave White privilege, positioning, and power out of the equation. Until educators acknowledge White to be a race, it is impossible to recognize the full impact of racism on student learning. Our deeper level of analysis points us toward understanding how neighborhoods that are all White, clubs that are all White, and the advanced placement or honors classes that are virtually all White impact *all* students' perspectives and performance.

Whiteness in the Second Condition

Once we have acknowledged that White is a race and Whiteness impacts each of us personally, locally, and immediately, we can then *isolate Whiteness* and determine how it impacts a given racial situation.

Consider the reactions of White educators to the Volkswagen advertisement presented in Chapter 6. Because White people can grow into maturity in this society without ever authentically interacting with a person of color, be it in their neighborhood, workplace, church, or the media, a White perspective on such negative representations of color is often lacking. Because the media in our society does not demonize White people in the same way it poorly represents people of color, the impact of a negative ad is minimized by White people. Typically, *white* is portrayed as the standard of beauty, intelligence, and moral correctness. Whiteness is indeed presented as the social, political, and economic yardstick by which everything and everyone is measured. When educators isolate these omnipresent occasions of racial standardization, they notice in their schools the pervasiveness of Whiteness and the overwhelming number of circumstances in which White cultural adaptation is required of students of color.

Whiteness in the Third Condition

We need to *normalize the social construction of Whiteness* to engage multiple White points of view and *surface critical perspective.* Once Whiteness is made visible and examined as a distinct and pervasive racial experience, White people will still offer a multitude of interpretations as to why Whiteness dominates in discourse and other interactions. Clearly, some White people adamantly and forcefully subscribe to beliefs of White supremacy passed on from previous generations. Although most educators would never admit to these beliefs, their low expectations and doubts about the ability of their students of color are revealing. For Glenn Singleton, growing up in a thriving Black working-class community and attending all-Black schools, churches, and social gatherings, notions of Black excellence were unquestioned. It was not until he attended the predominately White Park School that he began to embrace color inferiority and White supremacy. Today, many of his former teachers at Park would be heartbroken to discover that they helped instill these beliefs in their beloved student. Unfortunately, intention is not necessary to faithfully practice Whiteism and promote Whiteness.

A more sophisticated understanding of the social construction of knowledge prompts us to investigate how this phenomenon of Whiteness has been and continues to be constructed. Such inquiry leads us into developing critical perspective about Whiteness and how it plays out in curricular and instructional designs and decisions.

The Contemporary Social and Political Construction of Whiteness

In the Fifth Condition, we explored the historic progression of race in the United States. A sophisticated analysis of how Whiteness is socially and politically constructed today points us to conversations surrounding the sociology of a diminishing yet still dominating White population and the politics employed to maintain White power. The question of who merits White status remains a centerpiece discussion. Contemporary census takers struggle with finding the exact racial language to describe immigrants from Mexico, Latin America, and the Pacific Islands. White government officials and their supporters will embrace Latinos as part of the new White race, just as long as there are no requirements for Spanish-language acquisition or other non-White cultural adaptations. But if Latinos push for greater protections for and use of Spanish, they become racially Brown.

Contemporary Whiteness, as a sociopolitical construction, is far more focused right now on the movements of Latinos than on the traditional gauge of Blackness. Some suggest that this might be a way of avoiding the unresolved racial tensions between and among Black and White people. Others squarely see the new focus as the way White people can hold on to power and gain political insurance through forging alliances and granting a modicum of power to Latinos and other non-Black people of color. Institutionalized *White supremacy*—not the radical elements of the KKK,

Aryan Nation, and other White Supremacist groups—governs mainstream social institutions and is at the heart of exploring how Whiteness gets constructed in the current political and social contexts.

Multiple Points of View and Critical Perspective About Whiteness

After examining how we socially construct Whiteness, the challenge is to unleash multiple viewpoints to surface critical perspective. In doing so, what we discover is that White people tend not to be aware of who they are as *White* people. In addition, we have come to realize that people of color have discovered aspects connected to White culture and ways of being White that White people themselves have never recognized or fully understood.

The analysis of what it means to be White has traditionally been done only in contrast to what it means to be Black, Brown, Asian, or Native American. The challenge here is that Whiteness needs to be analyzed and understood on its own merits and not simply as a result of dissecting or diminishing other racial groups. What does it mean to be White, and what are the characteristics of Whiteness? These questions provoke our critical thought and are worthy of educators' time and focus.

Reflection

What does it mean to be White, and how has Whiteness been socially constructed in your own life? Without comparing White to other races, what are the characteristics of Whiteness? How does Whiteness impact you?

Whiteness in the Fourth Condition

The Fourth Condition invites us to *monitor the parameters of the conversation* and to use the Courageous Conversation Compass to determine how we are *positioned intellectually, socially, emotionally, and morally with respect to issues of Whiteness.* We need to determine the optimal parameters for examining and understanding Whiteness. Exactly how we determine groupings, prompts, and time allocations will have a great impact on how all people, but especially how White people speak, listen, and reflect on Whiteness. Given the predictable discomfort of such a process for many White people, all participants need to be prepared, supported, and continuously reminded to stay focused on Whiteness and stay engaged.

Consider again White Talk and Color Commentary:

White Talk	*Color Commentary*
• Verbal	• Nonverbal
• Impersonal	• Personal
• Intellectual	• Emotional
• Task oriented	• Process oriented

In the conversation on Whiteness, an understanding of these contrasting characteristics is necessary so that all participants can monitor their own engagement in the conversation. Typically, Whiteness is talked about only when it is threatened, for example, during conflict arising from school desegregation and affirmative action in college admissions or teacher hiring. White people tend to exempt themselves from having the characteristics of Whiteness rather than viewing Whiteness as a constant based on personal membership in the White racial group.

While a high degree of emotional disconnectedness from Whiteness exists for many White people, examining the presence and role of Whiteness, rather than launching into the typical dissection of color experiences, seems to stir deep emotional engagement among White people. Specifically, publicly naming White as a culture and challenging White educators to examine underlying desires to maintain racial privilege or advantage prompt feelings that are unusual and uncomfortable for most participants of Courageous Conversation.

If everyone is to travel deeper into this conversation and integrate White Talk with Color Commentary, it is important that White people get emotional about Whiteness and invest in challenging White cultural domination. Until White educators experience lasting emotions related to Whiteness, they will struggle to understand why their students of color exhibit such strong emotions around and connections to race.

The extreme emotions experienced in the Courageous Conversation are normal and necessary. The universal presence of these emotions signals to people of color that White people are willing to authentically engage in the conversation. Anger, guilt, and shame are just a few of the emotions experienced by participants as they move toward greater understanding of Whiteness. We have found that this full engagement and the difficult management of emotions eventually give way to feelings of liberation that only come with deeper racial understanding and clarity.

To fully understand Whiteness, White racial dominance needs to be intentionally and explicitly explored. To do this, however, White people need to listen to people of color describe the ways in which Whiteness is manifested and experienced. Likewise, White people should engage in a self-assessment of when and how Whiteness has benefited them in schooling, the community, the workplace, and their social interactions. This thorough and honest assessment helps White people feel less threatened by the presence and behaviors of people of color. When White educators no longer feel compelled to defend their racial privilege and power, they are more likely to address the racial inequities that exist in the school philosophy, structures, policies, and practices.

After working with Glenn Singleton for a couple of years and becoming more aware of his own Whiteness, Curtis Linton was faced with the opportunity to embrace his newfound awareness of racial inequity or retreat back into the arena of White privilege. Standing in line at John F. Kennedy Airport, Curtis was thrust into a situation where he could easily have engaged in the "silence dialogue." A White man at the counter next to him was demanding that the Latina agent check an additional bag at no extra charge. He badgered her incessantly, claiming that other agents had done it for him. As the agent continued to refuse, the man became increasingly upset. Eventually, the agent threatened to call over a security agent. In response, the man muttered, "Spanish bitch!"

With strong justification, the agent became quite upset and called over both security and a supervisor. Agitated, the man asked what he had done. In response, the agent said that she was proud of her heritage and that what he had said was racist and offensive. Shocked and surprised, the man said, "I'm not a racist—I'm Jewish!" What he did not realize is that before he is Jewish, he is White, and he was acting as such.

Curtis was the nearest White person, so the man turned to him and asked, "What did I do?" This was a moment of truth for Curtis. Fighting the urge to retreat within White privilege and remain silent, Curtis responded, "That was racist and very offensive." The man responded, "She wasn't showing me any respect!" Once again having to go beyond his comfort zone, Curtis said, "You are the one who showed no respect, and you were out of line."

After this, the man no longer wanted to speak with Curtis and turned to press his case—unsuccessfully—with the supervisor, another Latina. Curtis concluded this experience of having to move beyond the privilege of Whiteness by reassuring the supervisor that the agent was justified and that the man was out of line.

Reflection

Curtis described the aforementioned scenario as an act of racism. How do you see it?

As easy as it might be to redefine this situation in which Curtis engaged as one of gender or class discrimination, what if racism was the sole motive? White privilege allows White people to decide when and when not to address racial issues. White dominance allows them to continue to receive the benefits and opportunities associated with Whiteness, whether or not they acknowledge this additional assistance. For Curtis, race at this moment became personal, local, and immediate. He could easily have let the situation pass without saying anything, but the reality for the Latina agent is that race is always personal, local, and immediate. So, why should it be any different for Curtis? In this situation, White privilege became White responsibility. This response occurred, however, because of Curtis's continuous examination of White privilege and White cultural dominance.

Whiteness in the Fifth Condition

So much of this chapter has been focused on how Whiteness is lived—the *"working definition of Whiteness."* By virtue of the Fifth Condition, we can better understand how White skin signals cultural correctness and national legitimacy. In terms of nationality, White Americans often feel a unique sense of entitlement to "Americanism," partly because many never travel beyond the borders of the United States. Based on the number of passports issued, some demographers estimate that fewer than 34 percent of all Americans ever travel outside of this country (*The Economist*, 2005), and this fosters ethnocentrism and an expectation that others will observe and honor "our" cultural ways. Likewise, many White Americans are nearly oblivious to other national norms, cultural beliefs, and racial lifestyles. Domestically, this explains why White Americans rarely assimilate into another culture—they always exist and always expect to exist within the standard of American Whiteness.

Even more important, however, is acknowledging that many White people have a hard time dealing with the dominance of Whiteness because of White privilege. Consequently, the belief that White people are accorded advantage just based on skin color is foreign and threatening to their strongly held notion that White people achieved their superior status because they "earned it" exclusively through hard work. These tendencies are embedded in the White racial culture and perspective.

In terms of color, White people are seen as being White regardless of what their national or ethnic origin might be. People are identified as White before they are acknowledged as Jewish, Italian, or Scandinavian. This reality of being White in the United States today must be acknowledged.

Likewise, although it is often redefined as mainstream American culture or middle-class values, White culture is as racially distinct as Black, Latino, or Asian culture. Whiteness is also the dominant culture that governs the American school system. Rather than being defined as a separate and equal culture, it is most often understood as the "correct" culture or the "right" way of learning.

WHITE RACIAL IDENTITY DEVELOPMENT

The Sixth Condition of Courageous Conversation, examining the role and presence of Whiteness, enables us to discover the context in which all racial matters are judged. In this very specific investigation, we come to see how White functions not only as a color but also as a culture and a consciousness. But to deepen our inquiry into Whiteness, we can also look at how White identity development occurs and progresses for members of the dominant race and how this identity, at its various stages, might impact people of color.

Although several race scholars have attempted to explain the process of White racial identity development, no one has yet had significant impact on shifting the way White Americans think about their own raciality. This is partly due to White privilege and the ability of those who have it to simply avoid, ignore, or minimize the impact of race on their lives. Given that White people generally have difficulty seeing themselves as racial beings, it is no wonder that the notion of a psychosociological depiction of the White racial experience has been overlooked. Even so, we believe that understanding how White educators experience their own Whiteness, as well as how they view other White people and people of color through the lens of Whiteness, is critical to improving schooling. In short, until White educators understand their own racial experience, their interpretation of children of color's racial experiences will be distorted.

Janet Helms (1990) offers one such model for understanding White racial identity (see Table 10.3). Helms suggests that White people experience a progression from essential "color blindness" to a non-dominating stage of Whiteness.

Of course, no theoretical framework can precisely define the many complex and unique aspects of individual identity. What this model can do is affix language to some of the common racial experiences that many White people share. Like any developmental scale, White people might see aspects of their current experience in more than one stage on the continuum. This is an indication that people are probably never stationary or fixed in their racial identity development.

Table 10.3 Helms Model of White Identity Development

Contact: Whites pay little attention to the significance of their racial identity; "I'm just normal"; perceive themselves as color-blind and completely free of prejudice.

Disintegration: Growing awareness of racism and White privilege as a result of personal encounters. This new awareness is characterized by discomfort.

Reintegration: Feelings of guilt or denial may be transformed into fear and anger directed toward people of color. Whites may be frustrated if seen as a group rather than individuals.

Pseudo-independent: The individual gains an intellectual understanding of racism as a system of advantage but doesn't quite know what to do about it.

Immersion/Emersion: Marked by a recognized need to find more positive self-definition. Whites need to seek new ways of thinking about Whiteness, ways that take them beyond the role of victimizer.

Autonomy: Represents the culmination of the White racial development process. A person incorporates the newly defined view of Whiteness as part of a personal identity. The process is marked by an increased effectiveness in multiracial settings.

Reflection

If you are White, where do you locate yourself on the Helms Model of White Identity Development? Has your position changed over the last few years? If so, how and why? If not, what might have prevented your development?

If you are a person of color, where do believe your White colleagues—who believe themselves to be most racially conscious—are located on the Helms Model of White Identity Development? In the past year, have you seen evidence of their progress according to the Helms model?

An emerging consciousness surrounding Whiteness is critical to building racial equity. This is the purpose of Courageous Conversation—to engage, sustain, and deepen interracial dialogue about race, and especially about Whiteness. By acknowledging and understanding Whiteness, White people begin to see the way in which their culture subordinates other cultures. With consciousness comes action, and with action comes transformation.

Implementation Exercise

De-Centering Whiteness

Time required: 45 minutes

Materials required: Courageous Conversation Journal for each participant and the accompanying worksheet

1. Present the Sixth Condition of Courageous Conversation:

   Examine the presence and role of Whiteness, its impact on the conversation, and the problem being addressed.

   Based on your reading, define Whiteness according to
   • Color
   • Culture
   • Consciousness

2. Divide participants into small groups of three to four and distribute a copy of the worksheet to each group.

3. Have groups work on defining, unpacking, applying, and de-centering: Defining means to arrive at a common definition for the characteristic. Unpacking invites the group to explore how the concept plays out in each member's personal life. Applying is to find the connections between the characteristic of Whiteness and schooling. De-centering is to identify ways in which group members challenge or replace the characteristics of Whiteness with other contrasting ideals.
   • Universal perspective
   • Individualism
   • Avoidance
   • Decontextualization

4. Based on level of readiness, group members can construct the meanings of these terms on their own or refer back to meanings presented in this chapter.

5. Bring the groups back together and debrief on the experience.

6. Have participants reflect in their Courageous Conversation Journal on the concept of Whiteness and how it informs their understanding of race and their own personal racial identity.

Sixth Condition of Courageous Conversations

Examine the presence and role of Whiteness, its impact on the conversation, and the problem being addressed.

De-Centering Whiteness

This exercise assists educators in defining, unpacking, applying, and de-centering Whiteness. Participants should complete each column in Table 10.4 to develop a fuller understanding of how White consciousness impacts teaching and learning.

Table 10.4 De-Centering Whiteness

Whiteness	*Defining: What does it mean?*	*Unpacking: What does it mean in my life?*	*Applying: What does it look like in my work?*	*De-centering: How do I challenge it in my work?*
Universal perspective				
Individualism				
Avoidance				
Decontextualization				

RACIAL AUTOBIOGRAPHY: CHRIS

I am White suburbia. Growing up, I was what one might consider the all-American boy next door. In reality, I took pride in that comment. White, male, brown hair, blue eyes, tall, athletic, and very social seemed to be the perfect fit for the title. As I look back, it is not a title that is bestowed on many individuals of different races. At the time, I did not even stop to think what was implied by the title, but instead I just reaped the benefits. The product of a community that was predominantly White, I went to schools that were anything but diverse in their racial make up. Cupertino, California, in the 1980s was not known for its appreciation of all cultures. The schools that I attended through eighth grade were in school districts that were considered top-notch.

It is said that experiences shape the individual that you will become. I too believe this to be mostly true. The experiences and people you meet along the way create the lens through which you view the world. What experiences have I had with racism that have shaped my attitudes and beliefs about racism? My first experience dealing with race was my entrance into high school. I was supposed to attend a high school that had a track record of being a rough place to get through. The boundaries of the school extended to include some rough neighborhoods and an ethnically diverse community. All that I knew of these neighborhoods was that they frequently found their way into local newspapers and news reports (mostly negative publicity) and that my mother had asked me to stay away from them at all cost. When the time came to enroll in high school, I found myself taking entrance exams into such schools as Bellview, St. Thomas, and Johnson.

Not more than two months later, I was attending class at Bellview College Preparatory. The first thing I noticed while walking around campus was that there were only 12 Black people currently attending the school. At a school that was mostly White and Asian, there were few race-related problems. To me, racism did not exist at this school because I refused to see it as a problem and instead felt safe in classes with people that had experienced a similar cultural upbringing. This was the truth until one fateful football game when I became very aware of racism.

I was a member of the Bellview football team, which consisted of 40 White kids, 5 Latino kids, 9 Asian kids, and 1 Black kid. You could say that this team was not very diverse. We were scheduled to play a game against a team from inner-city Oakland. Needless to say, this was a school that was exclusively Black. Our bus arrived an hour and a half before the scheduled kickoff time, and class was still in session. As we walked toward the field, we were surrounded by hundreds of students starring at us as we walked by. For the first time in my life, I felt I was in the minority. I was scared and uncomfortable. As the students began to chant around us, I felt lucky that I had my fellow teammates to ease my rising anxiety. The attention of the students quickly turned as the only Black member of the team stepped off the bus. I remember the cruel comments made toward this teammate as he walked by. As I think back, I wonder what that individual had running through his head.

The next year, we played the same team but at our field. Having a year to reflect on the events that had taken place previously and understanding what it must feel like to get off of a bus and be the minority, I was excited to accept these players with open arms. Instead, what occurred next would shape my view of racism for years to come. I have never felt so embarrassed to be White as I did that day. For the first time, I witnessed racism first hand. In the locker room before the game, it was tradition to get fired up to take the field. Usually, this consisted of inspirational talks and a few words of wisdom, followed by a few head butts. This day it was different. I found myself in a huddle with a predominantly White team listening to my teammates say, "Let's beat those Niggers and send them back home." To this day, I am ashamed. I am not ashamed of being part of that team, but I am ashamed that I did not stand up and fight. It is one of the few regrets I have looking back at high school, and I wish more than anything that I could have that opportunity back.

I think my growing up was a scarier time for my mother than it was for me. My mother had worked for everything that we had received to this point. She took pride in the fact that nothing was ever given to us. She instilled a sense of fierceness and a competitive spirit in me. "There is nothing that is going to be handed to you, so get out there and get it" used to be her favorite bedtime story. I was raised with the understanding that if you worked hard enough for something, then it was possible. I think this statement is true, if you are White.

The American dream is a vision that is pitched to all—as if by a salesman— no matter the race or gender. It has to be because if people do not believe that there is a means to achieve their goals, it is human nature to give up. Capitalism fuels that hope as the rich continue to become richer at the expense of blue-collar workers with dreams of advancement. In reality, hard work can get you only as far as the color of your skin.

One of the most potent memories forever etched into my mind was one of helplessness, anger, fear, and confusion. I was born in Alabama, and my family often took vacations to the coast between Alabama and Florida. It is a beautiful place made mostly of white sandy beaches and cattail brush. Gulf Shores, as it was called, was a wonderful place to visit, if you were White. I say this now looking back on the experience. At the time, I was 18 years old trying to exert my freedom on the world. I decided to inquire about the local spots where I could chat with humans of the opposite sex.

One location that seemed to pop up in every conversation was the Gator Tail, a name that reeked of wit and sophistication. I found my way to this establishment only to find the most horrifying display of human indecency I had ever been exposed to. Every male in the place—all White—sported a shirt that portrayed a White man on top of a ship with whip in hand directing Blacks where to put cargo. This man used the whip to encourage fast and steady work by the chained Black crew. At the same time, something else about this shirt was somewhat confusing. It was Colonel Sanders of Kentucky Fried Chicken at the helm. It was not enough that these men had changed my whole view of racism in the 1990s, but they did it by destroying my image of a man who brought me a delicious serving of spicy chicken.

What happened next would continually replay itself in my dreams for several months. A Black man entered the establishment and found himself just as appalled as I was not two minutes earlier. The only difference is that he looked at me as one of "them." I remember the cold glassy stare. I was mad that he did not give me the chance to explain, angry that I felt involved, and confused as to why he would consider me, of all people, as the enemy. I know that if I had been in his position, I too would have passed judgment, but it is a feeling that has haunted me ever since. To this day, I wish I had the chance to explain to that man what I felt.

Individuals who tell you they are unaware of the problem of racism in the United States do not listen to the radio, watch television, or read. Racism is a part of our society, and if we do not address and talk about racism, it will continue to be institutionalized and continue to exist without being seen by the very culture that is maintaining it. It is for this reason that I get so passionate when talking about race relations. The burden of ending racism then falls on the White man. If there is to be a world free of racism, the White man must turn down and address privilege. The saddening fact is that we live in a country that thrives on capitalism, and no one in their right mind wants to give up the privilege that will enable them to become rich.

PART III

Persistence

The Key to
Anti-Racist Leadership

In American education, our beliefs have perpetually conflicted with our reality. For example, we say we believe that *all* children *can* learn, but reality shows that many are not learning. The perennial achievement gaps between White students and most student of color groups have been among the more reliable education statistics. Perhaps we have not expended sufficient time, effort, or resources necessary to close these gaps. Even clearer, however, is the fact that we have not maintained explicit focus on the way in which race impacts achievement. Thus, *persistence* is the third quality of equity/anti-racist leadership.

Persistence in this work means staying the course in pursuit of equity. Persistent educators consistently and collectively push forward with their transformation strategies. They take the time to learn what is needed to improve instructional effectiveness, and they commit to achieving the necessary results, no matter how difficult the challenges may be.

With the passage of the No Child Left Behind Act in 2000 and related accountability legislation, educators are now held to a higher standard—that *all* children *must* learn. The No Child Left Behind Act's statement of purpose explicitly requires schools to engage in "closing the achievement gap between high- and low-performing children, especially the achievement gaps between minority and non-minority students, and between disadvantaged children and their more advantaged peers." In a sense, federal legislation now mandates that educators must be persistent in efforts to close the achievement gaps, affording *all* students the opportunity to meet rigorous standards.

Key to closing the racial achievement gap is increasing teacher effectiveness with students of color in the classroom. Studies have shown the dramatic long-term effect on achievement when students consistently have effective versus ineffective teachers (Haycock, 2003). Educators have little control over students' background or the challenging experiences their students will bring with them to school. What school systems can impact, however, is the quality and preparation of teachers. Educators can also make decisions about class size, access to resources, and opportunities for academic enrichment, each judged through the lens of equity. When educators fail to provide an effective in-school learning environment for students, the uncontrollable, external mitigating factors have a more devastating impact on their achievement.

Some educators have been informed about the various types of reforms needed to eliminate racial achievement disparity. Unfortunately, systemic transformation is often thought of as simply a technical challenge that requires structural changes throughout the system. In other words, educators believe that by implementing some "silver bullet" strategies and perhaps a redesign in the schedule, program, or personnel, the gap will go away.

However, transformation is not merely technical or structural. It requires that educators first imagine a new way of delivering education—and then embrace it. Central to this type of transformation are cultural changes that engage educators in thoughtful examination of their own attitudes and beliefs about the ability of all students, but particularly the ability of students of color to perform. To eliminate racial achievement disparities, we believe educators must confront their own racial attitudes before they can facilitate classroom changes such as how to effectively engage students of color or how they teach to the standards and assess mastery of academic subjects.

Maintaining focus along this course of action is difficult, but persistence is the key to equity/anti-racist leadership precisely because cultural transformation is hard to orchestrate; it takes a great deal of time to achieve sustainable results. Without persistence, however, schools will continue to drift from one school improvement initiative to the next without developing capacity for lasting, systemic change. *With* persistence, educators will have the time and support they need to develop, apply, reflect, revise, and master the necessary knowledge and skills to guarantee success for all students.

How Anti-Racist
Leaders Close the
Achievement Gap

Adolescents of color really begin to think about their identities during adolescence. That's an important time to explore racial and ethnic identity. While White youth are also exploring their identity at this time, they usually aren't exploring the racial aspects of that identity. So, it's not uncommon to find adolescents of color actively exploring identity, which manifests itself in styles of dress, patterns of speech, music, and who they hang out with in the corridors of their schools.

All of this is happening in the presence of White teachers who have no personal history with that type of identity exploration, nor have they given much thought to their own identities, even in midlife. If one person is having an experience that another has not shared or even thought about, it's easy to see where there can be misunderstanding and conflict. This is particularly true when adults respond by telling youngsters not to do the things associated with their identity exploration: Don't wear those clothes, don't listen to that music, don't talk that way, don't sit together in the cafeteria.

—Beverly Daniel Tatum (Sparks, 2004, p. 49)

Critical to the academic success of students of color is having quality relationships with their teachers and the other adults in school.

As Tatum suggests here, it is important for educators to understand the cultural identity of their students. Likewise, educators need to empathize with where students of color find themselves, racially speaking, and what their experiences are. By giving their students the racial understanding, empathy, and compassion they need, educators begin to develop their effectiveness with students of color.

Now that we have explored the Four Agreements, Six Conditions, and Compass of Courageous Conversation, we want to briefly focus on some areas for their application in schools and districts. With Courageous Conversation as the prevailing strategy for discourse, educators are invited to examine more closely theories and practices aimed at closing the racial achievement gap. Courageous Conversation lifts the unconscious veil of color blindness and silence and requires educators to develop their color consciousness in a way that is humane and productive.

INVISIBILITY VERSUS HYPERVISIBILITY

Curtis Linton grew up in a White world where he never had to acknowledge his White racial experience. In contrast, at a very young age, Glenn Singleton encountered White people, which forced him to acknowledge his race and actively engage in his racial identity development. Most of the time, Curtis is racially invisible—he is rarely labeled or set apart for being White. For the most part, he is required to recognize his Whiteness only when he deliberately places himself in a racially diverse context in which race is acknowledged. On the other hand, Glenn has experienced hypervisibility ever since he ventured out of his Black community to attend a White independent school. Every day, he is forced to acknowledge his race. Whether he is vacationing, working, worshiping, or socializing, Glenn is defined first and foremost as a Black man, whether or not he chooses to be labeled as such.

To illustrate the hypervisibility Glenn experienced in school, imagine that the black dot in Figure 11.1 is a Black student, and the circle represents his school environment or context. Traditionally, the white space between the circle and the Black student has not been defined; in other words, when asked what surrounds the black dot, most people would say *nothing*. When nothing is noticed within the circle except for the Black student, the White context or White cultural backdrop is neutralized or made invisible, and all dark dots, by virtue of their color contrast, stick out or are hypervisible.

Rather than simply representing an empty circle, this space actually comprises a plethora of white dots—or White students and adults. But their Whiteness is only made apparent by the Black dot—or the student of color. When several students of color are grouped together amid the larger

Figure 11.1

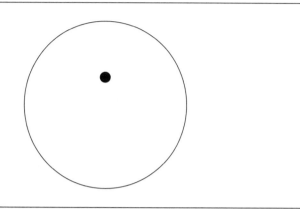

number of White people, they become even more noticeable and may even threaten the White dots' sense of entitlement to the entire space. As described in the book by Beverly Tatum, *"Why Are All the Black Kids Sitting Together in the Cafeteria?"* (1997), Black students grouped together become hypervisible and draw disproportionate attention to themselves, as illustrated in Figure 11.2.

When only the association of Black students is recognized or scrutinized, the larger group of White students is left invisible in terms of color, culture, and consciousness. This is not to say that we do not notice the White students' presence, but rather their color, culture, and consciousness are viewed as normal and appropriate. Thus, these factors are not scrutinized or examined.

To authentically understand and address the needs of the Black students, the White students and their culture must also be acknowledged

Figure 11.2

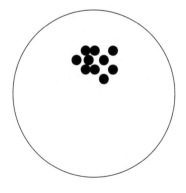

Figure 11.3

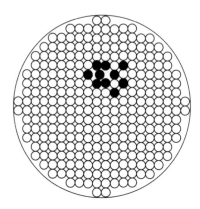

or made visible, as shown in Figure 11.3. Only then can we recognize the ways in which White culture impacts the student of color's educational experience.

Along with a pursuit of equity comes an emerging sense of empathy. A lone White student within a school of Brown or Asian students also becomes hypervisible, as shown in Figure 11.4. As unfair as it seems to single out this White student, it is equally problematic that educators continuously single out the Black students among the larger White student population.

A reality in schools, however, has been that the students of color and not the White students tend to be dealt with inequitably because of their race and racial culture. Experience tells us that many White Americans

Figure 11.4

find it painful to see that people of color continue to have it so tough in life due to racism. It is equally uncomfortable to acknowledge that White racial privilege remains a staple ingredient in American culture and that an informal racial support system affords every White person a little easier and more humane day.

When White privilege persists in schools without acknowledgment and when Whiteness in that school remains invisible, White educators may experience difficulty seeing how different life is for students of color, whose race and racial culture are hypervisible. With White privilege comes an unconscious skepticism about or dismissal of people of color's racial perspective or experience and an insensitivity toward the racial backdrop of American society. Understanding the concepts of racial hypervisibility and racial invisibility in schools is crucial as we build a system of educators who persist in their equity/anti-racism work.

Reflection

Have you observed hypervisibility among students of color in your school? How does recognition and scrutiny of them compare to the treatment afforded to White students?

UNDERSTANDING STUDENTS OF COLOR WITHIN A WHITE SCHOOL

People have often posed the question, If race matters in schooling, then why do Asian students do so well? We believe that expectations play a significant role in this regard. Asian people have been labeled by the dominant White race as the "model minority," and they are encouraged and supported by White people to act accordingly. Whereas White Americans, collectively speaking, use positive racial characteristics—intelligent, hardworking, quiet, and unassuming—to define Asians, Black and Latino students are often defined as "academically at-risk," gang-affiliated, and lazy, among other negative descriptions. The key concept, however, is that the achievement of all students is typically measured against White student performance. White students are considered to be the norm, reference group, or standard, and so their performance as a racial group is rarely examined or questioned. To understand why certain groups of students outperform others requires familiarity with phenomena such as *stereotype threat;* such understanding allows us to better interpret achievement disparities existing between student racial groupings.

Stereotype Threat

Researcher Joshua Aronson (2004) has stated,

Stereotype threat and the responses it elicits can play a powerful role in the relatively poor achievement of certain students—African Americans, Latinos, and girls in math-oriented domains. . . . Understanding stereotype threat has the potential to help educators narrow persistent achievement gaps. (p. 14)

Through the powerful research that he has done with Claude Steele, Aronson has not only discovered reasons for Black and Brown students' lowered achievement, but has also shown how stereotype threat diminishes the achievement of White students when they are placed in direct competition with Asian students.

According to Aronson (2004), students negotiate stereotype threat when they are made aware of any stereotype existing in an academic setting, whether negative or positive, and they will almost always perform accordingly. In their research, Aronson and Steele have administered tests to college students—primarily grouped by racial or gender identification. Before the examination, the researchers announce that they are administering a test that will disprove a stereotype, such as Asians are better at math than Whites, Whites perform better than Blacks, or males achieve higher than females in science, and so on. The same tests are administered to a control group, but with no reminder of the stereotype before the exam is taken. Comparing results, Aronson and Steele have repeatedly shown that the contrasted student groups—Asians and Whites, for example—can achieve equally well but will achieve according to the stereotype if they are reminded of its existence in explicit or even unintentional ways.

What their data suggest is that the stereotype threat can trigger acceleration or remediation in student performance; over time, this will determine the level of student engagement and success or the lack thereof. Educators, therefore, need to engage in conversation about how racial stereotypes "in the air" impact student performance and what educators might do to identify and mitigate these harmful messages.

Reflection

How have you personally been affected by stereotype threat? Have students with whom you have worked also been affected by stereotype threat? How might educators assist students in overcoming stereotype threat?

Third Culture and Racial Isolation

People of color who strive to conform to White culture often find themselves living in what we define as a *Third Culture*—always striving but never succeeding at fitting into Whiteness, and no longer culturally accepted within their own primary racial culture either.

When Glenn first arrived at the predominately White independent school, he realized that for the first time, all of his teachers were White. This was not Glenn's typical experience: All but one of his elementary school teachers were Black. When Glenn asked why this was the case, the principal asked, "Why does it matter?" Speaking from a White consciousness, the White educators had no correlating experience of being the only White person in an institutional context. However, Glenn—a young student who was quite conscious of his racial difference—needed to know who in this school might connect to the culture from which he came. Who would understand his references? Who would be able to accurately read his expressions? And who would be able to effectively communicate with his family? From the dominant White culture, the response "Why does it matter?" essentially puts the question back on the students posing it and informs them that their inquiry is irrelevant and their search for meaning, no matter how honest or personal, is basically wrong. Furthermore, Glenn essentially was being told "race doesn't matter," yet, he was constantly reminded of his social difference: White students would not date him, they told racist jokes around him, they sometimes would not invite him to their parties, and they investigated his culture as though it was foreign and inappropriate.

By the end of Glenn's first year at this school, he learned that he was not supposed to ask racially loaded questions, and eventually, he stopped thinking about race altogether. To deal with this setting, Glenn had to redefine his entire life in a White cultural way. What happened to Glenn—and what happens to other students of color in racially isolated situations—is that they begin to see themselves as inadequate. At school, the only Black adults Glenn saw were the custodians, cooks, and bus drivers, further reinforcing and affirming in his mind, as well as in the minds of his White classmates, notions of White supremacy.

Although their situation may not be as extreme as the one Glenn endured, students of color experience racial isolation in a White-dominated school context during the day and often find their own primary culture—say, their neighborhood—increasingly foreign and distant. This is what we mean by a Third Culture experience: racially speaking, neither here nor there. Glenn wasn't really gaining the privileges of White skin, but he was losing contact and connection with his Blackness on a daily basis.

In essence, he was forced to trade his kinship and alliance with people of color for scholastic success and high academic achievement.

Reflection

Can you think of people who have existed in a racial Third Culture? What can you recall about that their experience of negotiating two distinct racial cultures? In what ways have they attempted to reconnect with their own culture, or is their struggle to be viewed and accepted as White more pronounced?

UNDERSTANDING INSTITUTIONALIZED WHITE RACISM

In order for institutionalized White racism to persist as the status quo, it must be supported. As shown in Figure 11.5, institutionalized White racism can be pictured as a tabletop supported by four legs: internalized White racism, interracial White racism, intraracial White racism, and reverse White racism.

Internalized White racism presents itself differently in a White person than it does in a person of color. For White people, internalized

Figure 11.5 Institutionalized White Racism

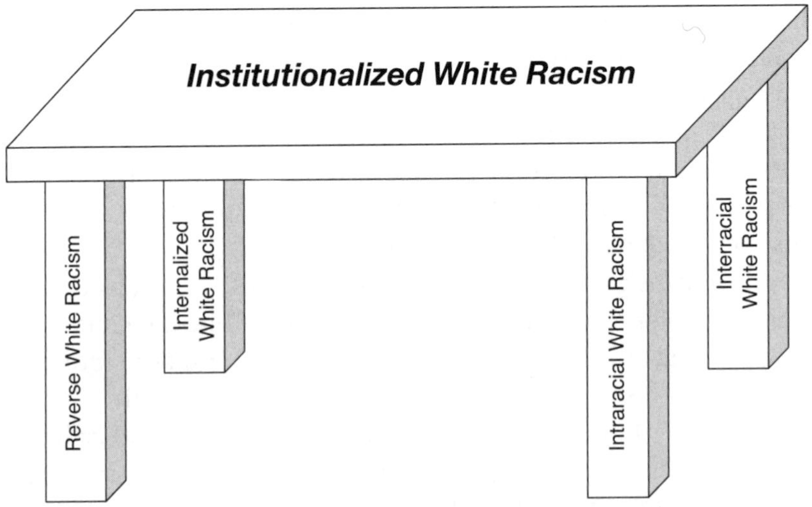

White racism may range from the radical White supremacy espoused by the Ku Klux Klan to a more passive White supremacy exemplified by someone who fails to notice when people of color, their ideas, or contributions are not present or sought after in professional meetings or social gatherings.

For people of color, internalized White racism appears in an active form as self-hatred as well as disapproval of other people of color because they lack White color, culture, or consciousness. For a time in his life, Glenn Singleton recalls believing that he was not attractive to others because of his hair texture and pigment. He wanted to look like the many White icons and images that his school held up as what is perfect and smart. Passively, internalized White racism presents itself as an unconscious, yet operating belief by people of color that White people are superior. In these instances, people of color fail to realize that they do not associate with other people of color and do not feel the need to seek the professional or personal company of members of their own racial group.

Interracial White racism occurs when different groups of color are in conflict with one another over their respective positions of power relative to the top of the table or to White culture. For example, when California's Black and Brown educators were battling each other for a share of bilingual funding, neither disempowered group had time to recognize that many White voters were quietly working to eliminate the entire budget. Interracial struggles between marginalized groups of color only diminish the power of the groups of color and increase White racial power. Thus, people of color who are in conflict are promoting or perpetuating White racism even without the presence of White people.

Intraracial White racism typically occurs among members within a particular group of color. For example, some Black people predictably will assimilate into the White culture to a larger degree than other Black people. These varying levels of assimilation or resistance to Whiteness may result in a clash between different Black people, which threatens solidarity among Black people as they work to collectively challenge White supremacy. Once again, we observe struggles among Latino and Asian students based on the time their family immigrated to the United States. Divisions among Latinos challenge their solidarity when they need to challenge White privilege and White cultural imperialism. Often, however, the racial implications of these intraracial struggles are masked because the formative topic seems to be language preservation and acquisition or immigration. The reality is that these issues are important only to White Americans because Spanish challenges the English-only culture that has held in place monolingual White leaders. Similarly, federal immigration policy will determine how quickly the country advances to a Brown majority. The rapid growth of the Latino population carries with it the power of numbers: the ability to vote into political office Brown people and Brown perspective. A racial group divided cannot threaten White privilege, presence, and power to the same degree. Thus, intraracial White racism defines yet another process through which people of color promote and perpetuate White supremacy.

Reverse White racism, which seems to get the greatest attention in this entire system of institutionalized White racism, is characterized by strong feelings of discontent, mainly among White people. It is here that White Americans collectively speak out against affirmative action or any programs that would funnel opportunities toward people of color that were once denied to them. Because Whiteness is characterized by a sense of entitlement, White people fail to recognize that White students also gain admission to college not because of individual merit but because they are children of alumni or because of other family connections to the institutional power. Reverse White racism seems to be somewhat a misnomer because many "qualified" White students do not gain admission to the college of their choice. But why are the relatively few admitted students of color the focus of White American scrutiny rather than the larger number of White students who gain admissions for reasons other than their personal merit or academic accomplishments. What confuses matters even more is the people of color who challenge the legitimacy of affirmative action because of the scrutiny and backlash they endure from their White peers on campus. In his former days as an admissions director at an Ivy League university, Glenn Singleton often told the students of color he advised, "If a light shined down on the campus and identified all students who did not 'earn' their way into this university, disproportionately and overwhelmingly illuminated would be White students. So often, the very students who did the least to gain admission to the university feel the most entitled to their coveted place in the class."

Reflection

Of the four legs of institutionalized White racism, which do you identify with most: *reverse, internalized, intraracial,* or *interracial?* Which do you identify with least? In what ways has your school system specifically addressed or challenged institutionalized White racism?

THE INJUSTICE OF GRADUALISM
AND INCREMENTAL CHANGE

In recent decades, some people of color have advanced into jobs and moved into neighborhoods where they were once excluded, thus creating a belief that with time and hard work, the American racial power imbalance will just disappear. This conclusion is challenged by critical race theorists, including Derrick Bell, Richard Delgado, and Gloria Ladson-Billings. Their racial critique is grounded in evidence that indicates important shifts in racial power are not gradual or unintentional. South Africa, for example, has had two Black presidents in the first decade since the end of apartheid, whereas no people of color have even been frontrunners for the U.S. presidency.

Presidents Bill Clinton and George W. Bush have claimed they hired the most diverse Cabinets ever assembled, asserting that progress is being made. Critical race theorists ask who is setting the schedule for achieving racial proportionality and balance? Real racial gains are painstakingly slow, both in U.S. government and in our schools. The comparative rarity of Black and Brown superintendents of schools is a prime example of slow transformation. Critical race theorists say that gradualism or support for incremental change is a major reason for the permanence of institutionalized White supremacy. While people of color are urged to be patient by those in power, leadership and excellence remain the property of Whiteness, no matter how much "progress" has been made.

Reflection

In what ways has gradualism and a preference for incremental change challenged the development and progress of educators and students of color in your school system?

In conversations focused around the themes of this chapter, the actual color of one's skin becomes less of a factor as one's knowledge about race, racial identity, and institutionalized White racism grows. Understanding how, when, and where race intersects with schooling allows educators to learn from each other and engage their students. Only through this heightened engagement of our students of color will school systems experience transformation that ensures success for all students. The purpose is not to accomplish gradual change in this work but to urgently and radically embrace the possibility of eliminating the racial achievement gap.

Implementation Exercise

Defining the Intersection of Race and Schooling

Time required: 30 minutes

Materials required: Courageous Conversation Journal for each participant, and chart paper, red and blue markers, and tape for each group

1. Re-create the invisibility and hypervisibility charts at the beginning of this chapter and present the concept to your staff.

2. Divide participants into small multiracial groups.

3. Distribute two pieces of chart paper, one red and one blue marker, and tape to each group.

4. Have groups label one sheet "Staff Barriers" and the other sheet "Student Barriers."

5. Have each group divide into two teams, one being White educators and the other being educators of color.

6. Have the White educators begin making a list on the "Student Barriers" sheet and the educators of color on the "Staff Barriers" sheet. Give them both five minutes to list as many barriers to closing the racial achievement gap that are imposed by staff or students, as they can.

7. After two minutes, have them switch posters and continue for five more minutes.

8. Have the White educators and the educators of color come back together in their small group and reflect on what was written.

9. Bring all the groups back together and reflect on the experience. What was discovered? What ideas emerged? What are the most common barriers that exist both for staff and for students? How did the race of the work group affect the responses listed?

10. Have the participants personally reflect in their Courageous Conversation Journal.

Exploring a Systemic Framework for Closing the Racial Achievement Gap

Solving the problem of racism is America's unfinished agenda, and it must be regarded by educators as a moral imperative.

—Gerald Pine and Asa Hilliard (1990, p. 596)

Think back to the circumstances of E. J., Glenn's cousin, which was described in the preface: a young Black student adrift in a White-dominated school. What would E. J.'s school look like if it were to become anti-racist and truly equitable? For that matter, pause and consider any student, particularly one who is African American, Latino, Southeast Asian, or Native American, with whom you have worked personally and who has struggled in school. Why do these students struggle? Is it simply because of the socioeconomic challenges they bring with them to school, or can their difficulty also relate to the known barriers that the school system has placed in the child's footpath to success?

Now reconsider these children as if they were your own. What would you want for them? Is that more than what is already available and accessible to them in school? Would the school—or you as an educator—experience the same level of expectation as provided for your other students? Would you want your own children to have the same relationship that your struggling students of color have with you and other adults in the school? Think of your school system in terms of equity, support, expectations, opportunity, and acceptance. Now ask yourself, is your school system adequate for our struggling children of color?

Reflection

Consider whether or not you feel that your school system is "good enough" for your own child. How many of your colleagues would choose your school system for their own children? How does this discovery impact your passion for, perspective about, and practice toward improving schooling for our most needy students?

A VISION OF EQUITY

If your school is truly equitable, all children arrive each day to a clean and inviting environment in which the educators are sure of their capabilities, excited about teaching *and* learning, and steadfast in their resolve to dismantle the barriers, such as harmful stereotypes and labels, that block children's freedom to learn. As students enter through the front doors, the principal and other members of the administration, faculty, and staff greet them by name and inquire about the well-being of a supportive family member or a recent personal challenge. Children feel safe and secure in this school, not due to locks, metal detectors, and security guards, but due to their understanding that school has their physical, emotional, and spiritual safety at heart.

As they continue into their classrooms, students again are warmly and enthusiastically greeted by the teacher. In class, students are exposed to a rigorous and demanding curriculum that challenges them fully. Students need not worry whether this or any other class is advanced or remedial because all students are placed in classes that push them to excel, regardless of their skin color, cultural background, or previous learning challenges. This class is not disproportionately White or discernibly Black, Brown, or Asian; it includes an equal representation of all the students in the school so that no student is isolated racially.

In facilitating learning, teachers are well aware of the individual talents of the students and provide the support that every child needs. The curriculum is respectful and reflective of the diversity of students' experiences, backgrounds, and cultures, both those that are represented in the classroom and perhaps some others as well. Furthermore, students see themselves in the curriculum and are encouraged to relate to it personally. Students can rest assured that every teacher will teach to standard and instruct from a common curriculum that is used throughout the school. Because learning goals and objectives are clear, students know that the teachers' aim is to promote their mastery of the subject matter. Students never worry that they will be shortchanged in terms of expectations, support, or opportunity to try, fail, try, fail, and try again until they achieve mastery.

Teachers have the freedom to use whatever teaching method, activities, or materials they may desire, but they also welcome being held accountable for each student achieving the standards on a regular and timely basis. In our equitable anti-racist school system, teachers know that the institution exists to support them in improving their teaching. There is no retribution or condescension directed toward teachers who attempt to take advantage of the support system and who suggest changes and ways of improving it. The teachers work closely as a professional learning community using disaggregated data and action research to determine how best to reach every child. When one teacher succeeds, methods that led to success are shared with the other teachers in an atmosphere of mutual support, void of turf protection and characterized by a desire to achieve excellence schoolwide.

The teachers in this anti-racist/equitable school know that they have a voice that matters in its governance. The administration is driven by the needs of the teachers, not by hierarchical positional power of "us versus them" or by mandates that overwhelm rather than support. The administration and faculty together set the standards that the teachers work to achieve. Through their collaboration, they experience the freedom, ownership, and accountability they need to accomplish the job. Administrators are not found in the office or behind a desk somewhere but are seen throughout the campus encouraging students, supporting teachers in classrooms, and addressing school-related problems quickly, efficiently, and completely.

Furthermore, the administration leads the effort to reach out to all parents and members of the community. The school sees the community as an asset, and the community sees the school as a part of the neighborhood. As family members enter the building, they know without a doubt that the school welcomes their presence. Parents and other community members do not feel disenfranchised, nor do they feel intimidated due to their own personal educational attainment, English language skills, racial description, economic status, dress, or perceptions of school derived from their own personal experiences. Families know that their voice matters in school affairs. They are invited, encouraged, and expected to participate in parent-teacher councils, teacher assistance, leadership teams, fundraising efforts, vision creation, school-improvement projects, and after-school activities. The families and community members feel ownership of the school and know that they are a vital part of their student's success.

As children excel in each and every classroom, they discover for themselves that education does indeed serve them. They begin to believe that they will receive every tool they need to succeed beyond the classroom. As they engage in activities after school, they are treated with respect and dignity. Above all else, they are expected to reach high and succeed often. When students graduate, they exit secure in their knowledge and their abilities. They have not been sheltered, coddled, and limited; they have been pushed to excel beyond their own expectations. Education has fulfilled its mandate with these students, and they are prepared to attain all their heart desires.

We believe that E. J. Singleton and other students like him deserve nothing less when they go to school each day.

Reflection

Compare your school to this vision of an equitable school. In what ways is your school system approaching, achieving, or straying away from this vision? Where is your school system strongest, and what is your most noticeable deficiency? Given the current attitudes, beliefs, and behaviors of your colleagues, does it seem possible that your school system could be transformed into the envisioned institution? Why or why not?

SYSTEMIC EQUITY ANTI-RACISM TRANSFORMATION

Closing the racial achievement gap begins with refocusing schooling on the children's educational needs rather than on the personal needs of the adults who inhabit the buildings. Next, a community of leaders from inside and outside the schools must cooperatively determine a set of core values that will guide relationships among and between the staff, students, and families. These values must exist at the heart of the school's educational philosophy, district policies, programmatic structures, and instructional practices. The cultural fabric is reinforced and sustained by Courageous Conversation, which ensures that all people and all issues are welcomed and addressed. Continuous improvement becomes a natural and normal state of affairs for all members of the community.

Transforming School Culture

The culture of a school system is based in its language and the styles and processes of communication that take place among its members.

Consequently, the way to transform school culture is to transform the language that is used. The racial achievement gap cannot be closed without talking about racial achievement disparities existing between White students and most student of color populations. But we cannot effectively talk about racial achievement disparity without first learning how to effectively talk about race. This is why the conditions, agreements, and compass of Courageous Conversation provide the structural and strategic foundation for having conversations about race that are truly transformative systemwide.

Simply talking about race, however, is insufficient. Courageous Conversation needs to fit within a larger effort aimed at total school improvement. Our model for *Systemic Equity Anti-Racism Transformation* presents three overlapping domains within which Courageous Conversation guides the dialogue. As illustrated in Figure 12.1, the three elements are community, leadership, and learning and teaching:

Figure 12.1 Pacific Educational Group's Systemic Equity Anti-Racism Transformation Framework

With children at the center and a set of core values surrounding them, Courageous Conversation will launch educators into deep and sustainable improvements focused around community, leadership, and learning and teaching. As you can see in Figure 12.1, Courageous Conversation is the strategy that encapsulates and defines systemic improvement. In addition, each domain is interconnected with the other domains. Consequently, systemic equity transformation occurs where it all converges: at the only place that touches the life and learning of *all* our children.

Our framework has evolved out of partnering with a variety of districts over the last several years, districts that are still striving today to eliminate racial achievement disparities. We have learned that addressing only classroom instruction, leadership, or community in isolation is insufficient for sustainable reform. Likewise, talking about difficult issues without focused discussions on how those issues impact teacher-student relationships will leave educators with a broadened perspective but little ability to translate meaningful dialogue into effective classroom practices.

Courageous Conversation holds this holistic transformation framework together. As educators develop their ability to participate in and then facilitate Courageous Conversation, they can better recognize and understand the linkages that exist between dialogue and the domains of systemic transformation. Following is a brief introduction to the three domains: leadership, learning, and teaching and community. To further illustrate the complete framework in action, Chapter 13 contains a case study of systemic equity work-in-progress in the Lemon Grove School District located in San Diego, California.

Reflection

What has been your experience with school reform efforts that focused solely on instruction, leadership, or community in isolation? What kind of dialogue took place during the effort, and how effective was it? What were the results of the effort in terms of improved achievement for all students and especially students of color?

Leadership

Systemic Equity Anti-Racism Transformation requires *leadership*. When only a few people in a school system are examining race, sustainable changes that impact overall results will not occur. If achievement is to improve for all student groups, school site and district office leadership need to establish a culture in which the agreements, conditions, and compass of Courageous Conversation are practiced and eventually internalized by all educators. If a vision for equity and anti-racism is only embraced in selected classrooms, departments, or schools, those educators who are disengaged will simply move to places in the district where fear, resistance, inequity, and racism remain unaddressed. Equity has to be systemic to buffer struggling students of color throughout the system from educators unwilling to examine their individual and collective roles in perpetuating racial achievement disparity.

Equity Teams

The district- and school-based Equity Teams or E-Teams include emerging leaders who wish to develop their will, skill, knowledge, and capacity necessary to support their colleagues in understanding race and deinstitutionalizing racism. This leadership development process begins with the leaders addressing their own beliefs, or mental models and then continues into careful examination of their instructional practices. Once this phase of development is in motion, then the leaders are poised to engage their colleagues in ongoing, job-embedded professional learning.

Members of Equity Teams are not necessarily the typical school leaders, as traditional leadership teams are often defined by seniority or popularity. E-Teams are developed using a different set of criteria. Equity Team membership is predicated on having the passion for understanding equity and the courage to lead the system toward anti-racist education. At the school level, the principal always leads the Equity Team, just as a superintendent must offer leadership to the district E-Team. The principal draws the members of the Equity Team from the various departments or grade levels, paying close attention to those who will bring to the team credibility, courage, confidence, and compassion.

The responsibility of the Equity Team is threefold:

1. Engage in a process of investigation to discover how race impacts one's personal and professional attitudes and behaviors.

2. Lead the school or central office staff in the examination of individual and institutional culture as it relates to equity and anti-racism.

3. Establish a professional learning community in which adults can effectively develop skills and knowledge necessary to improve student performance and eliminate racial achievement disparities.

Schools are not always ready to become places for healthy adult learning. In fact, a significant challenge to improving schools is that some educators are poised not to learn, but rather to posture as though they "know it all." Equity Teams, therefore, must create a community in which adults can learn, a community in which professional learning is repositioned as thoughtful, data-based inquiry rather than the source for disseminating quick fixes and trick strategies.

Anti-racist leadership is incubated and practiced by the Equity Teams. As an entire district staff begins to engage in developmental exercises and professional learning led by the E-Teams, its members discover ways of transforming institutional culture and appropriately reforming structures that impede student performance. The cultural shift is evidenced by a Courageous Conversation about race and an engagement of individual and organizational passion for achieving educational equity. This conversation and passion drive the innovative improvements in how educators organize to design and deliver instruction. Over time, anti-racist leadership becomes the standard throughout the district of schools.

Learning and Teaching

As a system moves toward effectively addressing *learning and teaching*, educators begin to examine their classroom practices through the lens of equity and anti-racism. Teachers will often say, "Give me a strategy," but there are two inherent problems with this request: (1) teachers are not situated to be learners, and (2) they do not understand equity and anti-racism. If a teacher is just handed a culturally responsive strategy without first establishing the language or ability to talk about race, that strategy will most likely be used ineffectively, if at all, because the teacher does not understand it or believe in its relevance.

The Equity Team can serve as the bridge between teachers' current understanding and skills level and the vision of quality instruction that is where they need to be. E-Teams work to support teachers in their preparation to engage in equity and anti-racism work at the classroom level. An Equity Team's goal is to develop the teachers' understanding of race through practicing Courageous Conversation and to guide their initial transfer of this conversation back to their classroom. This reflective practice or action research is the key component of the learning and teaching domain.

Educators cannot effectively implement a culturally responsive strategy if they believe themselves to be color-blind or are simply unwilling to examine race. The Equity Team is charged with moving a cadre of teachers to a level of readiness where they can more thoughtfully examine and change their classroom practice.

CARE Teams

Engaged teachers who demonstrate readiness to explore at a deeper level in the equity learning community are invited to be members of the CARE Team. CARE stands for Collaborative Action Research for Equity. Race impacts not only the lowest performing students—it impacts all students. Through CARE, teachers analyze a focus group of students to learn how best to teach and support them in their learning.

CARE is designed to support teachers in discovering the challenges that exist in their relationships with students of color and then to improve their instructional delivery accordingly. As a part of CARE, each teacher partners with a focus group of students of color to better understand aspects of teaching that positively impact student learning. Engaging student voices and examining student work are central in developing CARE teachers' ability to pinpoint how and when they are most and least effective.

CARE teachers meet every six weeks as a district collaborative and even more frequently as a school team to share what they have learned, observe one another's instruction, and talk about the progress or setbacks of various students in their focus group. Within CARE, teachers research and develop strategies that enable them to provide students with greater access to the curriculum and opportunities for meaningful learning.

Community

We define *community* as a network of effective and supportive relationships shared by all throughout the system. Although improving relationships between White teachers and families of color is central to this domain, community also incorporates interactions among administrators, teachers, and students. This work begins with everyone acknowledging that the school represents a community in and of itself and is also a part of an established community.

Typically, a school district functions apart from its community, especially in systems with large populations of families of color. The educators typically travel in and out of the community for work, but the students and families remain. Consequently, the entire school community as an entity needs to be engaged in conversations about how an appropriate education for the children in that community should be defined and be delivered.

This conversation—focusing on community education, awareness, and engagement—must take into account and give value to the resources that the community provides. One resource is that families have tremendous knowledge about how to be successful with their children in ways the school never sees: in the churches, homes, community organizations, and neighborhood—all institutions that are intricately a part of the established community. Another resource the community holds is the humor, contemporary idioms, and oral histories that educators must reference to connect academic disciplines to the students' real experiences. Likewise, the community is present for the joyous celebrations, rituals, and ceremonies that the students know and value. To the degree that their teachers relate to what is happening in the community, the children can view teachers as another integral part of their community.

PASS Groups

To facilitate the basic goal of developing and strengthening the institutional appreciation for *community*, the professional educators and community-based educators such as families, clergy, and government and law enforcement officials initially need to engage in a different kind of conversation that recognizes and values their disparate experiences. As the third branch of the Equity Team, leaders formalize the relationship between the institutional and established community members by organizing PASS Teams. Comprising both types of educators, PASS stands for Partnerships for Academically Successful Students.

The PASS Team recognizes that Courageous Conversation fortifies community. Therefore, members work to institutionalize the agreements, conditions, and compass of Courageous Conversation in the established community, just as it is in the institutional community.

School-based PASS Team members help the community-based educators understand the standards by which the children are measured. The community-based educators help school-based educators understand the community standards. Together, they develop standards that go above and beyond those of the district and state to ensure that students grow into respectful, contributing, and proud citizens of the community. The PASS Team focuses on engaging teachers and the community together in the best interests of the students. When either constituency is disengaged, the entire community experiences deficiency.

To build trust, the community needs to see teachers struggling openly with conversations about race rather than avoiding them. Furthermore, White teachers, especially those working largely in communities of color, need to witness families and clergy improving their effectiveness in the interracial conversation as well. This innovative form of dialogue is important because with few exceptions, the communities of color are segregated and have most likely not had favorable interracial interactions with White educators. Through PASS Teams, students ultimately benefit as deeper understanding and greater trust is built between institutional community and established community educators, leading to authentic support, improved instruction, and higher student achievement.

Role of the Principal

The principal is the guiding force behind equity efforts in a school. Without the principal's full and complete commitment, closing the racial achievement gap will be difficult, if not impossible. The principal leads the Equity Team, is supervisor of the CARE Team, and is a member of the PASS Team.

The Equity Team is a continuous and growing force until the school culture is permanently and profoundly transformed. The ultimate goal is for every school in the district to live that vision of schooling presented earlier in this chapter. The various teams actualize the equity goal and parlay the initiatives into a current reality of academic success for all children.

As the site leader, the principal specifically translates and transfers the learning of the CARE and PASS Team members to the larger staff. The principal should do this work in partnership with teachers and community leaders, perhaps sharing a demonstration lesson or modeling an effective teacher-student-family conference. Teaching adults differs from teaching students, and thus, it is the principal's responsibility to develop the skills set necessary to effectively facilitate adult learning.

Reflection

What do you perceive are some inherent benefits of simultaneously focusing on leadership, learning and teaching, and community transformation? In what ways is a principal in your system exhibiting effectiveness or ineffectiveness in terms of equity/anti-racist leadership?

Keeping the focus on student learning is the centerpiece of Systemic Equity Anti-Racist Transformation. Courageous Conversation is the strategy that enables educators from the institutional and established communities to focus their efforts on unifying community, developing leadership, and improving learning and teaching. As this framework is translated and transferred by site and district leaders—and particularly by principals—into everyday instructional practices by teachers, school systems will see the elimination of racial achievement disparities.

Implementation Exercise

Systemic Equity Anti-Racism Transformation

Time required: 45 minutes

Materials required: Courageous Conversation Journal for each participant and the worksheet that follows this exercise

1. Begin by sharing with the group the following quote:

   > Solving the problem of racism is America's unfinished agenda, and it must be regarded by educators as a moral imperative. (Gerald Pine and Asa Hilliard)

   Pose the following question to the group:

   > To what degree are the equity efforts under way in this school system a demonstration of our "moral imperative"?

2. Lead the group through developing a *vision of equity* for the school.
   - First, divide the participants into small groups of four to five people.
   - Hand out the worksheet to each group.
   - Present the diagram for Systemic Equity Anti-Racism Transformation.
   - Have the group develop an equity goal for each of the three domains.

3. Bring the groups back together, and list each of the goals they created for the three domains. As a whole group, determine for each of the three domains which goal will stand as the equity goal for the school or school system.

4. After the meeting, prepare a polished copy of the agreed upon goals for distribution so that all stakeholders groups who will benefit from these goals can have access to them.

Pacific Educational Group's Systemic Equity Anti-Racism Transformation Framework

- *Leadership*

_____

_____

_____

_____

_____

- *Learning and Teaching*

_____

_____

_____

_____

_____

- *Community*

_____

_____

_____

_____

_____

Using Courageous Conversation to Achieve Equity in Schools

The major challenge is to meet the need to generate new leadership. The paucity of courageous leaders . . . requires that we look beyond the same elites and voices that recycle the older frameworks. We need leaders—neither saints nor sparkling television personalities—who can situate themselves within a larger historical narrative of this country and our world, who can grasp the complex dynamics of our peoplehood and imagine a future grounded in the best of our past, yet who are attuned to the frightening obstacles that now perplex us. Our ideals of freedom, democracy, and equality must be invoked to invigorate all of us, especially the landless, propertyless, and luckless. Only a visionary leadership that can motivate "the better angels of our nature," as Lincoln said, and activate possibilities for a freer, more efficient, and stable America—only that leadership deserves cultivation and support.

—Cornel West (2001, p. 7)

W hen Cornel West wrote this, he was responding to national concerns about the lack of emerging leadership in the Black community. His words, however, ring true in education, where we have a pronounced need to develop powerful, dynamic, and engaged leaders who are willing to do what is necessary to build an anti-racist/equitable educational system where *all* students succeed. An effective force of anti-racist leaders can foster real equity transformation in America's schools and districts.

This leadership needs to exercise passion, be engaged in the design and delivery of innovative practice, and demonstrate persistence toward achieving equity at all levels of the system—from the district office to the classroom and throughout the established community. In this final chapter, we explore what anti-racist/equity leadership looks and feels like at the personal, individual teacher, whole school, and systemic levels. Included is a case study of the systemic equity anti-racism transformation work still under way in the Lemon Grove School District located near San Diego, California.

PERSONAL ANTI-RACIST/EQUITY LEADERSHIP

Each of us as individuals can begin a personal journey toward anti-racist/ equity leadership by recognizing that both White educators and educators of color have an equal amount to offer to the conversation on race and to the work of educating all students. As we begin, we must be introduced to or rediscover our passion for this essential work. Key to this discovery is examining within ourselves our current level of appreciation and need for people of races different than our own. Sustenance and depth of understanding in this work occur only when we make ourselves available to people of diverse racial backgrounds and perspectives. People who challenge our tightly held beliefs and those who encourage us to be introspective, self-critical, and self-corrective are our truest allies along the journey.

When Harvard legal scholar Derrick Bell (1992) suggests that "the faces at the bottom of the well" are Black, he encourages us to understand that until we all locate our deep and soulful need to know, to understand, and to be in the company of Black people, we will not have fully challenged our own deepest level of internalized racism. In schools, this need for connecting with Black people translates to the need to connect with our Black male students. Once we discover and act on our personal and professional connection to Black people in our daily lives, then members of the entire racial continuum of color populations—Brown, Asian, Native American, multiracial—gains presence, position, and power in our schools.

Graig Meyer, a district equity coach in the Chapel Hill-Carrboro School District in Chapel Hill, North Carolina, offers us the following reflection on his personal anti-racist work as a White male. We have chosen to include his voice over many other powerful voices of color and White voices specifically because White males not only continue to wield tremendous power in school districts but are also the most difficult group to engage in anti-racist work.

> The truly difficult work is looking deep within myself to recognize where my own reservoirs of Whiteness reside and what value or burdens they present to me. Every time I review Peggy McIntosh's inventory of White privilege I learn something more about myself, and—through attentiveness to my own experience— I think I could add a few more forms of racial privilege to her list. Frequently, I find myself examining my blind spots when a colleague of color expresses very different feelings about some experience we shared. This is fairly painless when it simply requires hearing about how they read between the lines of a presentation or caught a racist remark that sailed over my head. When the dissonance in our experience was in some way the result of my Whiteness, it's a little more painful but also more revealing.
>
> My White guilt tends to creep up most when I'm forced to reflect on the power I wield. For instance, I will spend weeks mentally reviewing an incident when one of my staff members bears the brunt of my ignorance or proclivity for dominance. I want them to trust me, I want them to like me, and I anger myself when I learn that I may have done something that makes it more difficult for them to do either.
>
> Perhaps even more important to our work are times when my power allows me to make decisions that negatively impact students of color. Although I often try to seek counsel of colleagues of color, it is inevitable that times arise where it's only after the fact that one of them points out some flaw in my reasoning. The flaws are often the result of my ingrained Whiteness and my own blindness to its perpetual presence.
>
> I suppose it's cliché to say that the work is never done or that none of us ever fully "get it." But I can't help feeling a strong desire to master this work, to learn all there is to know, and to do enough to become the "good White guy." Ultimately, it's probably the deepest vestige of my own White supremacy that feeds this need to know it all, to be right, and to be in charge. Paradoxically, the deeper I delve into this process, the more I feel called to lead other colleagues through the journey. My own capacity for leadership perpetuates the Whiteness within me, beckoning a return trip to look in the mirror. Perhaps I can't fully suppress all the Whiteness within me, and maybe that's for the better. The process is the task, the journey has no end, and I will always be White. (personal communication, March 2005)

> **Reflection**
>
> If you are White, in what ways do Graig's experiences and perspective as a White anti-racist leader align with your own? If you are a person of color, what connections do you see between Graig's personal journey and the racial triumphs and challenges experienced or expressed by your White colleagues engaged in this work?

Persistent in developing consciousness related to his own Whiteness, Graig tirelessly works to overcome the inherent and known challenges he faces in this work as an anti-racist leader. He is clear about the difficulty he experiences when it comes to listening to people of color. Thus, he can remain aware of his dominant viewpoint and actions in a way that challenges his White racial tendencies to define, take charge of, and master anti-racist equity leadership. This self-examination is at the heart of Graig's effectiveness in his school district.

INDIVIDUAL TEACHER ANTI-RACIST/EQUITY LEADERSHIP

Just as individuals like Graig can dismantle racism through developing a respect and personal need for people of all races whom they meet, every teacher needs to discover and communicate a personal need for and understanding of students and families of color. Until teachers develop classrooms that embrace racial diversity and place the needs of students of color on a level equal to that of White students, they will perpetuate and more deeply institutionalize racism on a daily basis.

Beyond developing a fundamental understanding of race, teachers must establish high expectations and implement more effective instructional practices to close the racial achievement gap. Teachers often claim to have high-level expectations for students of color, but then they demonstrate little surprise when their students perform poorly. This lack of disappointment reveals the true level of expectation that a teacher holds. To vocalize belief in the student's abilities but not act on or support those beliefs is not only hypocritical but also destructive to students.

When issues of race are thoughtfully addressed at the classroom level, teachers feel greater efficacy in terms of their ability to exact changes in their practice. This in turn reduces their anxiety related to known and unknown personal or professional deficiencies. Examining race openly and honestly encourages teachers to stop employing harmful practices and to replenish their toolbox with anti-racist, culturally responsive instructional strategies that support the success of *all* children.

Teachers who succeed with children of color do not describe their work as more difficult. Also, these teachers typically do not orchestrate quality student learning through the imposition of endless rules and regulations. They expertly focus on creating innovative ways to engage students in learning rather than seeking ways to punish them for not learning. Anti-racist educators clearly define what all students must know and be able to do; they develop multiple ways of assessing which students know it and are able to do it; and they have a repertoire of strategies to use when they discover that some students have not yet mastered the essential knowledge and skills. Ultimately, these anti-racist teachers take responsibility not only for what is taught but also for what is learned by every child, every day.

Reflection

Have you known a teacher who succeeds with children of color but would not describe his or her work as difficult? What was it about this educator's practice that allowed him or her to succeed without putting forth more effort or experiencing added stress?

WHOLE SCHOOL ANTI-RACIST/EQUITY LEADERSHIP

Every student who graduates not fully educated is another student whom educators have willingly allowed to escape unprepared to face the exciting, yet demanding challenges of our rapidly changing world. Students' lack of preparation and readiness comes at a great cost to society and to the reputation of the American education system. But mostly, their lack of requisite knowledge, skills, and capacities will cost the students future access to opportunities for success. The challenge for schools has long been to more effectively educate White, Anglo, middle-class students while simultaneously providing accelerated support for students who share few or none of those characteristics. As whole schools embrace the requirement for anti-racism and equity, educators will need to examine how the institution increasingly and almost naturally became an inappropriate and harmful environment for the growing number of students of color, as well as students from low-income and or English language-learning backgrounds.

According to Mary Montel Bacon (2005), what we have to work toward is making difference rather than likeness the norm in our personal lives, at school, and in our larger community. Individuals are inherently different, not just racially but in a variety of ways, including styles of communication, expressions of emotion, political opinions, religious thoughts, values, and traditions. When likeness is the norm, then White middle-class values will probably be the standard that is imposed on others, so that they are prevented from being present and empowered as who they are. When Whiteness is the standard, individuals are invited to participate to the degree that they will bend and conform to the experience of the racially dominant population.

By engaging in anti-racist/equity leadership, educators learn how to embrace differences and prepare all of our children to face a future of limitless opportunities. The goal of whole school anti-racist/equity leadership is not to gain accolades, recognition, or awards but rather to correct the current system of institutional White racial advantage, which should never have existed in the first place. Establishing anti-racist leadership for equity throughout the school calls for a courageous principal and the participation of all teachers, families, and students in the learning community.

Achieving equity requires that White educators engage as anti-racist leaders to the same degree as educators of color—or perhaps even more. As they increase their recognition of the reality and devastating impact of institutionalized White supremacy, White educators need to acquire additional skills and become more intentional and explicit in their anti-racist development and actions. The focus of anti-racism and equity is challenging White privilege by creating circumstances in which White people engage with people of color on a level playing field of access and opportunity that both desire.

Some White educators see themselves as "caretakers" for people of color, a perspective that emerges from a need to serve the "downtrodden" functioning beneath them. When this occurs, White educators understand their own *love and caring* for people of color far more than they actually understand people of color. In short, White school leaders initially will try to "take care of" people of color and "their race problems" in "the White way."

White anti-racist educators throughout a school and system of schools must embrace their leadership role as a way of *being* rather than a way of *doing*. Confronting racial inequities is an issue of deep personal and professional responsibility. Whenever White school leaders allow anti-racist work to move beyond continuous personal development and into the realm of self-importance, judgmentalism, or intellectualism, they will have abstracted and objectified the issue of racism and the difficult plight of their colleagues, students, and families of color. Such behaviors only serve to divide a school rather than unite it around a moral purpose that is educationally just.

Reflection

When we state that equity leadership is about *being* rather than *doing*, what response or reaction does this statement conjure up for you? Are you familiar with White educators who present themselves to children, families, and educators of color as their "caretaker"? In what ways might this mind-set and related behaviors demonstrate a potential lack of altruism that should arise from our pursuit of equality? How might such educators present problems for their colleagues and a schoolwide quest for equity?

SYSTEMIC ANTI-RACIST/EQUITY LEADERSHIP

It is clear why anti-racist/equity leadership must be present at the individual and school levels, but we must not mistake personal anti-racist leadership for Systemic Equity Anti-Racism Transformation. Individuals and schools must be part of an entire community of courageous, passionate, and mutually supportive leaders in the district.

Successful equity work systemwide demands anti-racist leaders at the highest levels who are willing to speak up, be honest, and challenge the privileges afforded to White people at the expense of people of color. In doing so, such leaders will recognize and examine the system of unaddressed educational inequities and vestiges of institutional racism.

The urgent requirement for anti-racist systemic transformation leaves no time for pointing out other people's racism. Instead, the process for sustainable change focuses educators, first and foremost, on uncovering and dismantling their own racism. After educators begin engaging in this work personally, they can collectively redefine and invent instructional practices that accelerate higher achievement of underserved student populations. Those with significant institutional power have the potential to challenge racism and inequity rather than merely identifying it and talking about it.

LEMON GROVE UNIFIED SCHOOL DISTRICT: A CASE STUDY

With effective anti-racist leadership, school systems can accomplish Systemic Equity Anti-Racism Transformation. As described in the previous chapter and illustrated in Figure 13.1, Courageous Conversation serves as the bounding strategy that brings depth and breadth to the three domains of transformation: leadership, learning and teaching, and community.

Through our emerging Courageous Conversation, educators throughout the system can embrace a set of core and common principles that guide them in examining and transforming each of these domains and thus ushering in improved achievement for all students.

Focusing on Equity

A focus on equity has been embraced at all levels in the Lemon Grove School District, located near San Diego, California. Now in its fifth year of focused work, the system has seen remarkable growth in student engagement and achievement as a result of using Courageous Conversation in the three domains of systemic transformation.

In 2001, Superintendent McLean King released a vision statement to the entire community. His leadership set the Lemon Grove School District on its journey toward anti-racism and equity. The response he sought was

Figure 13.1 Pacific Educational Group's Systemic Equity Anti-Racism
Transformation Framework

continuous engagement by all community members in support of equity and anti-racism transformation systemwide. Dr. King's (2001) vision statement follows:

Closing the Achievement Gap

A Vision for Students in a World of Diversity

Lemon Grove is one of the most diverse school districts in San Diego County with 34% of our students Latino, 34% White, 22% African American, and 10% representing other groups of color (CBEDS, October 2001). With such a high level of racial diversity, our schools benefit from a culturally rich environment for students, yet face the challenge of eliminating the achievement gap. Unfortunately, because of our history and existing inequities, issues of race more often divide than enrich.

Our mission is to engage and support all students in achieving high academic standards. To accomplish this goal, we must address the dramatic differences in student achievement, as reflected on multiple assessment measures. Disproportionate numbers of Latino and African-American students score in the lowest quartiles, and few are in the top quartile. Our challenge is to close the gap, which is no easy task. Our concerted efforts are needed to address this complex and difficult task.

Through staff commitment, professional development, and support, our district can create an environment that provides for the following:

- Equitable access to curriculum standards, programs, and materials regardless of race or achievement level.
- Equal success for all racial groups.
- A school community where multiple cultural perspectives and experiences are valued and people of color feel respected and welcomed.
- The challenge and elimination of practices that encourage bias.
- The showcasing of Latino, African-American, and other images of color through the curriculum.

School site administrators exercise authority and positively influence the attitudes of students, staff, parents, and the community in setting high expectations for all students. School leadership is also essential in the systemic change towards a culture that embraces diversity, respects all cultures, and ensures the development and implementation of educational programs that maximize academic achievement for all students regardless of race, color, or creed.

It is equally important that all school leaders are personally aware of the role race plays in perpetuating a system of bias, prejudice, and inequity.

Such awareness and each individual's personal commitment are critical to the creation of a school environment that is free of racism.

I charge the entire staff and educational community of the Lemon Grove School District to take risks by closely examining the role we each play in changing a system that has allowed this unacceptable achievement gap to emerge within the district. All educators in Lemon Grove will make a personal commitment and be held professionally accountable for the achievement of this vision.

We have the capacity; however, we must have the will to make a difference!

—L. McLean King, Ed.D.
Superintendent
December 2001

Source: Used with permission of Lemon Grove Unified School District.

Reflection

What resonates for you in Dr. King's vision for Lemon Grove Schools? To what degree does this vision correspond to the stated vision of your school/district? How would you expect such a vision to be received by various constituencies and stakeholders in your school community?

With a focus on equity and anti-racism established from the top, Lemon Grove has been able to stimulate dialogue on race, create leadership structures that maintain an explicit focus on equity, help teachers to reflect on and transform their practices, rebuild relationships, and create coalition between the institutional and established communities.

In fact, Dr. King has established three areas for long-term district-wide focus for Lemon Grove: (1) closing the racial achievement gap, (2) improving literacy for all children, and (3) accelerating the daily use of technology in the classroom by teachers and students. In all regards, the district has been nationally recognized and commended for its efforts. Dr. King would be the first to indicate that the recognition is gratifying but certainly not what drives the important work in the district.

A Brief Racial History of Lemon Grove, California

In Lemon Grove, addressing race has been a healing process for the community. In 1931, one of the first desegregation court cases in the nation occurred in Lemon Grove. Known as the "Lemon Grove Incident," it was a precedent-setting case that demonstrated the inherent racism and implausibility of separate but equal education.

Roberto Alvarez was a student in the Lemon Grove schools in the early 1930s. At that time, Lemon Grove had a large citrus-packing house that was staffed mostly by Latino immigrant workers. The workers' children lived in the community and by law were entitled to a "free and appropriate" education. As the local school became more crowded, the Lemon Grove community decided to provide separate schooling located in a barn for the Latino children.

A lawsuit was filed on behalf of Roberto Alvarez and the other Latino children in the school district, asserting that separate was not equal, and the eventual ruling supported Latino families and their children. Lemon Grove schools were required to provide equal facilities, and the district was ordered to place the students back in the public buildings. This ruling was one of the first to suggest that separate was inherently unequal, and it contributed to the legal precedent that eventually led to the U.S. Supreme Court decision, *Brown v. Board of Education,* which desegregated schools across the nation.

The 1930s' decision was indeed a turning point. Aware of its racist history, the Lemon Grove School District today has dramatically shifted its culture toward embracing diversity and anti-racism. Superintendent King said in a recent interview with author Curtis Linton,

> We probably have a greater appreciation of the Lemon Grove Incident because of how it fits in with what we're trying to do today. When you look at San Diego County, when you look at the state of California, when you look at the cultural pluralism of California, and you look at the diversity that this state embraces, Lemon Grove is truly a microcosm of all of this. If we cannot address the racial achievement gaps, who can?

Lemon Grove's present work on equity began several years ago when some of the teachers at Palm Middle School took their students on a day-long trip to the mountains in an attempt to build school unity. It did not work, however, because there was strong racial tension among the student body. As a result of this, some teachers joined school board member Robbie Montgomery in registering for Beyond Diversity, Glenn Singleton's training, which was being offered by the San Diego County School Leadership Center. The key focus of this seminar was to introduce Courageous Conversation to educators.

Convinced that Courageous Conversation was the key to addressing their racial tensions and achievement gap challenges, these teachers and the board member lobbied the superintendent to bring Singleton to Lemon Grove the following summer for the first in what would become a series of Beyond Diversity seminars. For the first time, all district administrators were required to attend summer professional learning sessions.

Upon completing the Beyond Diversity seminar, Superintendent King got to work on what eventually became his statement on equity as a vision for the district. Teaming with his director of educational services, Jere McInerney, King encouraged the understanding and implementation of Courageous Conversation throughout the district by allocating the resources and extending an opportunity for every stakeholder—teachers, administrators, secretaries, bus drivers, custodians, and parents—to attend the Beyond Diversity seminar. Soon, the superintendent expected all district employees to attend Beyond Diversity.

Current Demographics

Lemon Grove School District has a highly diverse student body enrolled in six elementary and two middle schools, all in an urban community situated on the edge of downtown San Diego. The district has succeeded with limited funds, spending less per student than the state average. More than two thirds of the Lemon Grove student body is Black or Brown, almost two thirds of the students are eligible for free or reduced-price lunches, and one in four students do not speak English at home. The challenges faced by this district are similar to any highly diverse, urban school system (see Table 13.1).

Academic Performance

In five short years, Lemon Grove School District has shown impressive academic growth. When compared to school districts with similar demographics in California, it consistently scores at the top. Two measures in particular show the growth that has taken place in the district, the California Standards Tests (CST) and Adequate Yearly Progress (AYP).

The California Standards Tests (CST). The CST show how well students are doing in relation to the state content standards. Student scores are

Table 13.1 2003–2004 Facts and Demographics of Lemon Grove School District

	Number	Percentage
Student population		
Total elementary	2,957	64.5
Total middle school	1,631	35.5
Total enrollment	4,588	
Student population according to race		
Hispanic	1,617	36.4
White	1,295	29.2
African American	1,046	23.6
Filipino	174	3.9
Asian	169	3.8
Pacific Islander	90	2.0
American Indian/Alaskan	44	1.0
Multiple ethnicities	6	0.1
Total minority population	3,146	68.6
Number of English language learners		
English language learners	784	17.7
English proficient ELL	345	7.8
Total of English language learners	1,129	24.6
Number of students receiving free or reduced-price meals		
Free	2,058	44.9
Reduced price	838	18.3
Total free or reduced-price meals	2,896	63.1
Funding per pupil		
Lemon Grove	$4,489	
State average	$4,508	
Use of technology		
Ratio of students per computer	2:1	

Source: Information obtained from district Web site, at http://www.lgsd.k12.ca.us. Used with permission of Lemon Grove Unified School District.

reported as performance levels. Students scoring at the proficient or advanced level meet state standards in that content area. Data reported in Table 13.2 are the percentages of students achieving at the proficient or advanced level (meeting or exceeding the state standard).

Table 13.2 Scores on California Standards Tests

Subject	District			State		
	2001	2002	2003	2001	2002	2003
English language arts	30	30	34	30	32	35
Mathematics		36	35		31	35
Science			0		30	27
History/Social Science			23		28	28

Source: Used with permission of Lemon Grove Unified School District.

Adequate Yearly Progress (AYP). The federal No Child Left Behind Act requires that all students perform at or above the proficient level on the state's standards-based assessments by 2014. To achieve this goal and meet annual performance objectives, districts and schools must improve each year according to set requirements. Data reported here show whether all groups of students in the school made AYP.

Groups	District in 2003
All students	Yes
African American	Yes
American Indian or Alaska Native	N/A
Asian	Yes
Filipino	Yes
Hispanic or Latino	Yes
Pacific Islander	N/A
White (not Hispanic)	Yes
Socioeconomically disadvantaged	Yes
English learners	Yes
Students with disabilities	No

The district is clearly experiencing great success in terms of closing the racial achievement gap. In 2004, Black students in five of the eight schools and Latino students in four of the eight schools improved at a rate greater than that of their White counterparts. While the racial achievement gap still exists, it is closing rapidly, while at the same time, all students are improving in performance. The transformation occurring in the district follows our equity definition:

Raise the achievement of all students while

- narrowing the gaps between the highest and lowest performing students; and
- eliminating the racial predictability and disproportionality of which student groups occupy the highest and lowest achievement categories.

Reflection

How does this definition of equity compare with your own? To what degree is our definition of equity operable in your school system? What elements are missing in your own definition that you find in Lemon Grove's adopted definition?

District-Level Equity Transformation

After the first summer of Beyond Diversity training in Lemon Grove, Jere McInerney created a broad-based District Equity Advisory Team, which met for a year to develop a plan for implementing Courageous Conversation and Courageous Leadership districtwide. One outcome of this District Equity Advisory Team was to provide Beyond Diversity training for every teacher in the district.

Later, that emphasis was extended to every board member and every principal attending Beyond Diversity training. As a result of this, the school board adopted a district policy in support of Systemic Equity/Anti-Racism Transformation. Subsequently, every principal crafted a vision for equity in his or her own school while participating in comprehensive, ongoing equity/anti-racism leadership development training.

Courageous Conversation has been the key element in everything the district has done in addressing equity. According to the superintendent, in a recent interview with Curtis Linton,

Courageous Conversation really captures the heart of what we're looking at. People shy away from talking about race. They can comfortably talk about wanting to address student achievement. They can talk comfortably about closing the achievement gap. But, they stop short of looking at what the gap really reflects—inequity. The fear is that when we begin talking about inequity, we begin assuming guilt as opposed to saying we need to do something about it. This is unacceptable when it's something where we can make a difference. Courageous Conversation has probably made the greatest difference in Lemon Grove School District.

School-Level Equity Transformation

Initially, the work toward equity in Lemon Grove began at the district level. But, for real impact to occur, it needed to move quickly to the school level. With the encouragement of district leadership, principals attended Beyond Diversity training and began to examine their own site-level racial challenges. According to Dr. Donn Griffits, principal of San Altos Elementary, "We have seen our achievement gradually decline over time. It wasn't until we recognized that our declining achievement scores were due to the fact that we had a huge achievement gap that was not closing that we attacked the problem" (interview with Curtis Linton, 2004).

One of the first assignments from the district was for the principals to attend ongoing Principal Equity Leadership Institutes, where they reflected on their own understanding, related beliefs and attitudes, and current efforts aimed at achieving equity in their schools. Rather than criticize principals, the Equity Institutes were aimed at helping them fortify their will, skill, knowledge, and capacity to courageously lead their schools toward equity/anti-racism.

Reflecting on his evolution as principal of Palm Middle School, Glenn Heath said, "I hadn't really thought much about equity work at all. I always felt that I was fair to kids and consistent to kids and always did the right things for kids. But I only looked at it from the perspective of a White male principal." These reflection exercises lead to change. Looking at data also became a critical part of the impetus for real school improvement. As Mr. Heath continues, "It took me a couple of years of [achievement gap] data—a hundred point difference between our White students and our students of color—for me to realize that there was something wrong" (interview with Curtis Linton).

Heath, Griffits, and other Lemon Grove principals began embracing equity work at different rates and with varying levels of enthusiasm. Eventually, they all introduced Courageous Conversation to their staffs as a way of supporting the district's Systemic Equity Anti-Racism

Transformation efforts in the three domains: leadership, learning and teaching, and community.

Leadership

From the beginning, the district administration communicated that equity work was a primary focus. According to Jere McInerney,

> First of all we acknowledged that there's an achievement gap. That our Black kids and our Brown kids are not doing as well as our White kids. You look at our data and you can very well see that there is a problem. And when you start looking at the problem, then what are you going to do about it? (interview with Curtis Linton, 2004)

As part of the district's leadership efforts, a top-level district administrator always attends any district-level meeting or training related to closing the racial achievement gap. Furthermore, Jere McInerney reports annually to the school board on progress toward systemic equity while the board itself revisits the issues and reforms the district policy so it supports the vision for equity. The district also focused resources and efforts on principal development and support by hiring an executive coach who works directly with the building administrators keeping them attuned to equity/race issues and clear in their communication of the vision.

Much of the district's anti-racism/equity work is guided by the District Equity Team, which includes Dr. King, Dr. McInerney, board members, principals, teacher-leaders, and community members. Together, with the support of Glenn Singleton's staff at Pacific Educational Group, Inc., the Lemon Grove District Equity Team establishes the tone, communicates the message, and ensures that the focus on eliminating racial achievement disparities remains a top priority.

According to principal Don Griffits, leadership at the school level is about "helping our teachers see that the work they do everyday in the classroom needs to reflect an equity paradigm that will allow all of our students to learn and to achieve to the utmost of their ability" (interview with Curtis Linton).

Equity Teams (E-Teams) are a primary and essential component of an anti-racist school community. In working with his E-Team, Don Griffits says, "Every curricular piece that we do needs to revolve around equity. Every resource we utilize is focused on not only serving the needs of children, but also looking at our children with sensitivity and finding what we need to do" (interview with Curtis Linton).

Glenn Heath, another Lemon Grove principal focused on equity, feels that

> it's easier for me to deal with students and parents of color now because I'm looking at it through a whole different lens. It is the equity lens that we're trying to use when we make decisions about programs and staffing. I think it's easier to deal with and support parents when I'm not looking at it in a way that's White centered. I need to expand what I do and look at it from another side of the coin. (interview with Curtis Linton)

Key to these principals' success is modeling equity in their own beliefs, decision making, and other leadership actions. It is critical that the principal provide both formal and informal opportunities for the staff to have Courageous Conversations about race. When the E-Team facilitates an equity activity at a staff meeting in Heath's school, it is usually the first agenda item rather the last so that all other issues are viewed through the lens of equity.

Daily Equity Walk-Throughs by principals and E-Team members provide an opportunity to observe teacher practices and notice inequities and positive deviance in classroom climate, culture, and teacher instruction. Equity Walk-Throughs rely on brief observations and are designed to discover patterns in instruction, both positive and detrimental to students. These emerging patterns observed in classrooms become the focus of schoolwide teacher professional learning.

A substantial part of equity leadership involves the principals' process of transformation into effective instructional leaders. According to Mr. Heath, "I think it's very important that I be out and visible wherever and whenever possible" (interview with Curtis Linton).

The primary role of a teacher in terms of leadership is to serve on the school Equity Team. Frank Wulftange, a member of his school's Equity Team, discusses his work with other teachers:

> Most of the time I don't go head on with the equity message. I first develop a relationship with somebody and then the equity issues come about as a natural progression in that evolving relationship with the person. If I have an established relationship with somebody, I can talk about race issues, "Oh, by the way, this is how I'm addressing this issue in my teaching . . ." After this, people will come to me rather than me having to go and pound it into them. (interview with Curtis Linton, 2004)

Teacher leaders also engage other teachers in Courageous Conversation. In doing so, they help teachers arrive at a better understanding of the needs of their students of color. According to Palm Middle School teacher Tracy Tyler, when working with her colleagues, "I would try to express that there's nothing I can give you—it's just all about reflecting and really looking at what you do from the perspective of your students. Think about the students being willing to change" (interview with Curtis Linton).

Learning and Teaching

In addressing learning and teaching, Drs. King and McInerney communicated to all teachers that ensuring equity and closing the racial achievement gap was a primary focus in Lemon Grove School District. According to the superintendent,

> Diversity is embracing differences. There is a different life experience that goes on with children of color that we should be very sensitive to and not ignore. Being blind to race was probably one of the first challenges we faced. Some teachers thought that since they treat all children equally they did not need a different perspective or a different sensitivity. Saying "Everyone is treated equally in my classroom" is absolutely unacceptable as a professional educator in today's society with a diverse population. (interview with Curtis Linton)

To reinforce their need to address racial inequities in the classroom, the district provides trainings that equip teachers with data, research, and literature highlighting the racial achievement gap and how to address it. The focus is always on the district's goals, objectives, professional development, and resources in achieving equity.

School-based learning and teaching in Lemon Grove begins with the principal, who is the instructional leader in the school. The principal leads the CARE (Collaborative Action Research for Equity). Team and drives schoolwide improvement in learning. At San Altos Elementary, according to Dr. Griffits,

> We are not going to have a real good understanding of what we need to do and the work that needs to be done if we don't spend the time and effort to help our teachers understand the population of kids they're serving. We've spent a tremendous amount of time in staff development guiding our teachers toward not only improving their own instructional practices with students of color, but also understanding more about themselves. (interview with Curtis Linton)

The CARE Team works to identify and understand culturally responsive strategies that engage all students in rigorous learning, especially for African American and Latino students. Lemon Grove provides CARE teachers with the time and resources to engage in collaborative action research focused on their own teaching practices.

CARE members in their first, second, or third year of focused inquiry examine the components of effective instruction and then assess the quality of their own lessons by examining student work and engaging in dialogue with focus groups of five to six students of color. Throughout this process, teachers learn what does and does not work with students of color. In Year 3 of CARE, teachers begin using data more extensively as part of their research so they can more intensely analyze how to teach students of different races and how to set and reach learning goals with all of their students.

Frank Wulftange believes his teaching practices at Palm Middle School have evolved as a result of CARE. He comments,

> For me, the practical aspect has been my evolving teaching practice. I've been in the classroom for 9 years now and it's really been an evolution for me as a teacher with CARE. I'm remembering in particular one of the very first exercises we did in CARE where we told stories about ourselves and our names. That was such a powerful experience for the adults sitting in this conference room. Even though it's sort of a formal setting, it was liberating, at least from my perspective, to tell these stories. I couldn't help but feel like my students also had these stories. I think I knew that all along, but CARE reinforced that for me. (interview with Curtis Linton)

One of the more positive aspects that teacher-leaders in Lemon Grove have experienced as a result of CARE is the improved relationships with students. According to Tracy Tyler,

> I didn't want to come across as an authority. I wanted them to know that this was something that I'm working at, that I want to be better at in my profession. That way they would be better students and hopefully they could help me be a better teacher. I think they liked that. I think it really broke down some walls that are always involved in education between the role of the teacher and the role of the student. (interview with Curtis Linton)

CARE has also encouraged Tracy Tyler to examine her own level of assumed responsibility for her teaching.

It is a lot more about the environment you set up and how you work with the students. They make or break your day. I think we have to be better as teachers at working with our students. So many of our challenges go back to the fact that we are just not connecting with kids—we can't blame the text book for everything. (interview with Curtis Linton)

Expounding upon this new found responsibility for teachers, Frank Wulftange comments,

When something goes wrong in your classroom, look not to the student and point your finger at them. When I point the finger at them, I've got three pointing back at me. Look first to your practice and what procedures and routines you have or have not implemented that need to be changed. (interview with Curtis Linton)

Community

This is an often avoided domain of Systemic Equity Transformation, however, Lemon Grove School District puts forth significant effort to build relationships among stakeholders found in the institutional and established communities. According to Dr. King,

When I came here to Lemon Grove, I embraced the diversity as one of the true assets that it had. For me, this was the spot I wanted to be. It was a community that I felt we could do a lot of good in by working hand in hand with families and community members. (interview with Curtis Linton)

After analyzing parental involvement data disaggregated by race, district and site leadership discovered that the parents who visited schools were disproportionately White. To increase engagement in school affairs among parents of color, district and site leaders formed PASS (Partnerships for Academically Successful Students) Teams and began to reach out to established community members of color in Lemon Grove, using innovative and creative methods. For example, they opened the doors of the schools to Latino community groups so that they can meet for English classes and other cultural events. Similarly, they invited local pastors of African American churches to co-host parent outreach programs at the churches, where families already feel safe and supported.

Site administrators in Lemon Grove also focus on creating alliances between the school-based educators and the established community. One way they do this is by providing phones in every classroom and encouraging teachers to contact the families of all their disenfranchised students of color. More than just calling home to discuss problems, teachers communicate with families about their children's progress and successes as well. Furthermore, school-based educators actively seek the opinions, knowledge, and cultural wisdom of families so they can better relate to and educate their African American and Latino students.

At Palm Middle School, Principal Glenn Heath says, "We are providing more opportunities for our families of color. When we offered the parent institute on site, we had 65 Latino families who were involved in that and graduated after nine weeks. It just has to be an ongoing mission" (interview with Curtis Linton).

Teachers as well as the principal actively participate on school-based PASS Teams. In this capacity, they function much like a CARE Team, but with the emphasis on discovering how to successfully engage families and community members in the process of improving student achievement. These efforts within the established community have impacted Tracy Tyler.

> I think for me, part of it comes from being a parent. It is a tremendous amount of responsibility but knowing that I have a son in school, I hope his teacher realizes the responsibility and the impact she has on him. As a teacher, you do have to take that responsibility. Parents are sending you their kids because they expect you to take on that responsibility. You don't have a choice. You shouldn't have a choice. (interview with Curtis Linton)

Reflection

Based on this case study of Lemon Grove School District's efforts in equity transformation, what have you learned that you can implement in your own school or school system? Where should you begin? Who else should you engage in this work around equity?

As a result of these comprehensive, ongoing, long-term systemwide efforts, Lemon Grove School District is realizing the significant improvement the superintendent once only envisioned. The racial achievement gap is quickly closing as Latino students and Black students are experiencing significant success in the classroom. Furthermore, as more teachers document substantial growth in student achievement, other teachers are inquiring as to how this is being accomplished. Lemon Grove is well on its way to achieving equity throughout the system. Understandably, the district's reputation is flourishing throughout San Diego County, as expressed in the following editorial:

Two East County School Districts Are Setting the Pace

East County school district—Lemon Grove—has considerable reason to be proud of its scores on the state's Academic Performance Index. The Lemon Grove School District, meantime, continues to exceed academic expectations. Five of its eight schools scored at or near the top in the API when compared to similar schools across the state.

Superintendent McLean King cites an ongoing commitment to bring all 4,600 students up to proficiency as measured by California and district assessments. That's quite a challenge given the diversity of learning styles including 65 percent qualifying for free or reduced price lunches, and 20 percent having limited ability to speak English. Lemon Grove teachers, however, are rising to the challenge and their responsibility to educate all children. . . .

Historically a low-performing district, Lemon Grove is more focused on making a difference than making excuses. King is a firm believer in early intervention to help get children up to speed. The district's Reading Recovery Program dovetails with a concentrated emphasis on literacy.

Like most districts, Lemon Grove is looking to close a chronic racial achievement gap, which is exacerbated by a high degree of mobility among low-income students of color. Still, Lemon Grove's reputation for getting the most from its students persists, which is why about 400 of its students voluntarily choose inter-district transfers from neighboring school districts. Lemon Grove proudly accepts students from neighboring communities and educates each as one of their own.

Lemon Grove embraces a can-do attitude that other districts would do well to emulate.

Source: San Diego Union-Tribune (2003).

ANTI-RACIST LEADERSHIP

Effective anti-racist/equity leadership goes beyond working to address obvious examples of institutional racism and inequities. This work is necessarily personal and far-reaching. Marching toward equity emerges as a life purpose for many educators as they focus on eradicating the racial caste system that exists in their classrooms, schools, and larger community. It appears insufficient, however, just to believe in and support anti-racism on a personal level. Systemic transformation requires that individual anti-racist efforts actually translate into improvements in pedagogies that positively impact colleagues' work and improve students' learning. Success is measured one system at a time!

In explaining his anti-racist leadership in Lemon Grove, Superintendent McLean King has said,

> [Equity is] the core of the work we do in schools. Our society counts on education to teach the whole child. It counts on us to perpetuate our culture within our society. If our culture is truly to be inclusive, this work is critical and essential in everything we do. I believe strongly in academics, and standards, and student achievement, but it can't be done by excluding the issue of access, equity, and compassion for the human condition. Compassion means empowering people to be successful by doing things differently to make that happen. (interview with Curtis Linton)

To be equity centered is to internally convert personal racism to anti-racist leadership. In the absence of this conversion, the individual will be left with a persisting dilemma of a transformed conceptual framework with little practical application and tangible results. Anti-racist leadership is not just playing a role; it is a deeply transforming personal experience. This work impacts everything an educator is and all she or he does.

Frank Wulftange sums up the purpose of his equity work in this guidance he received from a trusted adviser:

> My mother's advice to me as she was retiring after 35 years in public education wasn't about the small things that would bother me. Her only words of wisdom were, "You don't just teach your subject, *you teach who you are as a person.*" And that's the challenge. That's what we need to do as a profession. (interview with Curtis Linton)

To not be involved and engaged in equity work is to perpetuate institutionalized racism. There is no non-racist place—you are either anti-racist or perpetuating the racism that already exists. All potential anti-racist leaders must find within themselves how racism is affecting them, personally, on a daily basis. They must then create their own personal and internal strategy that provides instruction on how to address their own individual racism. Having satisfied these prerequisites, they can engage with colleagues in discovering strategies to examine and eradicate inequities and racism at the classroom, school, district, and institutionalized levels.

Finding passion for equity, developing equitable classroom practices, and being persistent in this work are the key components of and guiding strategy for anti-racist leaders. We wrote this book to provide you with the tools you need to close the racial achievement gap. Remain true to yourself in this work, fight for the sake of your students, and use an equity lens to determine appropriateness in all you do and become. We wish you the best of luck. Stay courageous and remain hopeful that systemic transformation offers us a journey to the possibility. Our children deserve nothing less!

Journal Reflection

Commit to paper your personal thoughts about the journey you have made throughout this book. Where did you begin in your understanding of race? Where are you now? How will your increased will, skill, knowledge, and capacity to examine race impact your personal and professional experiences? How will you continue your learning? What new commitments can you make to engage in equity/antiracist work?

Resource

Racism and the Achievement Gap

Julian Weissglass

Most educators, politicians, and educational institutions are concerned over the disparities between different ethnic/racial or socioeconomic groups in national and state test scores, attrition rates, enrollment in advanced courses, and degree attainment. Educators frequently state their commitment that "all" children will learn. One might think that this commitment and the considerable resources of the richest country in the world would result in change.

> Many of the assumptions, values, and practices of people and institutions hinder the learning of students of color.

But there has been little progress. A report this year analyzing National Assessment of Educational Progress results for the 1990s, for example, showed that only two states reduced the gap between white students and black or Latino students in 4th grade mathematics, and no state did so in 8th grade math. Although our society has made substantial progress in gaining civil rights for people of color, the achievement gap persists.

Julian Weissglass is the director of the National Coalition for Equity in Education and a professor of education at the University of California, Santa Barbara. He will be a nongovernmental delegate at the United Nations World Conference Against Racism this month in South Africa, and can be reached at weissglass@education.ucsb.edu.

Source: Reprinted with permission of Julian Weissglass, Director of the National Coalition for Equity and Education at the University of California, Santa Barbara, http://ncee.education.ucsb.edu.

I contend that although no one is born prejudiced, many of the assumptions, values, and practices of people and institutions hinder the learning of students of color and students from low-socioeconomic classes. Race and class biases in particular are major causes of differential success. For the sake of brevity, I will only address racial bias.

> Although our society has made substantial progress in gaining civil rights for people of color, the achievement gap persists.

Racism is the systematic mistreatment of certain groups of people (often referred to as people of color) on the basis of skin color or other physical characteristics. This mistreatment is carried out by societal institutions, or by people who have been conditioned by the society to act, consciously or unconsciously, in harmful ways toward people of color. Racism is different from prejudice. A person of color can hurt a white person because of prejudice. The difference is that in this country, people of color face systematic and ongoing personal and institutionalized biases every day. Shirley Chisholm, our country's first black congresswoman, wrote that "racism is so universal in this country, so widespread and deep-seated, that it is invisible because it is so normal."

Racism can be subtle or blatant, conscious or unconscious, personal or institutionalized. Unconscious personal bias occurs, for example, when teachers have low expectations of black or Latino students, or don't interact with them as much or as thoughtfully as they do with white children.

Institutionalized racism includes: (1) the incorporation into institutional policies or practices of attitudes or values that work to the disadvantage of students of color (for example, differential allocation of resources, or tracking practices that consign many students of color to low tracks with less experienced teachers, from which they can seldom escape); (2) the unquestioned acceptance by the institution of white-middle-class values (for example, the scarcity of authors of color in many secondary schools' English curricula); and (3) schools' being passive in the face of prejudiced behavior that interferes with students' learning or well-being (for example, not addressing harassment or teasing, or meeting it with punishment instead of attempting to build communication and understanding).

Since schools are the primary formal societal institutions that young people encounter, they have enormous responsibility in combating all forms of racism. What schools do, or don't do, has a significant impact on the future of society.

Racism persists in the United States for several reasons, including the following:

Lack of information, as well as misinformation. White people lack information about the history and nature of the oppression that people of color have endured. They learn little, for example, about the genocide of indigenous peoples, the kidnapping and slavery of Africans and the oppression of their descendants, the military seizure of the Southwestern U.S. territory from Mexico, or the imprisonment of Japanese Americans during World War II. The media promote stereotypes and neglect peoples' real lives. Given the lack of information and the spread of misinformation, it is not surprising that white people do not always understand the feelings of Native Americans, African Americans, Mexican Americans, or Asian Americans.

The tenacity of belief systems that advocate superiority and inferiority based on race. Theories of racial superiority and inferiority were common (and publicly stated) in the early part of the 20th century. The Harvard geneticist Edward East, for example, wrote this in his book *Heredity and Human Affairs* (1929): "Gene packets of African origin are not valuable supplements to the gene packets of European origin; it is the white germ plasm that counts."

A very prominent group of psychologists, educators, and geneticists from leading American universities believed in the superiority of certain racial, national, and social-class groups and attempted to influence government policies through what was called the eugenics movement. Current standardized tests are based on the theories and models developed by those men.

Eugenic organizations disappeared after the Nazis took the belief of racial superiority to a horrific conclusion in the early 1940s. But the ideas persist, often in subtler and more sophisticated forms, and affect our society and our schools.

Many people's expectations and attitudes are still influenced by these discredited racist theories. Let me be clear: The eugenics movement was based on untruths. Human beings are one species. Although there are significant cultural differences, biologically we are much more alike than we are different. Each human being is valuable beyond measure. Each deserves to be treated with complete respect.

Lack of opportunities to heal from hurt. Human beings experience considerable hurt (physical and emotional) when they are young—from accidents and from mistreatment or neglect by adults or other young people. Although, as adults, we may

> Unconscious personal bias occurs, for example, when teachers have low expectations of black or Latino students.

have forgotten many of the experiences, they still affect us. People who are "feeling bad" as a result of being hurt sometimes act in ways harmful to others. They may make misguided attempts to feel better by hurting someone else or by bonding with a group (informal or organized) that discriminates against (or even actively harasses) other people. They may exclude or marginalize others, or act in patronizing or condescending ways.

It is obvious to most people that it is hurtful to be the target of racism (or any form of bias). It is less obvious that any oppressive attitude is harmful to the individual who holds it. Oppressive attitudes limit one's potential, actions, relationships, and emotional health. Humans can heal from hurts that cause racism to persist, but it will take some effort.

The internalization and transfer of racism. This is the process in which people of color believe and act on the negative messages they receive about themselves and their group. Internalized racism causes people to give up, become hopeless, or believe that they are not as intelligent or as worthwhile as whites. Internalized racism undermines people's confidence and, as a result, their ability to function well.

The patterns of internalizing and transferring racism (insults, criticism, slurs, and violence) are rooted in genocide, slavery, subjugation, conquest, and exploitation. When people are hurt and not allowed to heal through emotional release, they are pulled to re-enact the hurt on someone else. Since people of color have rarely been able to act out their hurt on whites, they tend to act it out on family members and other people of color. These behavior patterns tend to get passed on from generation to generation.

The processes of racism and internalized racism help explain why some Asian-American groups outperform blacks, Latinos, and Native Americans. Although Asian Americans experience racism, they do not usually get stereotyped as less intelligent than whites, so they internalize and transfer messages about themselves that are different from those of blacks, Latinos, and Native Americans. Teachers who have made progress in closing the achievement gap have undoubtedly, through encouragement, high expectations, building caring relationships, and instilling self-confidence, overcome some the effects of internalized racism.

Good intentions and hard work are not sufficient for eliminating racism in schools. Neither will excellent curriculum and pedagogy in themselves be enough to eradicate the achievement gap. We need communities where it is safe enough for the invisible to be made visible, where whites can listen to people of color talk about how they and their ancestors have experienced racism, and where people of color can listen to whites talk about how they saw racial prejudice in operation and how it affected them. Listening to one another's stories and emotions helps people identify what needs to change within their institutions, their colleagues, and themselves. Being listened to helps us heal.

Although educators cannot, by themselves, solve all the problems caused by racism in society, it is possible for us to construct "healing communities" in which people can learn how to listen and give attention while others heal. Professional therapists are not necessary, nor are there enough of them to do the job. It is part of our responsibility as educators to do this work.

There is a tendency among educators to dismiss healing from hurt as too "touchy-feely" to belong in academic institutions. Consider, however, that this country has spent hundreds of millions (perhaps billions) of dollars in the last two decades on attempts to decrease the achievement gap without any major change on the national level. It is clearly time to risk new approaches—ones based on addressing the root causes of the achievement gap.

Building and sustaining healing communities to end racism is challenging. The issues related to racism and other forms of bias are complex and often emotional. People often deny that racism interferes with relationships or affects institutional policies ("I don't see color." "I treat everyone the same."). They may be fearful of talking honestly about racial issues, or feel hopeless or cynical about the possibility of change. It is easier to have one-day workshops celebrating diversity, to develop new curricula, buy "test prep" programs, write reports, and pressure teachers, than to talk about personal experiences with racism.

But without the ongoing and persistent attention of a healing community to the elimination of racism, it will not go away. Furthermore, any reform effort designed to reduce the achievement gap that does not help whites and people of color heal from the hurts of racism will not be likely to succeed over time.

Achieving healing communities will require leaders with exceptional commitment, understanding, persistence, and sensitivity. These leaders will need to understand not only educational issues and subject disciplines, but also the personal, social, and institutional roots of inequities. Leaders will be able to raise controversial issues while building unity, to relate well with people from diverse backgrounds, and help people deal constructively with their and others' emotions. A substantial effort will be required to develop these leaders, since the necessary skills and knowledge are not routinely developed by colleges of education or in professional development. But it can be done.

In healing communities, a wide range of anti-racism work will be going on. Educators will be identifying how their unaware bias affects their students, challenging any attitudes of low expectations, working with parents to help them support their children's learning, and identifying how racism becomes institutionalized in policies and practices. They will be questioning their curricula and pedagogy and working to make them more engaging to students of different cultures.

Schools will teach the history of how oppressed peoples have been treated in this country and support students of color and their families to challenge and heal from internalized racism. Schools will move beyond the celebration of diversity and create communities in which it is possible for students to talk about and heal from how they experience unfairness and discrimination. A healing community will have as its highest priority adults caring about students and their learning.

> If, as a nation, we develop communities in which people can speak honestly and productively about racism and heal from its hurts, we can change biased practices and attitudes.

If, as a nation, we develop communities in which people can speak honestly and productively about racism and heal from its hurts, we can change biased practices and attitudes. If we can communicate love and caring to all our students and help them recover from racism and internalized racism, they will be much more likely to achieve their full academic potential. If we do all this, we will accomplish more than reducing the achievement gap. We will create a better society.

References

Adelman, L. (2003). *Race—the power of an illusion* [Video]. San Francisco: California Newsreel/PBS.

Arciniega, T. A. (1977). The challenge of multicultural education for teacher educators. *Journal of Research and Development in Education, 11*(1), 52–69.

Aronson, J. (2004). The threat of stereotype. *Educational Leadership, 62*(3), 14–20.

Bacon, M. M. (2005). *Working with students from the culture of poverty.* Sandy, UT: Video Journal of Education.

Barnes, J. E. (2004, March 22). Unequal education. *U.S. News & World Report,* 66–75.

Barth, S. R. (2004). *Learning by heart.* San Francisco: Jossey-Bass.

Bell, D. A. (1992). *Faces at the bottom of the well: The permanence of racism.* New York: Basic Books.

Chapel Hill-Carrboro School District. (2004, July 19). *Chapel Hill-Carrboro School District achieves Adequate Yearly Progress (AYP) on national goals* (news release). Retrieved June 4, 2005, from http://www.chccs.k12.nc.us/news/news1.asp?ID=377

Chapel Hill-Carrboro School District. (2005). *District report card on African American and Latino student progress.* Chapel Hill, NC: Author.

Darling-Hammond, L. (1997). *The right to learn.* San Francisco: Jossey-Bass.

DeCuir, J. T., & Dixson, A. D. (2004, June/July). "So when it comes out, they aren't that surprised that it is there": Using critical race theory as a tool of analysis of race and racism in education. *Educational Researcher,* pp. 26–31.

Delpit, L. (1995a). *Other people's children: Cultural conflict in the classroom.* New York: The New Press.

Delpit, L. (1995b). The silenced dialogue. In L. Delpit, *Other people's children: Cultural conflict in the classroom* (pp. 21–47). New York: The New Press. (Original work published 1988)

DuBois, W. E. B. (1970). The freedom to learn. In P. S. Foner (Ed.), *W. E. B. DuBois speaks* (pp. 230–231). New York: Pathfinder. (Original work published 1949)

DuBois, W. E. B. (1996). *The souls of black folk.* New York: Random House. (Original work published 1903)

Economist. (2005). The unfriendly border. *The Economist.* Retrieved August 25, 2005, from http://www.economist.com.

Hale, J. E. (2004). How schools shortchange African American students. *Educational Leadership, 62*(3), 34–37.

Haycock, K. (2003). *Learning from "frontier" schools and districts.* Retrieved February 5, 2004, from http://www2.edtrust.org/EdTrust/Data+Tools+and+Presentations.

Helms, J. E. (Ed.). (1990). *Black and White racial identity: Theory, research, and practice.* Westport, CT: Greenwood.

Henze, R., Katz, A., Norte, E., Sather, S., & Walker, E. (2002). *Leading for diversity: How school leaders promote interethnic relations.* Thousand Oaks, CA: Corwin Press.

Herrnstein, R., & Murray, C. (1994). *The bell curve: Intelligence and class structure in American life.* New York: Free Press.

Hilliard, A. (1995). Do we have the will to educate all children? In *The maroon within us: Selected essays on African American community socialization.* Baltimore, MD: Black Classic Press.

Hoffman, F. L. (2004). *Race traits and tendencies of the American Negro.* Buffalo, NY: William S. Hein & Company. (Original work published 1896)

Jefferson, T. (1996). *Notes on the State of Virginia* (W. Peden, Ed.). Chapel Hill: University of North Carolina Press.

Johnson, R. (2002). *Using data to close the achievement gap.* Thousand Oaks, CA: Corwin Press.

Katz, J. H. (2003). *White awareness.* Norman: University of Oklahoma Press.

King, L. M. (2001). *Closing the achievement gap: A vision for students in a world of diversity.* Lemon Grove, CA: Lemon Grove School District.

Kivel, P. (2002). *Uprooting racism: How White people can work for racial justice.* Philadelphia: New Society Publishers.

Landsman, J. (2004). Confronting the racism of low expectations. *Educational Leadership, 62*(3), 28–33.

Lindsey, R. B., Nuri Robins, K., & Terrell, R. D. (2003). *Cultural proficiency: A manual for school leaders.* Thousand Oaks, CA: Corwin Press.

Marzano, R. J., Pickering, D., & Pollock, J. E. (2001). *Classroom instruction that works: Research-based strategies for increasing student achievement.* Alexandria, VA: Association for Staff and Curriculum Development.

McIntosh, P. (1988). *White privilege and male privilege: A personal account of coming to see correspondences through work in women's studies* (Working Paper No. 189). Wellesley, MA: Wellesley College Center for Research on Women.

McIntosh, P. (1989, July/August). White privilege: Unpacking the invisible knapsack. *Peace and Freedom,* 10–12.

Pine, G., & Hilliard, A. (1990, April). Rx for racism: Imperatives for America's schools. *Phi Delta Kappan,* pp. 593–600.

San Diego Union Tribune (2003, February 27). East County Opinion: Two East County school districts are setting the pace. *The San Diego Union Tribune,* p. B15.

Singham, M. (1998). The canary in the mine: The achievement gap between Black and White students. *Phi Delta Kappan, 80*(1), 9–15.

Singleton, G. (1997). *White is a color!* San Francisco, CA: Pacific Educational Group.

Singleton, G. (2002). *Closing the achievement gap* [Video]. Video Journal of Education.

Sparks, D. (2004). How to have conversations about race, an interview with Beverly Daniel Tatum. *Journal of Staff Development, 25*(4), 48–52.

Tatum, B. D. (1997). *"Why are all the Black kids sitting together in the cafeteria?" and other conversations about race.* New York: HarperCollins.

References

Trumbull, E., Rothstein-Fisch, C., Greenfield, P. M., & Quiroz, B. (2000). *A practical framework for understanding cultural differences: Bridging cultures in our schools: New approaches that work.* Berkeley, CA: WestEd.

University of California. (1998, June 7). Study of 1995 SAT scores. *San Francisco Examiner.*

West, C. (2001). *Race matters.* Boston: Beacon Press.

Wheatley, M. (2002). *Turning to one another: Simple conversations to restore hope to the future.* San Francisco: Berrett-Koehler.

Weissglass, J. (2001). Racism and the achievement gap. *Education Week, 20*(43), 49–50, 72.

Wiggins, G., & McTighe, J. (1998). *Understanding by design.* Alexandria, VA: ASCD.

Williams, L. (2000). *It's the little things: The everyday interactions that get under the skin of Blacks and Whites.* New York: Harcourt.

Wise, T. (2000). *Membership has its privileges: Thoughts on acknowledging and challenging whiteness.* Retrieved from www.zmag.org/sustainers/content/2000-06/22wise.htm

Wise, T. (2002). White like me: Race and identity through majority eyes. In B. Singley (Ed.), *When race becomes real: Black and White writers confront their personal histories* (pp. 225–240). Chicago: Lawrence Hill Books.

Woods, T. (1997). *Tiger Woods on Tiger Woods.* www.tigerwoods.com.

WRAL. (2003). *Some parents upset over proposed merger plans.* Retrieved October 13, 2003, from www.wral.com/education/2551687/detail.html.

Index

Index

Index

CORWIN PRESS

The Corwin Press logo—a raven striding across an open book—represents the union of courage and learning. Corwin Press is committed to improving education for all learners by publishing books and other professional development resources for those serving the field of PreK–12 education. By providing practical, hands-on materials, Corwin Press continues to carry out the promise of its motto: **"Helping Educators Do Their Work Better."**